HERVÉ RYSSEN

THE BILLIONS OF ISRAEL
Jewish swindlers and international financiers

Hervé Ryssen

Hervé Ryssen (France) is a historian and an exhaustive researcher of the Jewish intellectual world. He is the author of twelve books and several video documentaries on the Jewish question. In 2005 he published *The Planetary Hopes*, a book in which he demonstrates the religious origins of the globalist project. *Psychoanalysis of Judaism*, published in 2006, shows how intellectual Judaism presents all the symptoms of hysterical pathology. There is no "divine choice", but the manifestation of a disorder that has its origin in the practice of incest. Freud had patiently studied this question on the basis of what he observed in his own community.

France is home to one of the largest Jewish communities of the Diaspora with a very intense cultural and intellectual life. Hervé Ryssen has been able to develop his extensive work on the basis of numerous historical and contemporary sources, both international and French.

Israel's billionaires
Jewish swindlers and international financiers

Les milliards d'Israël, Escrocs juifs & financiers internationaux,
Levallois-Perret, Baskerville, 2006.

Translated and published by
Omnia Veritas Limited

www.omnia-veritas.com

© Omnia Veritas Limited - Hervé Ryssen - 2023

All rights reserved. No part of this work may be reproduced in whole or in part without prior written permission from the *copyright* holders. Infringement of such rights may constitute an intellectual property offense.

PART ONE 13

THE BIG SCAMS 13

1. VAT fraud 19
The Eurocanyon case 22
The Rubens Lévy case 23
The great carbon dioxide (CO2) scam 26
The beginning of the scam 27
The impunity of the enarcas 32
Fabrice Sakoun, absent at the time of the verdict 39
Lyon police are in good hands 42
The "Flacucho": the greatest of them all! 47
Small settling of scores among friends 50
On the trail of CO2 53
How to silence anti-Semitism? 56

2. Advertising fraud 61
The 800 victims of fake gendarmes 61
The victims of the "Franco-Israeli" 62
The 544 victims of Jonathan Zeitoun 63
Jacques Benayoun scammed farmers 64
The Monte Carlo Police Golden Book 67

3. False transfer orders 69
The monstrous impudence of Gilbert Chikli 75

4. Diverse and varied scams 79
The Badache-Apollonia Case 79
Money embezzled from charitable associations 84
Bank card number traffic 86
Market hucksters 87
King Solomon's good business 92
The counterfeiters 96
Memory fraud 103
Oscar Friedman's revenge 110
The Talmud and the Jewish Mentality 114

PART TWO 119

THE SHARKS OF FINANCE 119

1. Pyramid fraud 119
Bernard Madoff, the absolute champion 120
A financial shoah 122
Between negligence and complicity 124
The supposed victims were actually his accomplices 127
Compensate victims 133
The death of the goy 134
The little Madoffs 136
Scott Rothstein and his billionaire 137
Bruce Friedman, a Californian Madoff 138
Eliyahu Weinstein scammed his community 139
Tzvi Erez, the little "Canadian" Madoff 139

Nevin Shapiro relaxes in Miami 139
Philip Barry and the porn business 140
Barry Tannenbaum: A South African Madoff 140
Ezri Namvar, the Madoff of the West Coast 141
Two Madoffs commit suicide 141
Seymour Jacobson: a Swiss who loved Belgium 142
Claire Arfi, a "Madoff in a skirt". 142
Fast, easy and effective cash 145

2. *The great stock market frauds* 146
Sadly, Abraham Hochman has passed away. 146
Michael Milken and junk bonds 147
Jordan Belfort: a Leonardo DiCaprio with a kippah 153
The dotcom bubble scam 164
Insider trading 166
Ivan Boesky: the reference in this field 166
Steven Cohen: "You eat what you kill". 167

3. *The Federal Reserve Heist* 170
Predatory lending and the subprime crisis 172
The CDO scam 179
CDS: weapons of mass destruction 183
The foreclosure scandal 192
Make the taxpayer pay 194
Synthetic CDOs, fruits of love 203
Complaints against Goldman Sachs 212
Criminals at the top of the State 215
The awakening of anti-Semitism 219

4. *The Super Predators* 223
Goldman Sachs in Greece: financial magic 224
George Soros and speculation 227
Cosmopolitan billionaires 230
Visible and influential" billionaires 234
Cosmopolitan bankers and socialist revolutionaries 236
The Federal Reserve Fraud 241

5. *A singular mentality* 246
Blessed are the gold coins 247
On the suffering of being a banker 251
Purchase of protection 254
Interest-bearing loan 259
Pathological rapacity 264
Terrible prejudices 268

THE COSMOPOLITAN PROJECT **277**

OTHER TITLES 287

Jews have a very particular relationship with money. This is not a hateful "anti-Semitic prejudice", but a tangible reality, as Jews are vastly overrepresented among the world's billionaires[1]. Since time immemorial, scattered in all countries, they are famous for having dedicated themselves to the great international trade. They are also, for centuries, the masters of banking and speculation. Naturally, all speculators, all the masters of finance and international trade are not Jews; and conversely, all Jews do not exercise these trades. But it is undeniable that they have played and continue to play a crucial role.

To explain their predominance in the financial system, Jewish intellectuals repeat over and over again that since lending at interest had been forbidden by Christianity and Islam, the Jews had somehow been driven in this way in spite of themselves. But this is forgetting a bit quickly that Jewish bankers were already the masters of the profession, and that long before the advent of Christianity, and a fortiori of Islam.

Moreover, Jewish historians often claim that in Christian lands, for centuries, the practice of other trades was forbidden to them and that they were therefore forced to engage in activities related to money. In reality, there was never in history any prohibition for Jews to exercise a productive trade. As far as is known, no one ever prevented a Jew from being a carpenter or a cabinetmaker, a blacksmith or a farmer. But, on the other hand, the Jews are forbidden in their code of law to cultivate foreign soil. They preferred in any case to exercise professions that allowed them to exploit their intellectual abilities and financial skills, always keeping in mind the possibility of fleeing in case of shocks in the host country.

---

[1] *Milliard* in French corresponds to 1000 million, i.e. the billion in Spanish. Although this word appears in the RAE dictionary, it is rarely used, which is why we only use it to translate the original title of the book. Thus, in French, a *"milliardaire"* is a multimillionaire individual with more than 1 billion (Translator's note, NdT onwards).

And the fact is that the Jews were expelled from everywhere, from all countries, in all epochs, when they were not directly massacred: by the Egyptians, by the Babylonians, by the Greeks, by the Romans, and by the Christians and the Muslims; always and everywhere. And every time—as we have shown in our *History of anti-Semitism*—the main reason given was usury, that is, lending with interest at an abusive rate that ruined the peasants and merchants, and enriched the Jewish communities of all the cities immeasurably. Receiving stolen goods was another of the frequent accusations mentioned in the texts, as well as their manifest hatred towards the Church and the goyim in general. Throughout Europe, they were seen to engage in smuggling at the frontiers, to cut up currency, to wash gold ducats in acid, to use arsenic to give brass the color of gold, to "betray and deceive the Christians" in a thousand ways. Nothing has changed in this respect, but the swindles, since the beginning of this millennium, have acquired an unprecedented scale. The fact is that big swindles are their almost exclusive specialty. And here, too, no one has ever led them down this path. For, to tell the truth, they find in themselves, in the Talmud (their holy book containing the teachings of the rabbis[2]) as well as in their ancestral traditions, the psychological, moral and intellectual resources to embark on such ventures.

---

[2] Read about the Talmud in Hervé Ryssen, *Psychoanalysis of Judaism (and Appendix I)*. (NdT).

PART ONE

THE BIG SCAMS

The biggest scams in history have taken place at the beginning of this century, to such an extent that records have been smashed; not simply surpassed, but actually smashed. In our previous book on the cosmopolitan mafia, published in 2008, we evoked some cases that may now seem to be from another era:

Let us recall for example Claude Lipsky, who had been described as the "swindler of the century" when the case broke out in September 2000. Since 1987, Claude Lipsky had been offering investments to retired French soldiers or those still serving on the African continent. Officers and NCOs had amassed comfortable incomes thanks to their salaries as soldiers on mission abroad, and these savings had caught the eye of the swindler, who had offered them an annual return of more than 10% with capital inflows of 50,000 francs. Around 175 million francs (or 26.7 million euros) had evaporated, and several hundred soldiers had formed an association to denounce the swindle. On May 21, 2007, before the court of Versailles, the 75-year-old "French-Israeli businessman" still claimed his innocence. He had not embezzled the funds: *"They were lost. As in all financial companies, sometimes it works very well, and sometimes there are problems,"* he had told reporters. Claude Lipsky had in turn promised juicy investments in the metropolis to businessmen and retirees. This was the testimony of Suzette, a 54-year-old restaurateur in the Loir-et-Cher: *"He was introduced to us by our banker. So, although I had some doubts, I gave him 750,000 francs. When I later felt that I had been deceived, I went to see Lipsky in the Var, where he has a sumptuous property. The interview was fruitless and I denounced him."* For Pierrette and Louis, 73 and 77 years old, the script had been identical: *"We have handed over 900,000 francs, the result of the sale of our frozen food business when we retired. We have nothing left,"* they declared, devastated.

It is also worth remembering Jacques Crozemarie, the president of the Association for Cancer Research (ARC). The man appeared regularly on television, in commercials, in order to convince viewers to send him their money. Ordinary people were unaware that hundreds of millions of francs were siphoned off by the swindler to finance his luxurious lifestyle. The scandal had erupted in January 1996. The Court of Auditors' report had revealed that only 26% of the donations received by the ARC actually reached the scientists. 327 million francs (30 million euros) had been embezzled between 1990 and 1995, as revealed by the trial that had been opened in May 1999, i.e. 8,000 euros in cash per week. Jacques Crozemarie had resigned from the management of the association, but continued to claim his innocence, and, sure of himself and his right, he appeared in 1999 before the correctional court, "telling the president *off*", accusing her of "*not doing anything against cancer*", even going so far as to question the competence of the magistrates of the Court of Auditors: "*They can't count*", he would say in front of everyone. With phenomenal brazenness, he had then declared before the television cameras: "*I would be a criminal if I had pocketed something, but look at my representation fees, they are nil! They don't even reimburse me for the restaurant bills!*" Emmanuel Cohen's report, in the program *Secrets d'Actualité* of March 26, 2006, presented him weak, entering with difficulty with his cane in court. But a few hours earlier, photos taken behind his back showed him at a gas station walking without a cane. It was also discovered that his white blouse was nothing more than a disguise of circumstance: the ARC chief had never been a doctor. He had never studied medicine, which did not prevent him from often presenting himself surrounded by eminent scientists, posing in his white coat. With his *honorary* doctorate degree from the University of Tel-Aviv, he had managed to control all the gears of the main association that solicited the generosity of the French and to swindle 3.5 million donors.

The case of the Sentier was more important. The Sentier, in the center of Paris, was the garment district. 5000 manufacturers and wholesalers worked every day alongside their employees, almost all of them clandestine immigrants who were exploited "the old-fashioned way", sometimes fifteen hours a day. They worked at sewing machines or on the street, unloading trucks and loading rolls of fabric. These countless wage slaves from poor countries, who accepted a thankless job in exchange for a miserable salary, made the happiness of the cosmopolitan bosses.

In 1997, Sentier was at the epicenter of a gigantic scam. This consisted of a *"cavalerie"* system: a "bill of exchange" allows the supplier to be paid by his customer immediately instead of three months later. The bank, which pays instead of the customer, simply charges a commission. The customer will pay the contracted debt to the bank within three months. This is a win-win situation for all parties. However, if the customer immediately resells the goods at a profit, he can also be paid by another bank using the same system. Between what he will pay in three months to the first bank, and what the second bank pays him immediately, he generates a profit by reselling the more expensive product. The second customer only has to do the same thing again with a third, and the third with a fourth, etc. And since no one is going to check if the deliveries are real, it is not even necessary that the goods are actually delivered. At the maturity of the bill of exchange, the customer does not pay his debt to the bank, and the bank then turns to the supplier ... who has disappeared and declared bankruptcy. The customer then claims that he cannot pay because the supplier has not delivered the goods, which in fact never existed. This is the "cavalerie"[3].

Between April and June 1997, 2,700 bills of exchange had been issued in the Sentier, a prelude to numerous bankruptcies in a chain. 93 companies had stood up bankers and suppliers to the tune of 540 million francs, *"but if the investigation had covered the 768 companies potentially involved, the billion-franc barrier would have been surpassed."* (*Libération*, February 20, 2001). The companies were set up for this purpose, managed by unemployed individuals recruited for the scam.

To the *"cavalerie"* was added the *"carambouille"*. *Carambouille* is a slightly more primitive procedure that consists of buying goods without paying for them, selling them at a discount and disappearing at the right time. There had also been insurance fraud. Fires had destroyed warehouses in Aubervilliers. Warehouses of fictitious goods had supposedly burned down and the insurers had to pay out 16 million francs. All this made a policeman say: "*I have never seen so many*

---

[3] In this system, a fictitious window dressing is often used to simulate business transactions in the eyes of the bank or other lender in order to pass off the amount of the new loan as profit. Through this façade, the borrower feeds his appearance of respectability and solvency, and with it the lender's confidence, and thus his propensity to obtain new funds from him. The technique lends itself easily to snowballing: the fraudster can use the money to present himself as a solvent client of an accomplice, who in turn will obtain a larger loan, and so on. (NdT).

Rmistas [beneficiaries of the Renta Minima d'Insertion, NDT] circulating in BMWs". When the banks decided to alert the public prosecutor's office in July 1997, it was too late. In November 1997 and March 1998, two spectacular police raids had resulted in 188 arrests. The mastermind of the operation dubbed "leaving the bank planted" was Haïm Weizman, who was in the habit of wandering around the Sentier district dressed in Tsahal fatigues, as a reminder of his rank of sergeant-chief in the Israeli army. His own network had mobilized 23 of the 54 "active" companies around which the swindle was organized. 31 members of his team were indicted, but he had preferred to flee to Israel with other accomplices. The Sentier case had taken eighteen months of judicial investigation. Fifteen people were still on the run, and thirty-three banks had joined the case as civil parties. The trial took place in Paris from February 20, 2001, and lasted about ten weeks, given the magnitude of the proceedings. 124 defendants had taken the stand, all accused of organized fraud. In addition to the prison sentences, the charge of racketeering, which had been retained, required the defendants to jointly and severally reimburse the banks and suppliers. The sum they had to pay was 280 million francs: *"They want us dead"*, lamented Samy Brami after the hearing. *"They want to kill us with the money!"* he finally cried in despair.

On May 10, 2004, the investigating chamber of the Paris court examined the "Sentier II" file, which focused on money laundering networks between France and Israel. 142 persons were charged with money laundering: 138 individuals and four banks. The Sentier II trial began in February 2008 and was scheduled to last until July. The traffic consisted in "endorsing" the checks, that is to say to modify the name of the beneficiary with a simple mention on the back with a bank stamp. Endorsement has been forbidden in France since the 1970s, as it is almost everywhere else in the world except in Israel. The check was given to a "cashier" in exchange for cash (minus commission). The moneychanger would then deposit the check in his Israeli bank and the latter would have the account credited by the French bank. The cash made it possible to defraud the French tax authorities or to pay salaries under the table. The Financial Investigation Brigade (Brif) had meticulously examined all the checks of more than 20,000 francs circulating between France and Israel, and it turned out that the traffic of checks recycled into cash amounted to more than 1 billion francs. The banks could certainly not verify everything, considering the number of checks in circulation—several tens of thousands per day. But the investigators had well-founded suspicions when they found that a bank would agree to transfer a check made out to the order of the Treasury or the URSSAF[4] in favor of a third party with a simple mention in Hebrew on the back. With this system, it was effectively possible to recycle any stolen check, which explained the disappearance of numerous postal sacks in the postal sorting centers of the Post Office. Sometimes, the beneficiaries of the stolen checks were simply called "Mr. Urssaffi" or "Treasury publicity". The hundreds of Sentier checks were collected and then sent to Israel instead of being cashed in French banks. Hasidic Chabad-Lubavitch Jews[5], in traditional dress and unlikely to be searched at the airport, were responsible for crossing the border, suitcases full of checks on the way to Roissy and cash on their return from Israel. Six rabbis of the Chabad-Lubavitch movement and more than twenty association leaders were involved. They supplied the merchants of the Sentier with suitcases of cash.

The false advertising scam, which began in August 2003, consisted in selling advertisements in specialized publications published by police, gendarmes, firemen and finance ministry associations. The fraudsters proposed these advertisements to small businessmen, making them believe that an advertisement in a police magazine or in a Treasury yearbook would help them to avoid a fine or a tax adjustment. The advertising spaces did not exist, but the checks were cashed in Israel. In eighteen months, the fraudsters had amassed a haul of 55 million euros. Wiretaps had made it possible to trace the mastermind of the operation: Samy Souied, who had a business relationship with the head of Hapoalim bank in Israel. After this case—as we shall see—the scam became even bigger, and Samy Souied was once again in the limelight.

In March 2008, another scandal broke out. A gigantic VAT fraud network had been dismantled. Some fifteen individuals were accused of having stolen 100 million euros from the State. A record in France for this type of fraud. After two years of investigation, the mastermind, Avi Rebibo, a 38-year-old French-Israeli, and his gang were charged with organized fraud. Once again, since 2008, this type of fraud has taken on gigantic proportions.

---

[4] In France, the Unions for the Collection of Social Security Contributions and Family Allowances (URSSAF) are private organizations with a public service mission that are part of the "Collection" branch of the general social security system.
[5] On the mystical Jews, in particular the Chabad Lubavitch Chassidim, read *Psychoanalysis of Judaism (and Appendix V)*. (NdT).

Similarly, the "fake transfer" scam, or "chairman's scam", which consisted of phoning the address of a large company's financial department and pretending to be the chairman and demanding a bank transfer, gained considerable importance. The first example of this type of scam occurred in July 2005. With his formidable brazenness, Gilbert Chikli had manipulated an agency manager over the phone, persuading her to hand over 23 million euros in cash in a suitcase. Gilbert Chikli had then retired to Israel, leaving behind many followers and imitators.

All these cases, and some older ones, were described in detail in our 2008 book on the Mafia[6]. We will see below that they are rather small compared to the huge scams that have occurred in France, Europe and the United States since 2008.

---

[6] *The Jewish Mafia*. See also in *The Mirror of Judaism* (2009) and in *History of Antisemitism* (2010).

1. VAT fraud

VAT (value added tax) fraud has been little publicized since the carbon tax (CO_2) fraud scandal broke out in 2009. Billions of euros have been volatilized, or rather—to put it bluntly—stolen from taxpayers' pockets by unscrupulous fraudsters. Although other cases of VAT fraud had already occurred before the big CO_2 scam: especially with cell phones, but also generally with expensive, small, easy-to-carry products: computers, microchips, video games, not to mention gas, electricity or prepaid telephone cards.

The operation of these frauds was very simple. Let's take an example: a company A based in France buys €100,000 of cell phones without VAT from a company B located in Belgium. Company A does not pay VAT in Belgium, as there is no VAT on sales between intra-Community countries. It then sells the products more cheaply to an accomplice company C, also French, which makes a good deal (€90,000, for example, excluding VAT + €18,000 VAT, i.e. €108,000; we take here for example a VAT rate of 20%).

Once VAT has been charged, company A should be loss-making since it has paid €100,000 on the purchase and sold the goods for €108,000 including VAT, from which the €18,000 of local VAT on the sale must be subtracted: i.e. a loss of €10,000. However, if the company does not pay VAT to the French State and disappears, it makes a profit of €8,000. It is what is called a shell company, or "cab", or "defective", or, in Sephardic French, *"petadora de IVA"*. Company C, for its part, is going to invoice the VAT to the final consumer. It has therefore purchased cheaper goods, which has enabled it to lower its cost price and to take advantage of a competitive advantage that allows it to increase its sales and profits.

What is called "VAT carousel" is not very complicated. Let's imagine that company C, instead of reselling the goods to the final consumer, resells them to company B in Belgium—without VAT, since it is an intra-community sale. In this case, the goods return to their point of departure, and are ready to circulate again. This fraud is thus nicknamed "carousel", in reference to the famous revolving merry-go-round of wooden riders. In this case, the State's loss is twofold, since first it does not receive the tax collected by the "defective" company A, and then it loses the same tax from C, since the goods have been exported to a European Union country.

Several shell companies can thus be interleaved between the various players. Company C, for example, instead of reselling the telephones directly to company B in Belgium, can resell them to a company D in Luxembourg, which will in turn resell them to company B. And the cycle starts all over again when company B will resell them for 100,000 euros to French company A. When the scheme is perfectly set up, the goods that have circulated through several Member States return to their point of departure and resume the same circuit. And instead of delivering the expensive and not very bulky goods, it can also be limited to fictitious deliveries.

This intra-Community VAT system was established in 1993 with the Maastricht Treaty, which abolished fiscal borders and therefore also customs controls at the borders within the Union. So, since Maastricht, it is no longer necessary to check whether the content of a truck matches the invoice accompanying it, so why deliver goods when you know that they will return to their point of departure anyway?

In a report published in April 2004, the European Commission seemed concerned about the rise of this fraud, *"worrying for many Member States: it can represent up to 10% of their net VAT revenue."* In France, net VAT revenues reached[7] 127 billion euros in 2006. And for that year 2006, according to a report of the Court of Auditors of March 9, 2012, the fraud rate was estimated at 7%[8]. In 2011, according to a report of the Finance Committee of the National Assembly, VAT fraud as a whole reached 10 billion euros per year, while only a hundred or so customs agents were involved in its surveillance.

The business daily *L'Expansion* had unveiled a huge scam at the beginning of November 2005. Charles-Emmanuel Haquet had titled his article *The impunity of VAT scam professionals*: *"Phantom trucks loaded with cell phones. Dozens of corrupt companies. A gang leader*

---

[7] VAT accounted for 51% of total tax revenues at that time.
[8] This report had been followed by a law (art. 7 bis of the 2012 amending finance law) which aimed to create a VAT self-assessment device for supplies of natural gas, electricity and electronic communications, *"made by a supplier established in France for purposes other than consumption or use by the purchaser subject to VAT in France."*

hiding in Argentina. A haul of 60 million euros... It took a four-year investigation, tracking and wiretapping by the authorities to put an end, last August, to one of the biggest VAT scams of the century." But we have known for decades that records in this area are regularly broken, as we will see below.

"How many such networks operate in France?" wondered Gilles Duteil, a judicial expert in Aix-en-Provence. "In France, no one is aware of the magnitude of the phenomenon. However, it is a serious crime. More important, in total, than the sum of drug trafficking."

In that article it was a question of "Pakistani and Italian mafias". They won't tell us more about it... The crooks "circulated the goods through several European countries". It was mainly "products with high added value and low volume, such as cell phones or electronic components". We were informed that the products often made "several dozen tours, the absolute record being a pallet of ink cartridges seized by the Belgian police after having been sold six hundred times!" For the criminals, the profit is twofold: they steal astronomical sums from member states, while selling the goods at a loss so that they can dispose of them more quickly.

The Directorate General of Taxes, in charge of intra-Community VAT collection since 1993, was very discreet on the subject. All that was known was that its investigators were overwhelmed by the scale of the task. *Every month, we report the appearance of new carousels to our French counterparts,"* declared Yannick Hulot, tax coordinator within the OCS (Belgian cell for the fight against carousels). We never heard about it again. As if they didn't have time to deal with the files".

Vincent Drezet, national secretary of the Snui (National Unified Tax Union), confirmed: *"There are 3.5 million companies subject to VAT in France, and we carry out only 51,000 controls per year. Our means are insufficient."* The tax agents did not have an easy job, as the procedures were cumbersome: *"To carry out a search, the person in charge of the file must provide tangible proof of the fraud, explained Vincent Drezet. He must prove who the accomplices are, what the fraud scheme is and which companies are involved in the traffic... Only then can he send a registered letter to the suspect. Needless to say that the latter has already put his foot in powder a long time ago".*

It was therefore necessary to hurry to catch the criminals in the act. "First of all, *the judicial actors should be fully aware of these fraud schemes. This is rarely the case. Investigations are therefore slowed down,"* lamented Gilles Duteil, founder of a professional master's program at the University of Aix-Marseille entitled "Prevention and Repression of Financial Crime". Gilles Duteil felt that it was necessary to *"create a multidisciplinary platform"* to *"bring together customs, fiscal and judicial competencies."*

In France, the fight against carousels is the exclusive responsibility of the tax authorities. But Belgium, which has set up this type of structure, has succeeded in reducing fraud by 80%. At the end of 2001, the Belgian government had indeed decreed the fight against VAT fraud as a "national priority". A cell had been created. It brought together police and tax experts, and was equipped with a computer program that scanned databases day and night and alerted when a suspicious scheme was detected. *"Where we used to need two years, we have reduced the intervention time to three months."* As a result, the fraudsters ended up settling in neighboring countries.

The Eurocanyon case

In our book on the Mafia (2008), we mentioned that case in March 2008. A gigantic VAT fraud network had been dismantled, and some fifteen people had been charged with having stolen 100 million euros from the State. It was the biggest fraud of its kind ever seen in France. After two years of investigation, the mastermind, Avi Rebibo, a 38-year-old "French-Israeli", and his gang had been charged with organized fraud.

Avi Rebibo managed Eurocanyon, a Luxembourg company specializing in mobile telephony. He bought mobile telephones without VAT in England, and then resold them without profit to front companies (including VAT) which sold the equipment at a price below the market price to some fifty companies which in turn offered the batches of telephones to British suppliers. The money then left the system through a network of transfers between offshore accounts.

Avi Rebibo was particularly accused of having managed the "cab" companies. His lawyer, Sylvain Maier, categorically rejected these accusations. For him, Avi Rebibo had been the victim of his clients who had not declared the VAT. He had never violated the law, but *"since he lived in Israel, the managers of the accused companies had accused him"*, the lawyer declared. Since then, nothing more has been heard of the huge scam. No news in all the major media...

The Rubens Lévy case

In November 2009, the newspaper *Le Télégramme* d'Ille-et-Vilaine reported the opening of a major trial in Rennes. Forty-two defendants from all over France were charged with organized fraud, aiding and abetting, receiving, forgery of documents and use of false documents. The swindle, which had been partially assessed at more than 20 million euros in damages by the French tax authorities, had been reported by a company manager from Nantes. It took eight years of investigation to uncover the fraud.

The mechanism was simple: to make the tax authorities believe that goods were being exported from France to European Union countries in order to collect VAT. The fraudsters made fictitious sales thanks to real or newly created import-export companies, a compliant bank and accomplices in the ports of Le Havre, Dunkirk, Nantes and Brest. The companies issued false invoices in the name of fictitious companies. In total, 1128 invoices were found after several years of investigation and a thousand hearings of those involved.

The defendants were accused of having declared hundreds of millions of francs of false exports to the tax authorities. For four years, alleged suppliers, accomplices of alleged clients, had circulated invoices and transport documents for fictitious transactions which, once submitted to the tax authorities, had enabled them to charge VAT at 20.6%. The losses for the tax authorities, who did not verify the reality of the transactions: 200 million francs on a turnover of 1 billion francs.

The investigation had revealed the particularly ostentatious lifestyle of the main defendants: luxury cars, yachts, jewelry, works of art, palaces; however, the money diverted to tax havens had not been recovered.

The one who had organized the whole scam was called—sorry for the Jewish community, but it was one of their own: Rubens Levy. He was a businessman from Le Havre. *"He acknowledged having participated in the scheme, although he always denied having been the inventor and main beneficiary, his lawyer explained. In fact, during the investigation of the case, he had voluntarily come from Israel, a country from which one cannot be extradited, to give explanations."* After his arrest, *Le Parisien* of June 16, 2000 explained, *"While he acknowledges having recruited complicit companies and having had money transited from his accounts in Switzerland and Portugal, he claims that his role is limited to that of a simple agent or business broker and can barely sketch a description of his sponsors."* Levy, apparently, was a mere intermediary and not a limited partner.

Ten years later, on April 10, 2010, an article by Frederic Berg published in *La Charente Libre*, reported on the previous day's trial, which had taken place after a two-month deliberation. It was apparently *"the most important VAT fraud ever unveiled in France"*, which, in fact, was not the case. The defendants included company bosses, businessmen and retired people. The big fish (or "alma de cántaro"?) was a certain Daniel Berthelot, 65 years old, recently retired auditor, resident in Cognac. He was the former president of the French Judo Federation and above all a man of great influence, a member of Freemasonry, specifically the GLNF (*Grande Loge nationale française*). At the time of the facts, Daniel Berthelot managed three audits, in Argenteuil, Cognac and Guyane. His son Julian, 36 years old, had also been charged. Former departmental delegate of the RPR (former liberal party) youths in Charente, he was the manager of the Euro-consultant company, based in Cognac.

The whole crux of the matter was to find out who knew about the scam. Berthelot father and son swore they knew nothing about it. Julian Berthelot had even stated: *"The companies involved received a commission of 1.5 to 3%. As far as we were concerned, there was no problem. We also had all the invoices for the operations."* The account of an episode played in his favor: two defendants had arranged an appointment with him in London to give him some documents to authenticate some operations, and they had narrated in court the staging: rented office, false plaque on the door, etc. *"I was tricked,"* the young Berthelot had concluded.

His father Daniel Berthelot, who declared himself *"devastated"* by the media coverage of the case, also claimed to be *"unaware of everything"*. He explained having *"fully trusted"* Georges Toledano, the businessman who had introduced him to the system. *"He was looking for companies that generated VAT and that might be interested in charging a commission. He knew a few."* Daniel Berthelot had served only as an intermediary: *"He didn't receive commissions and thought the operations were legal. I was stunned."*

Georges Toledano, 48 years old at the time of the events, and still Sephardic, was the owner of OCV, a travel agency located on Rue Blanche in Paris. This company had long billed an impressive series of trips to Xavier Dugoin, Essone's general counsel. Until the day

Toledano was seized by an irrepressible desire for exoticism: in 2000, he sold his agency to buy an 18 million franc villa in Florida.

Rubens Levy, wanted since June 6, 2000, had decided to turn himself in after a year on the run. He had provided the judge with a heavy dossier full of invoices and photocopies of checks; he explained: *"When the scandal broke out, I was still unaware of its real magnitude. I had to flee to see things in perspective, to gather the files and to understand."* The newspaper *Le Parisien* of June 16 published this dialogue:

—What was your role in this case? —*I was paid by the organizers of this fraud to recruit companies likely to lend their name to these false exports. The money also passed through my companies in Portugal and Switzerland. As of today, justice has stopped at this point and designates me as the main responsible. I will prove that this money went back out without me touching it."*

—You seem rather naive. However, you entered voluntarily into the scam... *"These people used me just as they manipulated many people by stealing their identity photos to forge documents, to open accounts in Belgium or Switzerland. One of my close friends was asked for two photos, supposedly to offer him a PSG season ticket. He never saw his season ticket, but his photo was found on forged documents. The bosses of this racket are capable of anything. During my escape, men posing as policemen arrested me with a rogatory commission in hand. They tortured me and left me for dead. I owe my life to a passer-by who heard my screams and knocked on the door of the garage where I was locked up."*

—But who, in his opinion, are the masterminds of the fraud? And Levy answered: *"I think the case started with a small number of insiders who detected the flaw in the tax system. The world of Freemasonry has contributed to make it known among some businessmen with the capacity to finance the initial investment. A man like Georges Toledano proposed me to enter directly into a network and introduced me to important people, high officials, financial lawyers. There were also real swindlers like Christophe Lebesque, a businessman from Le Havre, whom I showed that I had signed numerous fund transfers with his hand, and Philippe Thomas, a smart guy who managed to go on television on the program "Y'a pas photo" on TF1 to complain about having been the victim of a scam. The last straw! Apart from that braggart, most of the protagonists of the scam have managed to put screens between them and justice."*

—How did they go about recruiting accomplices? *"Either they were real companies that received a commission, or they set up fake companies to organize fictitious exports. There are dozens of them in the files in France, in England, in Germany. They also had accomplices in the transporters and in the customs to get the necessary stamps to the declaration that was sent to the Treasury."*

Although Julian Berthelot was acquitted, Daniel Berthelot was sentenced to twenty-four months' imprisonment with six months suspended, and the seizure of the assets used to commit the offense. The amount he was ordered to repay was not disclosed in detail, but the thirty-eight convicted persons had to pay a total of 28.2 million euros to the State.

Rubens Levy, the main protagonist of the case, who had disrupted Daniel Berthelot's version, was sentenced to six years in prison ... but without a deposit mandate at the hearing.

The other main defendant, Christophe Lebesque, was sentenced to three and a half years in prison, as were six other protagonists[9]. Several of the condemned had expressed their intention to appeal and claim a new trial, and since no provisional execution had been pronounced, the appeal was therefore suspensive. In other words, Rubens Levy was free to return to Israel.

The *Ouest France* newspaper of February 18, 2013 informed us that the sentences had been confirmed on appeal: *"Rubens Levy, 51, the mastermind of the scam, sentenced to six years, has had his sentence confirmed."* But wherever he was, this news must have made him smile.

The great carbon dioxide (CO2) scam

The VAT (Value Added Tax) fraud in the carbon dioxide market (2008–2009) is probably the biggest fraud ever perpetrated, the biggest organized scam of all time; the new "robbery of the century". Despite being hundreds of times more voluminous than the scams that made the news in the 1930s and brought tens of thousands of patriots into the streets, the "CO2 fraud" scandal outraged no one, or very few people. This is due, once again, to the fact that the mainstream media remained

---

[9] There are almost always one or more goyim involved in these cases of swindling that they do not master.

very discreet on this issue. The little information we have, however, allows us to understand why journalists and public authorities kept a low profile.

In France, a robbery with violence, even for a few hundred euros in a supermarket, is punishable by 15 years in prison. On the other hand, a theft of billions of euros from the tax authorities, in the worst case scenario, is punishable by five years in prison. And, in any case, the risks are quite low, since, ultimately, there remains the possibility of fleeing to the State of Israel, which does not extradite its citizens. So it is worth trying your luck.

The principle of the scam

The scam was based on the existence of the new market for "pollution rights or emission rights" established by the "Kyoto protocol", which came into force at the beginning of 2005, but whose impositions were applied as of 2008. The aim of this international agreement was to set up a mechanism to encourage industrialists to reduce their carbon dioxide (CO_2) emissions in order to combat global warming. Each company was allocated a volume of emission allowances free of charge. If a company consumed only a part, it could resell the balance to companies that had exceeded their quota. The most virtuous companies made a profit, while the most polluting ones were penalized. In the European Union, 12,000 industrial sites were subject to this tax, mainly in the electricity, cement, steel and paper sectors.[10]

---

[10] *"The most important development in recent years for raw materials has been the carbon gas quota trading market, one of the instruments put in place under the Kyoto Protocol, which aims to reduce CO_2 emissions. Its principle? Each company is assigned an emission quota. If it exceeds its quota, it is obliged to buy emission credits from another company which, having emitted less than its quota allowed, has a surplus to sell on the market. The market is declined in various ways: spot (day-to-day), forward or by mutual agreement. Most companies go through intermediaries, banks and specialized brokers. It is a normal commodities market that already exists in an embryonic state in Europe and will see the light of day in the United States under the name of cap and trade. The stakes are enormous: according to the Obama Administration, on the other side of the Atlantic alone, $646 billion worth of carbon credits will be put up for auction over the next seven years, a figure that could be two or three times higher. The value of this new carbon exchange could exceed $1 trillion a year."* Marc Roche, *The Bank, how Goldman Sachs runs the world*, Ediciones Deusto, Barcelona, 2011, p. 209.

In France, carbon emission quotas were traded as bonds on the "Bluenext", the main stock exchange for emission allowances, whose main shareholder was an old public financial institution: the *Caisse des Dépôts et Consignations (CDC)*, which managed the emissions registry on behalf of the Ministry of the Environment. In Paris, it was enough to have a company and to present a photocopy of the identity card to be recognized as a broker on Bluenext. The filtering was made on the basis of the commission of opening of the account, about 1500 euros; and the 2500 that also had to be paid for the expenses of management. But the Ministry of the Environment, in agreement with the Ministry of Finance, had decided to subsidize registration, releasing some 450,000 euros to encourage candidates to come and participate in the large carbon market. In a way, the State was encouraging fraudsters to get their hands in the till. In 2009, Bluenext counted 1038 industrial accounts subject to the carbon tax, as well as 240 accounts of classic intermediaries ... including fraudsters. There were French, Chinese, Californian, Hungarian and, curiously, an over-representation of the city of Marseille.

In Denmark, registration in the CO2 registry was even simpler: the Scandinavian carbon market was accessible by simply registering online and sending a photocopy of your ID card by mail. Being listed in a registry made it possible to buy and sell CO2 emission allowances throughout Europe. Many French citizens had thus signed up for the Danish registry, as the VAT rate in that country was the highest in Europe: 25%. This was a real drawback for the VAT professionals, who used false identity documents and e-mails on Yahoo and Gmail. Most of the time, the fake ID cards were not even necessary: the fraudsters usually removed a letter from their first or last name. Hundreds of fraudsters had managed to sign up on the Danish register. The first of these had surnames *"of Sephardic, Arabic or Spanish origin."* Behind these, came *"several surnames of Pakistani or Emirati origin,"* and referring *"to British or Dubai addresses*[11]*."*

With a single computer click, the fraudsters, referenced on the CO2 exchange platform Bluenext, acquired tons of CO2 before taxes in the European Union, and then resold them at a VAT rate of 19.6%. The company disappeared a few months later without a trace, before the tax authorities became aware of the operation.

---

[11] Aline Robert, *Carbone Connexion*, Max Milo, 2012, p. 84.

Indeed, the European administration in Brussels had decided to subject CO_2 quotas to VAT because of their proximity to raw materials such as wheat, oil or nickel, for example. But these raw materials are traded by known industrial players, who do not disappear from one day to the next without leaving an address. It is therefore almost impossible to negotiate deliveries of wheat or oil cargoes without being a well-established and recognized company. Normally, only industrialists or financial institutions have the right to intervene in an organized market. Whether it is a stock, bond, oil, zinc or nickel market, the financial market is reserved for experts. But the carbon market was open to all, because environmentalists had thought of a global appropriation of the market by citizens, and that, in the medium to long term, they would all have "emission rights". Bluenext, the Paris-based CO_2 bond exchange platform, was widely open to all, whereas a stock market requires going through a recognized broker. And once registered on Bluenext, a company did not have to report the profile of its customers, who sold including VAT.

Moreover, with CO_2, deliveries were much simpler than with real raw materials, since CO_2 quotas were immaterial, let's say air. The fraudsters would therefore be able to sell, VAT included, and very quickly, goods bought 20% cheaper a few minutes earlier. And the payment and delivery of the bonds could be made in just fifteen minutes after the transaction, whereas in a traditional market it would take three days.

Thus, at the end of 2007, a Parisian had started to buy, with his French company and from an Internet café, 10,000 tons of CO_2, i.e. some 10,000 vouchers valued at just 4.2 euros each, on a small market place in the Netherlands. The vouchers were then sold to companies that were also registered accomplices and authorized to trade in carbon, in order to erase the trail. On the same day, after four different exchanges, the bonds were sold again by the company Monceau Trade on the Powernext market (which had preceded "Bluenext") at a price of 4.1 euros—a little less, therefore—but with a VAT of 19.6%. The morning investment of 42,000 euros had generated some 49,000 euros in the afternoon. The profit was immediately transferred by the Caisse des Dépôts et Consignations to an account opened for this purpose in Hong Kong. The test had been a resounding success. However, being a sale at a loss, there was a significant risk of being suspected of money laundering. The fraudster then avoided the risks of the Internet café and asked his cousin to place the buy and sell orders from… Jerusalem.

Hundreds of thousands of euros thus transited each day between his various bank accounts.

The scoundrels had then created a company in Luxembourg. Contrary to many European banks that investigate the origin of the funds, the banks of the Luxembourg enclave are less scrupulous; moreover, the constitution of a company under American law is possible. This would be the "Commodity Stock Market[12]". In order to remain anonymous, the fraudsters put a straw man at the head of the company to act as a front. Later, in exchange for a few thousand euros, pizza delivery men, drug addicts, pensioners or relatives of friends would be placed at the head of companies whose addresses referred to post office boxes created by company domiciliation companies[13]. It was not necessary to inspire confidence in the banker to open an account: in case of refusal or refusal of the bank—the swindlers knew this very well—it was enough to ask for a "refusal to open an account" and send it to the Bank of France, which would then designate another bank to execute it. Thus, a certain Moktar, in Marseilles, who hardly spoke a word of French, was able to open a bank account for his new company. The straw man can also be someone in the family, whose good faith cannot easily be doubted: a very young or very old person, a housewife, a distant relative. In France, the straw man is almost never incriminated or charged; and the fraudsters know this perfectly well.

In the fall of 2008, the Caisse des Dépôts had received dozens of requests to open accounts in the carbon market from companies that had nothing to do with the chemical, paper, steel or cement industries. They were newly created brokerages. As in the Danish register, the names of the companies, which were rather sober at the beginning, became more and more fanciful later on. Names such as "Tradewell" (trade well), "Great Luck International", "I Play Ltd", "I Vanish", etc., whose e-mail addresses were also ridiculous, such as "dancoco8@gmail.com", appeared in the register.

---

[12] Cosmopolitan spirits often use English names for their businesses and companies, thus flaunting their globalist convictions.

[13] Companies' domiciliation companies offer very useful services, mainly adapted to companies in the process of incorporation or new creation or to those who have a reduced budget and do not necessarily need commercial premises. They allow them to have an administrative address quickly and cheaply. But that's not all: they also offer many other services, such as: reception, secretarial services, workspace rental, etc. (NdT).

Curiously, the exchanges were mostly one-way: the players sold bonds on Bluenext, but bought very little. French experts then asked themselves: is it possible that French industrialists have received too many quotas in relation to their needs and are therefore reselling them? Obviously, the huge volumes sold were going to cause problems for the cash flow of the small Bluenext company. Since April, the amounts of anticipated VAT had skyrocketed: from 2607 euros in March, the volume had risen to 663,723 euros in April, 50 million euros in August, and 181 million euros in December. 181 million in December. For a company with a turnover of less than 10 million euros, these sums were disproportionate[14]. For each bond sold, the marketplace paid 20% more to the seller-scammer (VAT advance), which then had to pay its own VAT. In the meantime, the State reimbursed Bluenext every quarter. The State was advancing the VAT through Bluenext, so it was not a matter of lost profit (loss of profit) but directly of clear cuts in the budget. Fortunately, the new shareholder covering Bluenext's cash flow was the Caisse des Dépôts—which no bank would ever do.

The network thus formed would eventually number 35 companies, causing several billions of euros to evaporate. The ultimate irony was that the Caisse des Dépôts et Consignations, a 40% shareholder of Bluenext, which also managed the registration of CO_2 quotas for the latter, directly carried out *offshore* transfers of sums of up to six figures to Latvia or Hong Kong. For several months, these huge transactions did not set off alarm bells, precisely because of the venerable financial institution's reputational guarantee. Bluenext, a partnership of about twenty people, had become the State's first debtor in a few weeks.

"At the time, we thought the market had exploded because of the new rules and because some countries like Poland had been slow to put their quotas on the market, explains Serge Harry, former president of Bluenext. In the end, when we noticed recurring volumes by small companies we sounded the alarm[15]*."*

---

[14] Aline Robert, *Carbone Connexion*, Max Milo, 2012, p. 62. Bluenext, which received one cent commission for each ton of CO_2 sold or purchased, had realized a profit of 15 million euros.
[15] *La Provence*, January 4, 2012.

Between October 2008 and June 2009, the State bank had transmitted to Tracfin [16] (the anti-money laundering service) twenty-two "suspicious declarations" concerning 80 companies. The accounts of one of the companies showed several transfers of funds to Montenegro, Cyprus and Georgia. But Tracfin preferred to wait to gather more information and was slow to react. Four months had elapsed between the date of the declaration and the submission of the file to the Paris prosecutor's office on April 29, 2009; four months during which the company in question had carried out most of its fraudulent transactions worth some 200 million euros.

The impunity of the enarcas[17]

The cabinet of Christine Lagarde, then Minister of Economy, had been alerted on January 30, 2009 by a letter from the general manager of the Caisse des Dépôts, Agustin de Romanet, who had detected several anomalies: many brokers were reselling large amounts of CO_2 at a loss—which was logical when the scam was known. With a margin of 19.6%, they could afford to skimp in order to resell faster and put their feet in the powder. But it took several meetings between the Caisse des Dépôts, the cabinet of Eric Woerth, then Minister of the Budget, and that of the Minister of Finance before they reacted. The decision to abolish the tax was taken on May 15, 2009, but it took another three weeks to become effective at the beginning of June. An unfortunate slowness, since between May 15 and June 9, the date of the effective abolition of VAT, 1240 million tons of CO_2 had been exchanged on Bluenext.

In its 2011 annual report, the Court of Auditors pointed directly to the responsibility of the Caisse des Dépôts (CDC). Each account holder on the French carbon register was in fact required to have a bank account

---

[16] Tracfin (acronym for *Traitement du Renseignement et Action contre les Circuits Financiers clandestins*) is a French intelligence service in charge of combating money laundering, terrorist financing and also tax, social and customs fraud. (NdT).

[17] *Enarchs* are the graduates of the prestigious Ecole Nationale d'Administration (ENA). Founded in 1945, it was the school responsible for ensuring the selection and training of senior French state officials. It was dissolved in 2021 and replaced by the National Institute of Public Service. Over the years, the ENA became the focus of criticism, due to its role in the reproduction of elites, bureaucracy and over-centralization of the country. Many came to consider that a large majority of *enarcas*, alumni of the school, control political and economic life in France. (NdT).

with the CDC in order to buy and sell bonds (quotas); and instead of transferring their funds to another French account, the fraudsters took them directly out of the country through the State bank. In any other banking agency, any transfer from one country to another of more than 10,000 euros would have been subject to a customs declaration. But the State bank offered an unsuspected guarantee. It was all the more surprising that the transfers came from micro-companies with personal names, and that the destinations were in countries not subject to CO2 emission limitations. According to the registry regulations, the registered companies were indeed entitled to make money transfers anywhere in the world, but on condition that they had subsidiaries domiciled with a bank account abroad. In the largest French case, prosecuted in Marseille, the company RIDC had a branch in Panama. 380 million had been transferred directly there, several times. Tens of millions of euros had been paid to a company called Atlas Capital, in Montenegro, without any alert being raised...

After the sudden abolition of the tax at the beginning of June 2009, the volumes traded went from 20 million tons of CO2 per day to only two or three million tons. It could therefore be inferred that 90% of the exchanges were due to fraudsters. With an average price of 14.31 euros per ton of CO2 in the period under consideration, the losses for the Treasury exceeded 300 million euros, and this in less than three weeks[18]. In total, between autumn 2008 and September 2009, the fraud had enabled the fraudsters to take 1.8 billion euros out of the French State's pocket.

The journalist Aline Robert, who published a book on the subject entitled *Carbonne Connection*, stated in an interview published in September 2012: *"The public administration was slow to understand. Even the Caisse des Dépôts, which saw astonishing flows of money between April 2008 and June 2009 to tax havens, did not react. It could have blocked the fraudsters' accounts and stopped the money transfers. It did not do so and simply alerted Tracfin (the Ministry of Finance's anti-money laundering agency[19])."* No sanctions were imposed on the public body.

At Bercy (the Parisian headquarters of the Ministry of Finance), the Directorate General of Companies, within the Tax Directorate, did not

---

[18]*La Tribune*.fr, November 26, 2010.
[19]*Les Échos*. fr, September 3, 2012.

even ask about the hundreds of millions of euros that it reimbursed each month to a small emerging market player, Bluenext, which had become in a few months the State's first VAT debtor. Bercy's services had once again shown a certain laziness by waiting several months for the case to be investigated before becoming a civil party.

No director of the services involved had been reprimanded or dismissed, be it from Tracfin's management, from the Tax Directorate or from the cabinets of the Ministers of Budget or Finance. *"Alina Robert wrote that the Ministry of Finance did not see fit to respond to the questions and written requests from the magistrates of the Court of Accounts. The impunity of the State services is such that no official of the ministry assumed responsibility for the case: none was sanctioned in that ministry so prized by the enarcas and which is supposed to host the elite of the Republic*[20]*."*

The prosecutor then reproached Bluenext for not having verified the reliability, no longer of the registered companies, but of its clients. After the negotiations, Bluenext had to pay 31.8 million. The Caisse des Dépôts, for its part, paid its proportional part of the fine, i.e. some 12.8 million euros: ridiculous amounts compared to the State's losses[21].

At the end of 2009, Europol estimated the scale of the fraud at the European Union level at 5 billion euros. The British state, which had been just as badly affected as France by the carbon VAT fraud, was on the lookout for dozens of people in the area from Malta to Pakistan via Dubai. Journalist Alina Robert wrote here that Pakistan played *"the same role as Israel for the French fraudsters, that of a refuge. In the case of Israel, the non-existence of extradition agreements between most countries and Israel makes the fraudsters safe from justice*[22]*."*

In England and Germany, the men who had been arrested were reportedly mostly Pakistanis, but no names had been released. During the trial in 2012, the English judge had ordered the entire proceedings to be held in camera, so that no information had emerged from the interrogations. It simply emerged that three men of "Pakistani" origin had been sentenced to prison terms ranging from 5 to 15 years. In Germany, six straw men had been sentenced in 2011. It is good to know on this point that French fraudsters also used Englishmen of Pakistani

---

[20] Aline Robert, *Carbone Connexion*, Max Milo, 2012, p. 72.
[21] Bluenext closed its doors in December 2012 and laid off its twenty-five employees.
[22] Aline Robert, *Carbone Connexion*, Max Milo, 2012, p. 77.

origin as front men for their companies. In Denmark, where numerous fraudsters had registered, only a few men had been convicted, three years after the fact. In Paris, case instructions were being carried out with the utmost secrecy.

The amount of the bill had subsequently increased: although fraud amounted to more than 2 billion in the United Kingdom, and as much in France, to which the 850 million declared by Germany had to be added, Europol's estimate of 5 billion was therefore far below the reality, explained Aline Robert. Italy, the Netherlands, Belgium and Spain were also heavily affected; Greece, Austria, Hungary and Poland were also affected, but to a lesser extent. According to Marius Christian Frunza, a former employee of the Sagacarbon brokerage firm, the fraud amounted to 10 billion euros.[23]

Police and justice infiltrated

Five judicial investigations had been opened in France. They were distributed among four judges of the financial pole, out of the eleven members it had. Such was the magnitude of the case. Judge Jean-Marie d'Huy had taken over three investigations, while Judge Renaud Van Ruymbeke was in charge of one of the investigations. Judges Aude Buresi and Guillermo Daieff, from the "fight against organized crime" unit, created in 2009 and attached to the financial unit, were in charge of the "Nathanael" case.

The investigators' work had first consisted in locating the swindlers, whose names were nowhere to be found. The name "Frederick[24]", the Parisian swindler, for example, did not appear in the articles of association of his main Luxembourg-based US law firm, for which he had used his uncle. The customs investigators' strategy was to rely on wiretapping and email tracing to identify the IP addresses of the computers used. But the lists of information led them each time to Internet cafes, Starbucks and other MacDonalds, where the fraudsters connected via Wifi. The scammers thus remained perfectly anonymous and the data was untraceable. It was only after several weeks that they were able to find a fixed address ... in Jerusalem. That's where the

---

[23] Aline Robert, *Carbone Connexion*, Max Milo, 2012, p. 205.
[24] In her book, Aline Robert warns the reader at the outset that she has changed the names of the main characters. Their names appear here and there, but the reader has the impression of being confronted with a puzzle. We have had to recast the whole work with information taken from the press.

scammers called the "Smurfette", who was the cousin of the main protagonist, operated. She executed the orders and answered the e-mails. Within minutes of each other, the Smurfette had logged into her Gmail messenger and a Bluenext voucher account belonging to one of her companies. This was the beginning of the trail that would lead to the dismantling of the network. The money had transited through Lithuania, Cyprus, Montenegro and Georgia. These countries were not tax havens and should in theory have cooperated with the justice system of the other countries. But in practice, the international letters rogatory launched by the French judges never came to fruition.

A Versailles policeman also found an important clue thanks to a dubious check. Looking through the accounts of "Fabrice S[25]", he was surprised by the lifestyle of this merchant of the Sentier who drove a luxurious Aston Martin and owned a yacht in Cannes. For a man whose official activity was to sell jeans in the markets, it was a bit exaggerated. It should be noted that Fabrice S. had also specialized in money laundering for "the community". Together with his friend from Lyon, "Sebastian", he owned a luxury car rental company: Hummer, Ferrari, Maserati, Aston Martin, etc, which were rented on the Côte d'Azur. In reality, the rentals were mostly fictitious, and the money that came in cash was dirty money that came out clean in the company's bank accounts. Through a percentage of 3 or 4%, the money was then transferred to the account of the "friends of the Community". It was this friend of Lyon who implicated "Fabrice S." in the carbon scam.

Married, father of two children and very committed to the Jewish community of the suburbs of Paris, Fabrice Sakoun had indeed begun to boast a striking fortune since 2009. His business had taken off too quickly, according to investigators who suspected the man of having enriched himself by participating in the CO2 fraud. Sakoun was then accused of being the administrator of the Nathanael company, a textile company whose accounts showed impressive movements of funds: 263 million, in two months, transferred abroad. Between March and June 2009, he had deprived the Treasury of about 43 million euros. An accomplice of his bought 100,000 euros of bonds in the Netherlands in the morning, before taxes, and resold them on Bluenext, receiving about 20,000 euros which were immediately transferred to the United

---

[25] *The Tribune*. Fr of November 26, 2010 does not disclose the fraudster's last name.

Kingdom, and then to accounts domiciled in China, Macao and Hong Kong, from where they fed the accounts in Israel a few hours later.

On December 8, 2009, a first search took place in Paris, in a luxurious apartment on Avenue d'Iéna, in Paris, which "Frederick" rented for 4,000 euros per month. "Frederick" (according to Aline Robert)—who was actually called "Gregory Z", according to *La Tribune* newspaper—barely had time to lock himself in the bathroom and throw his cell phone SIM card in the toilet, while his partner argued with the customs officers. But the credit cards of some of his companies (CO_2 Limited, Twilight) were still in his wallet. Fortunately, there was only 20,000 euros in cash in the apartment that day. Son of a restaurateur, divorced, father of three children, Gregory Zaoui had started his fraudulent career selling jeans and cell phones. He had become considerably wealthy and had forged some remarkable relationships, since he had had lunch a few days earlier with a manager of the judicial police. So he was not expecting this sudden search, as he was probably counting on being tipped off in time[26]. Gregory Zaoui, who was accused by the justice system of having defrauded nearly 200 million euros, was now behind bars.

The investigation of the case by judge Jean-Marie d'Huy had allowed the customs officers to search the home of one of his associates, "Arthur" (according to Aline Robert), 38 years old, who lived in an ultra-secure apartment in Neuilly-Sur-Seine. Arthur" was actually named Kevin El Ghazouani, a restaurateur in Neuilly and a dealer in luxury car purchase orders.

Three weeks later, the second case moved to a second stage. On January 15, 2010, Fabrice Sakoun ("Raphael", according to Aline Robert) was arrested at his home. He should also have been warned of the bad move, but he had disconnected his phone the night before. In the morning, he barely had time to hide his phone's SIM card in his wife's bra. His friends and accomplices had received the tip-off during the night, and in the absence of evidence, documents or computers found in their homes, they were barely disturbed. As a result of the leaks, the investigation was transferred from the Versailles court to the judicial customs services in Vincennes, under the baton of the Parisian financial brigade.

---

[26] According to Aline Robert, he was the number three of the Parisian judicial police, who was later demoted for obscure reasons. Aline Robert. *Carbone Connexion*, Max Milo, 2012, p. 133, 178.

In the Santé prison in Paris, Gregory Zaoui had been sent to the VIP area, and his stay was probably not difficult to cope with. He was entitled to a visit from a rabbi and to receive kosher food, and, above all, the prison administration had given him a cellmate: Fabrice Sakoun, who had been arrested three weeks after him.

In prison, the rabbi had provided them with cell phones; although, of course, these were bugged by the police and the conversations of the two criminals could be enigmatic: *"Did you talk to the Londoner? He's got to give it a go, otherwise we'll get busted.— Well no, I still didn't get him ... but don't worry, I'll go through the blond, it will work ...— And we also have to tighten up with Belgium... And the spaghetti also[27]."*

The "Blondie", a dark-haired guy with blue eyes in reality, was "Sebastian" (according to Aline Robert), the Lionese. He was in fact a pimp named Esteban Alzraa. From their cell, the two swindlers passed their orders remotely to Belgium and Italy. In 2010, after the abolition of VAT on carbon in France, the Italian market represented the best place to sell VAT included. In the absence of evidence, the investigators did not add these new frauds to the fraudsters' debts, although the wiretaps had been added to the case file.

After a year of cohabitation, the detainees were separated. Sakoun was fortunate enough to conceive a child inside the prison[28]. He was finally released after two months, before the start of his trial in September 2011, due to a strange procedural error: apparently, one of his numerous requests for release had not been examined in due time. The prison administration had apparently not respected the ten-day deadline required to examine his request, which had been rejected belatedly on the eleventh day. Fabrice Sakoun's lawyers had thus obtained his release. It must be said that, in the prison world, this type of delay is extremely rare.

Gregory Zaoui was also released from prison. During his pre-trial detention in December 2009, he had confessed to everything. But later, his lawyers had succeeded in having his statements annulled on the grounds that the suspect did not have a lawyer at the time. Thus, all mentions of his pre-trial custody statements were erased from his file.

---

[27]Aline Robert. *Carbone Connexion*, Max Milo, 2012, p. 158.
[28]The newspaper *Libération* was careful not to mention any names. Let us recall that this "left-wing" newspaper had been in the hands of majority shareholder Edouard de Rothschild since 2005.

The bail initially demanded of him was two million euros; but the rate had been reduced, and he had managed to get out in exchange for 150,000 euros. Little, after all, compared to the 150 million euros stolen from the French public purse (four times more than Sakoun). The investigation of his case was still ongoing in the summer of 2012, due to a series of international letters rogatory whose answers the judge was awaiting. Gregory Zaoui was in judicial custody; but in his apartment on the Champs-Elysées, his life was unbearable. With his new partner, they used to privatize the Christian Dior store, avenue Montaigne, to do their shopping more quietly.

Fabrice Sakoun, absent at the time of the verdict

The first part of the case was tried in Paris in September 2011. The French judiciary had preferred to divide the case into a dozen separate criminal proceedings, thus depriving itself of an overall view that would have made it possible to establish bridges between the various networks. A mass trial with a hundred defendants was thus avoided, which would certainly have been called "Sentier III"[29], *"to avoid the risk of whetting the appetite of anti-Semites, since the vast majority of the protagonists were Jews"*, as the journalist of *Libération* wrote in the January 26, 2012 issue. *"And the cases are very different from one another,"* said the Paris deputy prosecutor in charge of the carbon file, Bruno Nataf[30].

The Nathanael case was the first to be judged in France, even if a dozen of judicial instructions were still in progress in Paris and Marseilles. The side of the case tried in Paris *"consisted of scenes that seemed to come straight out of the movie La Vérité si je mens*[31]*"*, wrote the *Libération* journalist. Like that scene of a young man rushing to the window during a search: *"If the police catch you, you throw all the papers out of the window and deny that they are yours"*.

Seventeen defendants were to appear; but as in the previous Sentier cases, which we examined in detail in our 2008 book on the *Jewish Mafia*, many of the protagonists had taken refuge in Israel where they

---

[29] The Sentier was the traditional Parisian Jewish quarter of the textile trade with a long history of financial scandals. Read about the Sentier I and Sentier II cases in Hervé Ryssen, *The Jewish Mafia* (NdT).
[30] Aline Robert. *Carbone Connexion*, Max Milo, 2012, p. 145.
[31] *La Vérité si je mens* (The *Truth if I lie*) is a movie from the late 1990s about the Jews of the Sentier neighborhood. It was a very popular comedy in France.

enjoyed almost total impunity. Before the XI Criminal Court in Paris, the main defendant, Fabrice Sakoun, had dressed in his navy blue Christian Dior suit. He was accused of "attempted fraud", "money laundering in organized gangs" and "complicity in the extortion of funds"; the justice system suspected him of having stolen 43 million euros from the State coffers.

A little more was then learned about the scammers' modus operandi. The swindlers had quickly smelled the trick. One of Sakoun's accomplices, David Illouz, had explained to investigators that in the morning he bought €200,000 worth of CO_2 emission rights (or bonds) from a company in the Netherlands, which he resold in the afternoon through the company Voltalia, recovering €220,000. *"It's like leaving a Ferrari with the keys in La Courneuve, it wouldn't last an hour there!*[32]*"*, said David Illouz metaphorically.

Cab drivers, clothing salesmen, secretaries who had never carried out a financial transaction had improvised themselves as brokers in CO_2. They had all obtained from the commercial court a Kbis extract[33] stating the characteristics of their companies. Almost everyone had been able to act as a broker in the CO_2 market.

Sakoun's secretary "Nadine", alias "the Smurf", who still pretended to ignore everything about the fraud, was questioned by the prosecutor: *"But still, between 2008 and 2009, you signed thirteen checks of 200,000 euros, thirteen of 150,000 euros and about forty of 100,000 euros"*. Her lawyer, paid by Sakoun, recommended her to maintain that she knew nothing about it.

However, Sakoun was not the inventor of this fraud. *"Sakoun intervened late, in March 2009, a few months before this tax regime was abandoned"*, recalled his lawyer, Martine Malinbaum. As for the amount of his fraud, 43 million, "it *represents only 2.5% of the swindle committed to the detriment of France."*

The defense lawyers had called the Minister of the Budget at the time of the events, Eric Woerth, to testify at the bar. He had not shown up[34],

---

[32]*Libération*, January 26, 2012
[33]The Kbis (or K bis) is an official document proving the legal existence of a commercial enterprise or company in France. The "KBIS extract" consists of an extract from the commercial and companies register (kept by the commercial court registry); it is the only official "identity document" of the company.
[34]Article by Aline Robert, in *La Tribune* of September 28, 2011.

but, surprisingly, one of the witnesses, Gregory Zaoui, caused a sensation by questioning the modalities of the ongoing proceedings. A cellmate of Fabrice Sakoun during his imprisonment in 2010, accused in another VAT fraud case and suspected of having defrauded 150 million euros, he had questioned the judicial procedure by comparing it with the ongoing investigation in Belgium.

The sentence was handed down in mid-January 2012. Sentences ranging from one to five years' unconditional imprisonment and a fine of one million euros were handed down by the Paris Criminal Court against five defendants, who were also required to jointly and severally reimburse the French State for the 43 million euros of VAT stolen from the State. Fabrice Sakoun was sentenced to the highest penalty: five years in prison and a €1 million fine. *"He has completely failed to realize the seriousness of the consequences of his behavior for the economic public order, said the verdict, since far from really assuming his responsibility, he constantly blames it on others, be it the State, the Caisse des Dépôts et Consignations (CDC), the Bluenext and Voltalia companies."* His Aston Martin and luxury yacht were seized, as well as several real estate assets.

But Fabrice Sakoun was absent at the time of the verdict. The swindler, who appeared free, had smelled the harsh sentence that the judges were going to pronounce against him, so between the end of the hearings and the reading of the deliberation he had vanished. He had fled to the refuge, in Israel, where he could quietly sip his Palestinian blood juice at the edge of his swimming pool. Although he had also not refrained from appealing the verdict, what was the point?

Of the 43 million euros of VAT claimed from Fabrice Sakoun and his accomplices, 23 million euros had been traced to Israel, in bank accounts belonging to close relatives and friends: those of his wife, his children and one of his partners. Part of the money (seven million euros) had already been invested in the purchase of a hotel and a beachfront property in Tel-Aviv. Sixteen million were missing, which the tax authorities had tried to repatriate without success. The Hebrew State, generally uncooperative in judicial matters, had agreed to block his bank accounts with his millions ... but not to return them to France. In her book *Carbone Connexion*, Aline Robert was forced to admit: *"By refusing to cooperate in such a clear case, since the money flows have been easily identified, the country seems to want to close the door to any restitution of the funds in the future*[35]." The remaining twenty million were unaccounted for, probably in Dubai.

Fabrice Sakoun's four accomplices were also sentenced: Haroun Cohen to four years in prison and a million euro fine. But he had also fled to Israel, and this conviction was the occasion for him to uncork the champagne. Seven of his buildings in the 19th arrondissement and in the Paris region still had to be seized, but the execution was complex because the buildings were managed by civil real estate companies of which Haroun Cohen was not the sole owner. Everything had been planned.

Elie Balouka was sentenced to 30 months imprisonment (6 suspended) and a fine of 100,000 euros. David Illouz was sentenced to three years' imprisonment and a fine of 100,000 euros and Sid Foudil to one year's imprisonment.

The civil parties, the brokerage Voltalia, the carbon exchange Bluenext and the CDC, which was a shareholder of Bluenext, received one euro for moral prejudice. Sakoun's lawyer, Martine Malinbaum concluded in all seriousness that the penalty had been *"particularly severe, especially the forfeitures*[36]*."*

Lyon police are in good hands

At the end of September 2011, 31 year old Esteban Alzraa, from Lyon, was arrested in his luxurious villa in Cannes. He had been involved in several drug traffics, but he was suspected above all of being involved in CO2 fraud to the tune of 50 million euros. One of his companies, located in rue Créqui, in the center of Lyon, had a surprising activity, to say the least: the production and wholesale trade of electricity.

---

[35] Aline Robert. *Carbone Connexion*, Max Milo, 2012, p. 212. It is obvious that Jews often feel unpunished in France. A customs officer friend assures us that at Roissy airport, the tacit instructions are not to check Israelis very often. On the other hand, the Lebanese must be checked frequently.

[36] In the month of March 2014, we learned (through the free newspaper *20 minutes* of Thursday, March 13, 2014) that about twenty cases of VAT fraud in the carbon market were being prosecuted in France, mainly in Paris and Lyon. This was twice as many as two years earlier. The trial of the Nathanael case was opening at that time before the Paris court of appeal. We went there in person: there was no one there, no journalist, except a real professional: William Molinié, from the free newspaper *20 minutes!*

Evidently, it was only a question of VAT fraud. Justice had finally succeeded in cornering him.

In 2009, Esteban Alzraa moved millions thanks to the carbon tax. He created companies and closed them after a few months of activity. Suddenly, his friends saw him living large. *"Nobody really knew what he was doing. But he made a lot of money and flaunted it,"* acknowledged one of his close friends. *"In fact, he was very generous and didn't hesitate to give nice gifts to his friends."* On the Presqu'île[37], everyone knew him. He drove around town in extraordinary luxury cars: Bentley, Rolls Royce, Aston Martin. *"In Lyon, there aren't fifty guys who can afford that kind of car. We knew right away it was him,"* explained a shopkeeper.

Esteban Alzraa often went to Israel, where several fraudsters counted on him. In addition to a luxury car rental company on the Côte d'Azur, intended for money laundering, he also shared a 23-meter yacht with Fabrice Sakoun. The boat was registered in the name of a Jersey-based company that disguised the names of the shareholders. Esteban Alzraa and Fabrice Sakoun often met at a kosher restaurant in the 17th arrondissement of Paris, Avenue Niel, which they used as a rear base for their trafficking. The drug money passed through there to be laundered. The owner of the restaurant had been detained for a few months, but had reopened the restaurant—she had managed to get out without paying the full bail—just when professional disqualification is usually the first measure taken by judges.

Esteban Azraa did not hide his sudden success, as if he was sure of himself and his impunity. *"He knew that some Jewish swindlers who had taken advantage of the carbon tax were going to take refuge in Israel, where extradition agreements are non-existent for that type of crime, although he did not understand why he stayed in France. Today he may have understood..."*, declared the correspondent of the *Lyon Capitale* newspaper.

This interlocutor alluded to the contacts that the fraudster maintained with the police. Indeed, the IGS (Inspectorate General of Police Services) investigators had wondered why Esteban Alzraa had no criminal record despite having been sentenced to one year of unconditional imprisonment for fraud and tax fraud in June of the same year. During the interrogations, Esteban Azraa had finally confessed to

---

[37] The neighborhood of *the peninsula*, the center of Lyon (NdT).

the policemen that the former number 2 of the Judicial Police (PJ) of Lyon, commissioner Neyret, was a "friend". He was finally prosecuted for corruption and influence peddling and imprisoned in Fresnes prison.

Gilles Benichou, 41 years old and first cousin of Esteban Azraa, was himself prosecuted for corruption and influence peddling on public officials. Michel Saragossa, 49 years old, a former robber converted into the automobile business, was himself being prosecuted for drug trafficking, money laundering and criminal conspiracy. Described as "high-flying swindlers" by police sources, these three—Alzraa, Benichou and Zaragoza—were linked to the Lyon "super cop" Michel Neyret, who was arrested and prosecuted at the same time as them.

In Lyon, Inspector Neyret and Esteban Alzraa had been seen several times together in the bars and nightclubs of the city. The ruffian, who rented a villa of 12,000 euros per month, in the Roquette-sur-Siagne, in the interior of the coast of Cannes, had invited him several times to his house and lent him high-end sports cars. He had also paid for two trips to Morocco for him and his wife. Questioned by the IGS agents, the commissioner had admitted having been invited to the Côte d'Azur and having benefited from a trip to Marrakech. According to him, it was not corruption, but rather *"an open friendship"*, and *"exchange of services"* for *"his professional needs"*. All this in exchange for information contained in the files of the persons under investigation.

Questioned thirteen times during his pre-trial detention, between September 29 and October 3, 2011, commissioner Michel Neyret implicitly admitted most of the facts. The divisional commissioner, knight of the Legion of Honor, key figure of the *"Who's Who* lionés", was suspected of passive corruption, influence peddling, criminal association and drug trafficking. He was tried and imprisoned on October 3 at the Santé prison in Paris, just when he had just been ranked 22nd in *Lyon People* magazine's "Top 100 most influential men", with this comment: *"He is the most mediatic policeman, as he is omnipresent in the fight against crime and also at all the parties."*

Gilles Benichou had *"a good pedigree in the narcotics files"* (parismatch.com). He had been officially recruited as a police informer before being removed from the lists in 2000, due to his "unreliability". He was, in fact, to inform the number 2 of the Lyon PJ about the "Jewish environment". The two individuals had previously known each other: *"I met Gilles through his brother Albert, who is still a source in the service"*, explained commissioner Neyret. Gilles Benichou and Michel Neyret had quickly become friends. They saw each other two or three times a week and called each other almost every day. *"Sometimes we go on vacation together,"* the commissioner indicated. The last time, it was at the end of September, in Essaouira, in Morocco, a week before his arrest. On that occasion, Michel Neyret had accompanied Gilles Benichou *"on a Jewish pilgrimage"*. The policeman, who did not hide the gifts of his "informer", did not care in the least. Indeed, Gilles Benichou had given his wife a gold Cartier watch worth 24,000 euros. *"He gave it to her out of pure friendship, he is a true friend"*, assured Michel Neyret, *"In my opinion, he has been the target of the Tunisian Jewish swindlers' environment, sighs one of his former police colleagues... With the carbon tax swindles, they have incredible sums of money that they have reinvested in drug trafficking by weaving a network with traffickers from Morocco."*

Gilles Benichou was asking more and more of him, so much so that the relationship between the two men had taken an unexpected turn: it was no longer the rogue who was the policeman's informer, but rather the opposite. At the end of 2010, Gilles Benichou had introduced his cousin Esteban Azraa to Michel Neyret. Since then, the requests for information from the national files or from Interpol became more frequent. On at least ten occasions, Michel Neyret had communicated to his friends information about persons under investigation close to Esteban Alzraa. Thus, in March 2011, the commissioner dusted off the file of Albert Benichou to find out if he was under investigation and under what identity. Some time later, he had consulted that of the Chikli brothers[38], known criminals from the Lyon region.

In November 2011, the weekly magazine *Paris Match* informed us that Michel Neyret had negotiated in exchange for retribution the seven Interpol files that he had extracted and delivered to Gilles Benichou. In total, Neyret had taken 108 PJ and 7 Interpol files. In a telephone conversation with Michel Neyrat, Esteban Alzraa had asked the latter to try to inform him why two of his foreign bank accounts had been blocked. He had specified to Neyret that it was an account in Portugal with 7 million euros deposited and a second one in Italy with a sum amounting to 4 million.

Michel Neyret had spared no effort; and in return, his friends were not stingy. In another wiretap, Esteban Azraa told an intermediary that he

---

[38]The Chikli brothers were involved in a swindle in 2005–2006 at the expense of the *Banque Postale*. On this swindle read in *Planetary Hopes*.

would soon be making a transfer from an Indonesian investment fund to five bank accounts, including one in his name. The others were in the names of Gilles Benichou, Daniel Kalfa (his stepbrother), Rudy Sitbon—another defendant in a cocaine trafficking case in Neuilly— and... Nicole Neyret[39].

Esteban Alzraa lent his high-powered vehicles to commissioner Neyret and paid for his trips. Michel Neyret had also received 40,000 euros worth of clothes from Gilles Benichou. Nothing was too good for the "supercop" who had pockets full of cash.

The policeman and his wife Nicole had been invited in April to spend a week at the *Koutoubia Gardens,* a large luxury Riad in the medina of Marrakech. It was there, in a peaceful and elegant atmosphere, that he met Albert Benichou, Gilles' older brother[40]. Fifty years old, Albert Benichou, born in 1961 in Oran, convicted up to fifteen times for swindling cases, was also a major drug trafficker. In November 2008, the Lyon public prosecutor's office had requested three to four years of unconditional imprisonment against him. The man, whose criminal record could fit on eight pages, had swindled the *Banque Postale,* which he estimated to have lost between 2001 and 2002 more than 155,000 euros, and the *Caisse d'Epargne* which, for its part, had suffered a loss of 130,000 euros[41].

In a video available on the Internet, the *Complément d'enquête* journalist, who had gone to the home of Commissioner Neyret's wife, in the Lyon region, stated that the latter, worried about her husband's new relationships, had repeated this statement by the Commissioner: *"Wait a minute! They are making me come in. They say it is very difficult to enter the Jewish mafia."*

The arrest and imprisonment of Commissar Neyret was a very high profile event. But everything was going to return to normal. At the end

---

[39] *Paris Match,* November 11, 2011, article by Delphine Byrka.
[40] *Paris Match,* October 12, 2011.
[41] In February 2002, at a time when his various companies were struggling, Jerôme Kuntz, 40 years old, met Albert Benichou, who suggested to him that he should become a cell phone salesman. Without the necessary funds, Kuntz had asked his brother, a financial advisor at the *Banque Postale,* to write him some bank checks, after which Albert Benichou gave his wife a Mercedes A-Class and his brother a Renault Scenic. Kuntz had then settled in Morocco with his wife Florence Kuntz, MEP and new hope of the political right in Lyon (*Le Progrès de Lyon,* November 15, 2008; *Lyon Mag* of January 6, 2009).

of October 2011, we were informed that a new commissioner had been appointed to the post of interregional director of the Lyon Judicial Police. "The *page has been turned. The Lyon PJ has our full confidence.*" The prefect of the Rhône, the Prosecutor of the Republic in Lyon and the head of the French PJ had guaranteed their full "support" to... Francis Choukroun. The Lyon police was once again in good hands[42].

The "Flacucho": the greatest of them all!

The biggest swindler was a Frenchman based in Tel-Aviv, a certain Alex Khann. In the world of VAT fraudsters, Alex Khann had become a legend, despite his unflattering nickname: "the skinny one".

Alex Khann was no rookie. In France, where he was still known as Cyril Astruc, he had appeared in June 2009 with his accomplice Michel Bensoussan before the correctional court of Toulouse for a cell phone VAT fraud. He was sentenced to three years in prison ... on probation, despite the fact that this fraud had cost the French Treasury 15 million euros. Who knows why...

He had then continued his activities from Belgium. The "VAT carousel" attributed to him by the Belgian courts had been operating at full capacity between September 16, 2009 and November 28, 2009, i.e. a little less than three months. He had not exceeded the quarter of activity in order to avoid the administrative control of the quarterly VAT non-declaration. The name he had given to his company was *"Groupe Energie One"* (GEO); with his straw man at the head. In fact, it was nothing more than a post office box on Rue de la Presse in Brussels— an address that housed many more companies, two blocks from the Parliament. GEO had bought €350 million of CO_2 bonds from Bluenext. As this was an intra-EU transaction, GEO had not had to pay the 21% VAT. The company had sold them, including VAT, to a company, IRM, which, in turn, had sought buyers at bargain prices. Electrabel quickly became suspicious of these low prices and severed its ties with IRM. At Fortis Bank, however, the alarm bells were only

---

[42]Commissioner Neyret was released in May 2012, after a little less than eight months of provisional detention in the Santé prison in Paris. He was dismissed from the police force in September 2012 by Socialist Interior Minister Manuel Valls. In 2014, the Neyret case was still under investigation in Paris. In June 2014, Esteban Azraa and his cousin Gilles Benichou were sentenced respectively by the Lyon court to thirty months and four months of unconditional imprisonment.

sounded after a dozen or so transactions worth around 400 million euros had taken place. When Fortis finally alerted the courts, it was too late, and 72 million VAT owed to the tax authorities had vanished in less than three months[43].

"El Flacucho? In the carbon business, he's the biggest of them all!" joked one expert. Alex Khann, who boasted of having earned more than 1 billion euros with this fraud, had in fact organized a big party in Israel to celebrate his success. In his Tel-Aviv discotheque, in front of the beach, champagne was flowing and Ukrainian prostitutes were wagging on every corner[44]. He also had yachts in Marbella, Spain, a helicopter, private planes and bodyguards armed to the teeth. He was very irascible, judging by this altercation without serious consequences: while driving his Ferrari in the company of an undesirable person, a passer-by had the misfortune to take a photo of the car. Alex Khann got out of the car to give him a copious beating, subsequently ending up in prison and under house arrest.

Its fashionable discotheque also served as a hideout for some Jewish mafiosi from the Russian community. The place was especially frequented by the former oligarch Michael Tchernoï, who had made a name for himself in the aluminum war in Russia, after the collapse of the Soviet system. Tchernoï had been the commander of many assassinations, before having to flee when Russian President Vladimir Putin began the great cleansing. This very rich mafioso intended to gather all Putin's opponents. In Russia, he was a democrat, a supporter of an "open Russia", tolerant and multicultural. But in Israel, in his country, he was the opposite: he was close to the "extreme right-wing" foreign minister, Avigdor Liberman. This mafioso was actively wanted by the Russian justice system, by the US FBI, and was the subject of an international arrest warrant issued by Interpol in a money laundering case in Spain. The Brussels examining magistrate, Michel Claise, had in turn issued an international arrest warrant for him, but the State of Israel refused to extradite him[45].

---

[43] *Lalibre.be*, January 21, 2013.
[44] Thousands of young Russian, Ukrainian and Moldovan women were literally kidnapped in the 1990s, after the collapse of the Soviet empire, after answering small fake job ads promising well-paid employment in Israel. On this sensitive subject, read our long chapter on the "White slave trade" in *The Jewish Mafia*.
[45] *Le Parisien*, November 18, 2011. About Tchernoï, *The Jewish Mafia*.

Alex Khann had been interviewed in November 2008 by *Global Vision*, an advertising supplement of *Forbes* magazine. He affirmed his commitment against the capitalist system and hedge funds. He explained to the African journalist, *"having always donated money to charitable organizations to help the third world"*, and *"having always wanted to do something with his own hands"* to help the underprivileged[46].

In that interview, conducted in his luxurious villa in Tel-Aviv, he expressed his admiration for Bob Marley, after discovering his music *"that filled the air with promise"*. He also explained his respect for Nelson Mandela, whom he would like to meet in order to present a check for his foundation. *"When I was a child, I used to share my toys with other children. In France, where I grew up, society is very mixed, and, for some reason, I always felt close to black children, wanting especially to share my toys with them."* He also insisted on the hope of the election of a black president—Barack Obama—in the United States. He told finally that he had returned to Israel because he was Jewish and because he wanted to raise his children in his environment and his religion[47].

The *Libre Belgique* journalist mischievously added: *"It is not clear, however, that this 39-year-old man, who has availed himself of the "Law of Return" to acquire Israeli nationality and change his surname, has landed in the Promised Land solely for religious reasons. There could be some judicial motives."*

On January 10, 2014, Cyril Astruc, alias Alex Khann, forty years old, curiously arrived at Roissy airport. He was immediately apprehended, charged and imprisoned. This arrest took place a little more than two months after the trip of French investigators in Israel. On that occasion, two operations had been carried out (from September 9 to October 4, and from October 20 to 29) by the Israeli customs and police, who had carried out about forty interrogations and about fifteen searches, especially in Herzliya Pituach, the opulent diplomatic district north of Tel-Aviv where many "Franco-Israelis" lived. But this did not explain the reason for Cyril Astruc's arrival at Roissy airport, since he knew that he would be arrested in case of control. It had to be understood that the situation in Israel was not as calm as he had thought. The day before,

---

[46]Aline Robert, Carbonne Connexion, Max Milo, 2012, p. 91.
[47]*Lalibre.de,* January 21, 2013.

on February 9, 2014, the explosion of a car bomb in Tel-Aviv had cost the life of his driver. It was the tenth such murder in Israel in just over three months, and each time, a link had been established with one of the country's great mafia families, the Alperon, Domrani, Abergil, Abutbul, and above all Amir Mulner, whose reputation as number one in organized crime was well established. Now, this Amir Mulner was closely related to Cyril Astruc. *"It is not impossible that Astruc thought that the atmosphere had become unhealthy, and that he would be safer in a French jail than in Israel, noted a French policeman to explain the surprising decision of the person concerned to travel to France[48]."*

Small settling of scores among friends

The "robbery of the century" was the headline on the front page of the newspaper *Libération* on June 1, 2013. The great carbon tax fraud was once again at the forefront of the legal scene with the trial of Michel Keslassy, 49, which opened at the Paris correctional court. The man was charged with "organized fraud and money laundering". With his company Ellease, he had stolen no less than 65 million euros of VAT. But the scams of his company Ellease were only one link in the chain. Other aspects of the case were under investigation, so that, due to its numerous ramifications, the case actually involved 283 million euros, or even more.

Michel Keslassy had been arrested in Belgium in April 2012. He claimed to have been duped by a man he had met in 2008 at Paris Charles-De-Gaulle airport (no pun intended), whom he presented as one of the main instigators of the scam. In short, according to him, he was nothing more than a straw man who had been duped. The mastermind was a certain Samy Souied, who was not unknown, as he had already appeared in another police investigation into the CO2 scam, among others. Samy Souied allegedly promised Keslassy a small percentage of his own profit in exchange for some facilities granted by the Ellease company.

Michel Keslassy was not alone in court. At his side was a young woman, 28 years old, to whom he had entrusted the management of his company since he was forbidden to manage companies in France. He had offered her financial assistance and shares in the company in exchange for

---

[48] *Le Monde*, February 11, 2014.

secretarial services. When the young woman burst into tears, Keslassy angrily declared, "*She has nothing to do with all this and should not be here.*" However, the company was indeed registered in her name. Moreover, she had agreed to travel abroad twice, to Cyprus and Hong Kong, to open bank accounts for Ellease.

Michel Keslassy was sentenced to three and a half years in prison and ordered to pay damages of 65.5 million euros to the state. His young accomplice was simply released. In November 2013, due to health problems, the swindler was released under electronic bracelet surveillance. However, after a few days, the device had *"stopped working"*. The Paris prosecutor's office had then issued an arrest warrant, but wherever he was the thing was no longer of much importance, as in mid-February 2014 his trial took place in his absence. *"According to sources contacted by 20 Minutes, he is currently in Israel."* This was truly surprising information! *"He says he feels threatened,"* reported a person close to the case. From Israel, he had written to the judges through the consulate. *"Other individuals, with the same degree of involvement, have never been apprehended or troubled by this court proceeding. It is very unfortunate"*, commented his lawyer Philippe Ohayon[49].

Samy Souied personified this Jewish environment quite well, 45 years old, father of four children, he had been involved in judicial investigations for more than 20 years: fraud and aggravated fraud, falsification of documents, money laundering. He had already been indicted for a major fraud involving false advertisements. With the help of the president of the police retirees' association, in the early 2000s, he had sold advertising space to large companies such as Peugeot, Renault and Casino in exchange for false promises of impunity for fines. The financial damage had been estimated at 50 million euros over two years. Evidently, no advertising had been published in the specialized police magazines. The money flowed to Israel through the Paris office of the Israeli bank Hapoalim, otherwise suspected of involvement in a massive money laundering network. The fraudsters had extorted money from the Chinese community by threatening them with an imminent hygiene inspection. Some of the money was laundered in horse racing. Samy Souied was later implicated in a money laundering case related

---

[49] Article by William Molinié in the newspaper *20 Minutes* on Thursday, March 13, 2014.

to the horse racing world[50]. He had long flirted with the wonderful VAT scam, first in the cell phone sector, before discovering the miraculous world of the carbon market.

Samy Souied was murdered on September 14, 2010. The scene took place at Porte Maillot in Paris at 8:30 pm. That evening, Souied had a date with a friend in front of the Palais de congrès, a common place for dates. Two men had approached him in a white scooter, one of them brandishing a gun with a silencer. Five 7.65 mm caliber casings were found on the ground. Hit in the chest and collarbone, Sammy Souied had managed to take refuge between two cars, while the motorcyclists fled in the direction of the Defense. The assassins, who had fulfilled the contract, had not taken the money that the victim was carrying: about 300,000 euros in cash. Undoubtedly, they were well informed, as Samy Souied had just arrived from Israel and was due to return the same night. Michel Keslassy did not take many risks by blaming his crimes on a dead man.

The CO2 scam was so lucrative that the sharing of the profits had ended in a bloodbath. The last man to have spoken to Samy Souied was a former son-in-law of one Claude Dray. This individual was a very wealthy 76-year-old businessman who had made a fortune in hospitality and real estate. The billionaire owned luxury hotels in Saint-Tropez, Jerusalem and Miami, and amassed works of art in his 1,000-square-meter mansion located in villa de Madrid, in the chic neighborhood of Neuilly-sur-Seine. The man had a reputation for being intractable in business, although he had never come to the attention of the police.

However, Claude Dray was found dead in his room. He had been killed on the night of October 24–25, 2011, with three 7.65 mm bullets in his neck. Apparently, nothing could connect Claude Dray to the account adjustments stemming from the carbon scam. But his murder raised many questions, as the safe full of jewelry had not been broken into, nothing had been stolen and there was no evidence of a break-in.

The victims were not all of Sephardic Jewish origin. There were also some "peripheral deaths". Amar Azzoug, for example, nicknamed "Amar blue eyes", was a criminal of Maghrebi origin. He had been

---

[50] About Samy Souied and the racetracks: *The Jewish Mafia* (2008).

liquidated on April 30, 2010 in Saint-Mandé, another upscale suburb of Paris where the Jewish community was very present. The ambush took place on Avenue Alphand. After entering the bar-restaurant *"Au Bois doré"*, two individuals wearing balaclavas pounced on him and shot "Loving Blue Eyes". Before becoming interested in the millions of CO2, Amar Azzoug was known to the police as a former robber and cocaine dealer in the exclusive districts of the capital, especially in the vicinity of the Champs Elysées. He lived in a luxurious apartment, frequented fashionable nightclubs and drove around in a Porsche cabriolet. Before his death, he had recorded several death threats against him in the registry of the Vincennes police station by a certain... Samy Souied[51].

On the trail of CO2

Yannick Dacheville was not yet dead in 2014. But he was actively wanted by the police in the case of 110 kilos of Colombian cocaine seized in an apartment in Neuilly-Sur-Seine in November 2010. *"A profile of a swindler who invested his dough in cocaine trafficking, noted a police source."* Around 10 p.m., a dozen policemen had brutally raided the second floor of a luxurious residence, in the empty apartment of a Saudi princess, where they found cocaine and hundreds of thousands of euros in cash. Other searches were executed, but the main traffickers had managed to escape from the police. And if they did, it was because they had been tipped off. The General Inspectorate of the police services immediately took action. After investigating Yannick Dacheville, nicknamed "the Fat Man" because of the roundness of his face, the Parisian policemen had revealed his links with Gilles Benichou and Esteban Alzraa. In addition, and thanks to the wiretaps applied in this case, the policemen had in turn been able to verify the links of commissioner Neyret with the Sephardic underworld[52].

In 2011, agents learned that Yannick Dacheville had commissioned one of his friends to recover $300,000 from a poker player in Las Vegas. The money had been deposited in a Los Angeles bank. His mother, Rosaria, and her friend, Alejandra, had gone to pick up the loot, but the two women were arrested by the FBI and the money confiscated. According to the latest information, Yannick Dacheville spent his life

---

[51] Article by William Molinié in the newspaper *20 Minutes* on Thursday, March 13, 2014.
[52] *Parid Match*, November 11, 2011; article by Delphine Byrka.

between Miami, Israel, Panama and the Arab Emirates, where he had invested in real estate.

In August 2012, an important figure of the Sephardic "environment" was arrested in Barcelona. It was a certain "Manu" Dahan, suspected of "attempted extortion of funds and kidnapping". The Spanish police officers had acted on information from the French Judicial Police who knew that Manuel Dahan, a refugee in Israel, was going to arrive at Barcelona airport. The man had been arrested in the framework of a procedure against organized crime involving an individual named Karim Maloum, imprisoned in Paris since July. Maloum and Dahan were described as *"old horses back in the saddle"* according to a source close to the case, as they were both in their sixties. They had become known in the 1990s during the robberies of cash-in-transit vans. Already at that time they had fled to Spain, their base of retreat, *"like numerous bandits of the same ilk*[53]*."* But Manuel Dahan was also the target of several police services, who saw his shadow looming in many cases of extortion, account adjustments, and carbon tax frauds. Dahan was extradited, but no other information about him came to light.

We could also look into money laundering cases. In September 2008, we were informed that the Belgian justice system had uncovered a major money laundering network. This shadow banking network, which had been operating for eight years, was a sort of underground bank for various criminal organizations. Hundreds of "clients"—fraudsters, traders, tax evaders and mafia dons—used it.

A man carrying a large sum of cash had been arrested a few months earlier at Brussels airport. The investigation had shed light on the modus operandi of a transnational organization led by a "Belgian" businessman, a certain Daniel Zalcberg, who divided his activities between Brussels, France and Israel[54]. Daniel Zalcberg had helped hundreds of people to launder their money by circumventing the control of banks, thanks to a traffic of false invoices and in exchange for a 3% commission on all transactions. The organization had extended its activity as far as China. The examining magistrate and his investigators had gone to the region of Wenzhou, an important textile center where Daniel Zalcberg paid local manufacturers with the money of his

---

[53]*Le Monde*, August 29, 2012
[54]*Le Monde*, September 16, 2008

European customers. On that occasion, the Chinese authorities had collaborated with the Belgian justice—which was the first time—allowing the seizure of 80 million euros.

In addition to Daniel Zalcberg, Belgian police officers had arrested Sissel Vielfreund, 61, a Tel Aviv resident, but the investigation also targeted six other suspects. Zalcberg and Vielfreund, who had confessed to the crimes, had nevertheless been released on "parole"!

A Belgian journalist, Gilbert Dupont, had tried to interview Zalcberg, who was living in Brussels at the time, in the "Millionaires' boulevard"—a private road located in front of the forest of La Cambre. But Daniel Zalcberg had left Brussels to settle in Paris, at 34 Avenue des Champs-Elysées. This is what the journalist wrote: *"Bruno is the concierge at 34 Champs Elysées: he explains that the building is actually used exclusively for offices and post office boxes for 800 or 900 customers. A building in which nobody lives. Now, Bruno has been the janitor of the building for twenty years, and the name and surname of M. Zalcberg, born on July 31, 1948, does not evoke any memories for him*[55]*."*

Since then, no information has been available about the aforementioned. If Daniel Zalcber fled from justice, where do you think he took refuge?

In Marseille, the most important case being prosecuted by French judges concerned 400 million euros stolen. The newspaper *La Provence*, dated January 4, 2012, had published an unbeatable article on the subject: *"At the forefront of the swindle are several Marseillaise families, brothers and sisters currently settled in Israel."*

These families had taken refuge in the "law of return", voted by the Knesset in 1950 (the Israeli parliament), which guaranteed to any Jew the right to emigrate to Israel and to be safe from extradition. The swindlers had settled in Herliya, a distinguished seaside resort near Tel-Aviv, more precisely in the Pituach district, considered to be the equivalent of the Parisian "Neuilly". They led, since then, a happy life, with yachts, helicopter rides, 20 million sekele (5 million dollars) villas, trips to Florida in private planes, etc. One insider enthused, *"Better than a robbery, it was like robbing a bank whose safe remains open, visit after visit, for months."*

---

[55]*Dh.be*, October 3, 2008

But the "Marseillaise" refugees in Israel experienced some unpleasantness with the local mafiosi who coveted their booty; particularly the powerful "Russian" mafia installed in the country who tried to extort money from them[56]. In Herzliya, one could see former military men who had been recruited as bodyguards and who accompanied their children to school. Suddenly, the small Marseillaise community became more discreet; in fact, it is impossible to gather more information about the protagonists of this case.

In the leftist weekly *Marianne* of January 15, 2011, one could read these lines, under the pen of Frédéric Plotin: *"For a few months now, Jewish gangsterism has been going through turbulent times again. Kidnappings, settling of scores, threats, suitcases full of bills bound for Israel… It seems that we have returned to the splendorous days of the epic of the Zemmour brothers, those black feet originally from Sétif who were in the limelight of the Parisian underworld in the 1970s*[57]*."*

How to silence anti-Semitism?

The article in the Marseille daily *La Provence* of January 4, 2012 had raised blisters. The Jewish community, which alone produces all the super-scammers, had felt attacked. The front page headline read: *"These Marseillaise, kings of the VAT scam. Hundreds of millions of euros evaded on the market for emission allowance bonds. The suspects have taken refuge in Israel."* Which was fully justified in this case.

After the publication of this article, Michèle Teboul, president of the CRIF[58] Marseille-Provence (Representative Council of the Jewish Institutions of France), had written to the newspaper a letter to the editor where one could read these lines written in a rather strange tone. We reproduce the text in its entirety:

"Let's be clear, while we deplore and strongly condemn criminal and inexcusable behaviors, on the other hand, we can only be hurt by the prejudices and expressions that emerge throughout this article,

---

[56] The *Tribune* article was by "Fred Guilledoux", who probably knew that it was frowned upon to mention the "Jewish mafia". In the *L'Express* magazine of October 4, 2013, all reference to the state of Israel and the Jewishness of the protagonists had disappeared.
[57] On the Zemmour brothers, read *The Jewish Mafia*, 2008.
[58] The CRIF is the powerful pro-Israel lobby of the French Jewish community. It is the official French affiliate of the World Jewish Congress (WJC)—the global umbrella organization of Jewish communities—and of the European Jewish Congress (EJC).

bordering on slippage and excess. The VAT scam "Jewish specialty": what environment is referred to here [sic]? Is it environment in the sense of mafia or in the sense of ethno-religious group? The ambiguity of this phrase draws our attention because of the stigmatization it may entail. The author of this article goes back to the times of the Zemmour brothers, to the Sentier case! Is Jewish delinquency so rare and scarce that it is necessary to bring up the old days of crime? Or are we proceeding [sic] here to establish a kind of affiliation or, worse still, to point to an organization that is inscribed in time with its counterpart of ramifications, of conspiracies? Sinister evocation, to gather [sic] some criminals and present them as a "small community". Words have a meaning and can have projective effects that we reject. Of course, the facts are the facts, but the whole of the Marseillaise and French Jews should not be confused with individuals who will be brought to justice. The men and women who make up our community, like all others, are workers, employees, retirees, the unemployed and the whole range of the French social fabric, even its deviations! Human, so human !!!" Readers of our book *The Mirror of Judaism* know that it should be read here, *"Jewish, so Jewish !"*

Philippe Minard, the editor of the newspaper, wrote the following reply: *"I read your text very carefully after our article on the VAT scam. Of course, words have a meaning, and we would never think of singling out this or that part of the Marseille community for public vindictiveness. The newspaper's editorial staff is particularly attentive and sensitive to the life of all communities in general, yours in particular. In reporting this unusual event, we have not mixed up your entire community with these professional criminals. We have mentioned the "Jewish environment" as we would have mentioned the "Corsican environment", the "Parisian environment", the "Russian environment". The milieu, as the dictionary specifies, is a group of people outside the law, who make their living from illicit trafficking*[59]. *In fact, there are*

---

[59] This meaning of the word *"milieu"* in French corresponds rather to the meaning of "hampa" in Spanish. But the word *"milieu"* in French, although it connotes the mafia, has a softer and more euphemistic character than writing directly mafia or hampa. We use the word *milieu* to translate the word *milieu*, and not *hampa*, which would not fit the sense of the protagonists' discussion. Neither does the word *medio*, which would be the literal translation of *milieu* but is not as pertinent as *ambiente*. The RAE provides this definition for *environment*: "Set of physical, social, economic, etc., conditions or circumstances of a place, a community or an epoch; Group or social circle in which someone develops or lives". (NdT).

such environments in all communities, with some specialties, of course. I would add that the journalist who wrote this article has always been a fervent defender of civic rights and freedom, and your Council has been able to verify this on many occasions. Your text cannot, in my opinion, constitute an answer, in the sense that the fact denounced has not been proven. It could be a precision after the use of a word that we have interpreted differently. But I fear that this precision would draw unfavorable attention to a problem not perceived by the community as a whole."

On Friday, January 6, 2012, CRIF President Richard Pasquier and Michèle Teboul sent the following email to Phileppe Minard[60]. At first, the Jews act indignant; the article apparently shocked them terribly. Then they went on to accuse: "You incite to murder," they said in essence. Then they warned the culprit, telling him between the lines that his words, described as "anti-Semitic", could be the subject of a complaint and a trial that could cost him dearly. Finally, he is made to understand that a public apology, preferably on his knees, could make everything right. Listen to this:

"Your response to the text sent to you by the President of the CRIF-Provence has left us perplexed. It was not only in Marseilles that the offensive article, by the terms used, the ambiguities and the insinuations it conveyed, deeply shocked the Jewish "milieu". Your dictionary search for the meaning of this word was very partial: are we to suppose, when we read the expression "in the medical milieu" [guild, NDT], that we are referring only to doctors "living outside the law"? And when he writes in La Provence: "in political circles..." [circles, NDT], are we to conclude that he is referring only to the politicians under investigation?

Obviously, no. You are referring then to elements representative of a whole group of individuals. So, when you read the expression "Jewish environment", it is the entire Jewish community that feels finger-pointed and stigmatized.

But this is not all. You write that evoking the Jewish environment is like evoking the Corsican environment, the Parisian environment or the Russian environment. Can you tell us how many Corsicans, Parisians

---

[60] The CRIF organizes every year in France a big dinner to which all ministers and political personalities, both right and left, are tacitly obliged to attend.

or Russians have been assaulted, persecuted or even killed in the past because of such accusations?

Accusations of criminal behavior against Jews have repeatedly led to pogroms and murders. Not so long ago, even in our country, newspapers were eager to describe "Jewish criminality". We are certainly no longer in that era, but the time has not yet come when jokes about Jews will have the same supposedly folkloric charm as jokes about Corsicans or Belgians.

If you had thought twice before writing, for example, that such and such violence against women is characteristic of the "Muslim environment", you would have been a thousand times right to refrain from doing so. Because any stigmatization of a group based on the criminal actions of some of its members is a call to hatred. As far as Jews are concerned, this is called anti-Semitism.

Sartre wrote that when one is robbed by a furrier who happens to be Jewish and one protests by saying that all Jews are thieves, when one could just as well have said that all furriers are thieves, one thus opts for anti-Semitism. Your article, by incriminating the "Jewish environment", has taken that direction. Perhaps you have done so unintentionally, but then you would deserve at least an apology. Unfortunately, we have not found it in your response. Perhaps it is not too late."

The message was very clear: it is strictly forbidden to denounce the actions of the Jewish mafia. And this message has been perfectly received for a long time by all the "journalists" of the press, radio and television. In such a way that the biggest financial swindle ever unveiled in Europe has been concealed from the great majority of the population. We are a long way from the time when a swindle like Stavisky's had provoked thousands of patriots to take to the streets of Paris[61].

Readers of our previous books know that if Jews are always innocent, it is because they practice accusatory inversion when it comes to dealing with a "painful" subject. In March 2013, for example, the Canal+ channel program, *Special Investigation* had programmed a documentary by Gad Charbit and Jean-Louis Perez entitled *CO2, the*

---

[61] Read the summary of the Stavinsky case in *The Jewish Mafia* (2008).

heist of the century (a typical example of this fraud). Listen to an excerpt from it:

"Paris. We have an appointment with a man who has participated in the heist of the century. It took us months to convince him to testify anonymously. We'll call him 'Christopher'." They could have perfectly well attributed a Jewish name to him, since the *jewrnalist*[62] specified that he *"had made his first steps here, in the Sentier district."* But in the name "Christopher", there is "Christ", which could suggest that the swindlers were good Catholics: an obvious accusatory inversion.

This documentary showed us how in Denmark a journalist *"had taken an interest in swindlers all over Europe. He mapped out all the companies involved in swindling. They were everywhere; essentially in Germany, in the Benelux, but above all in England. They were mainly in the hands of the Pakistani mafia. According to a judicial source in London, the CO_2 scam would have made it possible to finance Islamist terrorist groups."* Another accusatory inversion!

That is why Jews are always innocent: *"they are falsely accused by anti-Semites, who blame their problems on a scapegoat whom they accuse of all evils past and present."* We know the refrain!

---

[62]The author writes the pun *"Jew-rnalist"* for *"Journaliste"*. (NdT)

2. Advertising fraud

In this type of scam, the scammers contact small and medium-sized traders and craftsmen to convince them to sign a contract to publish advertisements in supposedly regional magazines or professional yearbooks. The victims think they are dealing with a serious company and pay the requested amounts. Later on, the fraudsters demand increasingly large sums.

The 800 victims of fake gendarmes

In February 2014, we learned that some scoundrels had pretended to be gendarmes to defraud 800 companies in the Tours region. The case had been highly publicized in October 2013 when the facts were revealed by the newspaper *Le Parisien*: a fake gendarme had sold false advertisements in the name of the Association Gendarmes et Citoyens (AG & C), which in fact really exists, and which is chaired by the former commander residing in Vendômois, Christophe Contini.

On October 9, 2013, the 57-year-old swindler had been arrested along with two accomplices by police officers of the Brigade for the Repression of Astonishing Crime (BRDA). *"Residing most of the time in Israel, the accused posed as a gendarme and sounded out numerous companies to sell them advertisements in the association's monthly magazine*[63]*."* He and his accomplices claimed to work for a "Central Agency for Administrative and Social Publications," specializing in the sale of advertising space. The investigation made it possible to draw up a list of 800 companies swindled for total losses of 1.5 million euros.

A restaurateur from Tours, Xavier Aubrun, recounted his case: *"In 2012, I wrote a check for 358.80 euros for a publication in a monthly magazine in favor of the orphans of the national gendarmerie. They played me well. What are we going to do... I didn't give it any more importance..."* But the restaurateur had decided to tell more details of the scam, because, according to him, other rogues had taken over. *"I*

---

[63]*La Nouvelle République*, February 20, 2014.

received a dozen calls during the last few weeks from supposed lawyers claiming 3600 euros for a dozen unpaid ads. But when I asked them for further explanations they hung up the phone... They called with hidden numbers. They threatened to send a bailiff to seize me. I guess they call people who didn't report after the first scam. I'm sure that kind of pressure works from time to time. I hope my testimony can be helpful to other victims..."

Xavier Aubrun, like a good goy, had consulted his lawyer, Abed Bendjador, and was considering filing a complaint. The restaurateur was waiting with a firm foot for the supposed bailiff who was to come to enforce the lien.

The victims of "Franco-Israeli".

In November 2011, three swindlers were indicted by an examining magistrate in the financial district of Paris. They had organized, between the summer of 2009 and the end of October 2011, a similar swindle. The criminals, hiding behind the company Info Service Multimedia (ISM), contacted small traders, craftsmen and even religious congregations to offer them advertisements in a professional yearbook for 400 euros. They then faxed the documents to be sent with payment by check. In reality, no advertisement was ever published, neither on the website, nor in the paper yearbook, which had never existed. Some time later, the litigation or accounting department would call the client to explain that they had made a mistake and that they had agreed to pay 20,000, 30,000 or 40,000 euros. Finally, a man introducing himself as the commercial director of the company called and was sympathetic to the situation. He understood the client's misunderstanding and only claimed about 10,000 euros. In general, the loss per victim was around 500-1000 euros.

The three defendants had thus succeeded in deceiving 500 small merchants, craftsmen and religious congregations in France and Belgium. The priest of a village had paid 40,000 euros out of his own pocket to publish an advertisement aimed at mobilizing his parishioners for good works. In total, the damage was estimated at about 700,000 euros.

On October 27, 2011, police officers raided the offices of the ISM company in Paris XIX. The newspaper *Le Parisien*, dated November 1, 2011, reported that *"the operations were led by a 44-year-old French-Israeli."*

The gendarmes had expected him to come to France for his vacations and arrested him after following him from the airport. This "Franco-Israeli"—more Jewish than French in spite of everything—worked with a 42-year-old lieutenant and a sexagenarian who served as a straw man. Two thirds of the loot had been *"transferred to an account in Israel"*. The two accomplices were released on probation, with a large bail; they were also lucky not to see their names and surnames published in the press and on the Internet.

The 544 victims of Jonathan Zeitoun

Another scam of the same type took place between July 2007 and March 2009. The swindlers were well organized: alongside young brokers attracted by easy money, trustworthy men were in charge of the most delicate missions (check cashing, money laundering). Most of the swindlers were unaware of the identity of their acolytes, each with his own pseudonym—"Hugo", "Monk", "Meetic", etc. The official address of the fictitious society was on the Champs Elysées, and all telephones were redirected to a number beginning with 01, a test of seriousness. Everything had been carefully planned to "fish" butchers, campground owners, driving school directors, gardeners and other craftsmen from all provinces.

The first phase consisted in locating recently installed managers, and therefore very interested in advertising that would make them known quickly. The brokers were in charge of the *"unpacking"*, an argument to convince the victims to sign "an insertion order" in a yearbook or in a fictitious directory. The victims did not really know what they were signing up for, since the fax sent to them afterwards contained the important passages in small, scratched and barely legible print.

One or two months after a successful sale, an "accounting" team would enter the scene, announcing the total invoice which was usually ten, twenty, even thirty times higher than the 900 euros agreed at the beginning. Convinced that their signature obliged them, the victims were relieved to receive, after endless telephone harassment, the "commercial discount": paying 12,000 instead of the 18,000 euros filled them with relief. The recalcitrant ones were threatened with prosecution by an alleged "debt collection service", even with being summoned to a non-existent court. This time too, more than 500 traders and craftsmen fell into the clutches of the swindlers. Some of them went bankrupt because they could not pay their debts.

In less than two years, this fraud had generated a net profit of more than 3.4 million euros. Bank accounts were discovered in Switzerland. Investigators from the Brigade de Répression de la Délinquance Astute (BRDA) had found a check for 600,000 euros during one of their searches, bringing the total to 4 million euros. But there was probably much more.

Of the 544 victims who had been robbed, 135 had been made civil parties, and no less than 32 people had appeared before the Paris court charged with swindling and "attempted swindling in an organized gang". *Le Parisien* of May 5, 2010 summarized the case as follows: *"After a full-blown clean-up, the various companies set up by Jonathan Zeitoun, the alleged mastermind of the entire network, collected nearly 4 million euros."*

The brothers Jonathan and Lior Zeitoun, imprisoned in the Santé prison since the end of 2009, had only been deprived of their freedom for a few months. They had been released and placed under judicial control. Since then, no further information about them was available[64].

Jacques Benayoun scammed the farmers

In December 2008, the public prosecutor of the Republic of Mont-de-Marsan declared that, so far this year, hundreds of complaints had been filed in connection with an electronic yearbook scam. The fraudsters solicited craftsmen, tradesmen and associations by telephone in order to place advertisements in fake online yearbooks. After a free trial period, the victims, who had signed a faxed contract that was difficult to read, received exorbitant invoices. To cancel the contract, they had to send a "guarantee check" of a variable amount. *"A guarantee check*

---

[64]This Thursday, April 10, 2014, I learned that I have just been sentenced by the 17th criminal court of Nanterre (president: Claire Lafoix) to one month of imprisonment—UNCONDITIONAL—for possessing (simple possession) a tear gas bomb while sticking some posters at night for a public meeting (which took place in Paris in the month of September 2013). This prison sentence was in addition to another two-month unconditional one (also unconditional) for a simple joke about the habits of Bertrand Delanoë, the mayor of Paris [notorious homosexual, NDT], which had been perfidiously interpreted as a "death threat". The difference in treatment between a cosmopolitan criminal and a French patriot demonstrates the degree of debasement of the judges of the Republic. [Note by Hervé Ryssen, NDT].

of 2,000 to 3,000 euros was demanded and finally cashed illegally," said the prosecutor[65].

The investigation had begun in December 2007 following complaints from two farmers in Dax, in the Landes. The Pau gendarmerie had taken charge of the case and for months an investigation cell composed of about ten soldiers had been trying to locate the victims. In total, some 422 complainants had been listed, of which only 12 in the Landes.

All the victims of the scam had the same profile: small traders, small self-employed, craftsmen, farmers and religious communities. The damages, for each of them, amounted to between 5,000 and 47,000 euros. They had been swindled by several companies, such as Net.com in Viry-Châtillon, Net. communication in Val d'Oise, Atout.com, Esperance Diffusion, etc. The gendarmes had traced the trail thanks to the telephone numbers indicated in the fax headers.

At the bottom of the contracts, onerous compensation payments appeared in small print, sometimes illegible. The victims would then receive an e-mail demanding payment of between 5,000 and 9,000 euros for one-year contracts. This was followed by phone calls, fake lawyers and fake bailiffs to put even more pressure on them. The fraudsters would eventually propose a fixed payment for the termination of the contract. Hundreds of people were swindled in this way all over France, although only 132 had filed a civil action.

In April 2008, five men were arrested in Paris. Two of them had been presented to the examining magistrate of Dax and placed in pre-trial detention until August ... before finally being released (as usual) and placed under judicial control[66].

Thanks to a kind of tracing of the transmitting faxes, the investigators subsequently discovered that the top of the pyramid of this organization was not in France, but in... Israel (surprisingly!). The French numbers on the telecopies were indeed redirected to Ashdod, an Israeli resort town near Tel-Aviv. Thanks to perfectly credible false accounting documents, the "Franco-Israeli" fraudsters managed to convince their victims that they were operating from French territory.

---

[65] *Sud-Ouest* newspaper, December 12, 2008.
[66] Most of the time, judicial control forces those who are subjected to it to go once a week to the gendarmerie or to the police station in their neighborhood.

The gendarmes of the Landes training center then contacted the Israeli authorities, and on December 8, 2008, thirty people were arrested in Ashdod and Tel-Aviv. During the searches, 700,000 euros in cash were seized, as well as four luxury vehicles and several pieces of jewelry. Within the framework of the international rogatory commission, two gendarmes from the Pau investigation section were able to go to Israel for several hearings and investigations. For once, the Franco-Israeli collaboration had worked well, and Jacques Benayoun, the head of the network, who had dual French and Israeli nationality, spent a year in Israeli jails before being transferred to the Fleury-Mérogis prison on December 25, 2009.

On May 4, 2010, before the investigating chamber of the court of appeal of Pau, *"a whole van was needed to transport all the documents of the case in Mont-de-Marsan—ten thousand estimates, six hundred victims, more than 130 civil parts*[67]*."* Victims had started to complain in 2007 in several departments of France: in Lorraine, then in Hérault and in the Landes. The case had been transferred to the High Civil Court of Mont-de-Marsan, while another judicial inquiry had been opened in Évry, in the Paris region.

Jacques Benayoun, 62 years old, had worked for 40 years as a representative in the textile industry. He denied everything categorically: *"It is false. I was only in charge of the financial system,"* he declared by videoconference from the Fleury-Mérogis prison. *"The company was run by the brokers and the salesmen's office."* Imprisoned on remand for seventeen months, he demanded his release; in vain. From the republican justice it was something unusual.

The trial took place at the Évry correctional court in October 2010. Twenty-two defendants appeared before 132 civil parties for damages valued at 3.5 million euros. In the courtroom, only Xavier, 61, and his wife, farmers in the Aisne, had had the courage to confront the fraudsters. In March 2006, they had received a fax requesting them to *"update their professional directory"* in order to be registered as farmers. The farmer had responded to the *"promotional offer"*. But a few days later, she was being asked for more than 8,000 euros. The phone calls multiplied. *"They put a lot of pressure on us,"* the farmer confessed. *We managed to reach an agreement to pay one month and terminate the contract. Then we went to see the agricultural union. It was at that*

---

[67]*La République des Pyrénées. fr*, May 5, 2010.

moment that we realized we had been cheated. Others like us had been contacted by the same network." Xavier and his wife hoped to recover what was owed and also compensation for moral prejudice. *"My wife felt guilty,"* Xavier recounted. She was *"on the verge of depression."*

Along with Jacques Benayoun, his son Boris, 34, had also appeared in court. Mikael Estanque, back from Israel, had taken the stand, but four other defendants remained at large. In the end, two defendants were released. The others were given suspended sentences of three months' imprisonment and a fine of 500 euros, five years' imprisonment and a fine of 200,000 euros: ridiculous sentences, therefore, compared to the damage they had caused. For Kaminski, the fraudster's lawyer, *"justice was even-handed. The request against my client was for six years in prison, four unconditional. He was only sentenced to one year. It proves that the indictment was not complete*[68]*."* With the sentence reductions, he would be free in a few months, assuming he actually went to prison.

At the beginning of July 2014, the president of the Dax court was less comprehensive: Jacques Benayoun was sentenced to 8 years of unconditional imprisonment and his son Boris to 7 years. They were incarcerated in the Mont-de-Marsan prison[69].

The Monte Carlo Police Golden Book

On July 30, 2008, a three-year unconditional prison sentence was imposed on a company manager and two commercial agents of the IMS company. These men were accused of having extorted funds from several traders and companies.

A few years earlier, in 2002, the company IMS (International Media SA) had signed a contract with an association of police officers called *"Circle of mutual aid and public safety forecasting"*, in order to raise funds to publish the golden book of the centenary of the Monaco police.

The commercial agents, Eric Souied and Esteban Fitoussi, had used aggressive sales tactics, clearly implying that the police would remember *"who gives"* and *"who does not give"*. Certainly, at 15,000 euros a page, some dealers had been reluctant. Prosecutor Claire Dollman had denounced their prospecting methods, which combined

---

[68]*Le Parisien*, September 15, 2010.
[69]The information was reported by the newspaper *Sud Ouest*, as well as the internet portal, but no other media echoed the news.

"threats and harassment". One merchant evoked a *"form of blackmail of this type: "With all that the police do for you..."* In short, to continue to be protected, one had to buy an advertising page. The criminals also boasted that they had *"the blessing of the prince's palace"*. The Algerian company Khalifa Airways, for example, had sent a check for more than 300,000 euros. IMS, based in Geneva, had thus amassed a haul of 1.8 million euros.

A principality labor inspector investigating other sides of the case had filed a death threats complaint, following an anonymous phone call from a man claiming to speak *"on behalf of the police"; "You would do well to drop this whole case, because outside Monegasque territory you never know what might happen to you."*

Forty-six complaints had finally been registered in 2003, but the two men had fled and an international arrest warrant had been issued for them.

The head of IMS Monaco, Jean-Dominique Ktorza—another "Franco-Israeli"—remained deaf to requests for a judicial hearing: *"Ah, but I'm sorry,"* he replied from Geneva, *"I have not been summoned so far, and as we are a Swiss company, we have to rely on the rules of international justice. I will give you such clear answers that you will wonder why you have come all this way. This will all deflate like a balloon."*

Jean-Dominique Ktorza claimed that the policemen had not participated in the commercial canvassing, carried out by his agents in a *"healthy manner, without any kind of pressure"*, adding, *"If two clients complained, out of several hundred, I would like to meet with them and find out what their complaints and grievances are. This is pure slander."* No further information about the trial transcended... As for the head of the Aid Circle, Maurice Albertin, instigator of the golden book, he had claimed his right to a just retirement pension[70].

---

[70] Whenever a case of swindling appears in the press and the names and surnames of the criminals do not appear or have been modified, you can legitimately harbor great suspicions about the Hebraic-Talmudic origin of the swindle.

3. False transfer orders

This type of scam first appeared in 2005, but complaints multiplied in 2011 and cases have exploded since 2014[71]. This new form of scam, also known as the fake international transfer orders (Foti), is again a "French" specificity.

"The phenomenon has become rampant: we count several dozen attempts a day; our services are in demand everywhere. It seems that new networks have appeared using an identical modus operandi, which works very well and causes significant damage," explained Sophie Robert, police commissioner at the Central Office for the Repression of Major Financial Crime.

The targets are subsidiaries of large companies: a fraudster calls pretending to be the head of the company and gets a financial or accounting manager to make a bank transfer to an account abroad, outside the European Union.

"The discourse is very well elaborated and the swindlers have a lot of lip. They are very persuasive and do not hesitate to exploit the naivety of their interlocutors. In addition, they are able to adapt to the situation and change the script very quickly[72]*",* explained Sophie Robert.

To be successful, you obviously need to know the target company very well. Before going into action, the scammers conduct a thorough research on social networks and the company's website. They buy all available "open source" information about their future victims, taking great care to remain anonymous. It is enough for them to pay with prepaid cards, recharged with cash and not linked to a bank account, or with hacked payment card numbers. They can thus access websites such as *Infogreffe* or *Société.com* to obtain data such as company statutes, minutes of general meetings, organization charts or the annual accounts of the companies they are targeting, explained OCRGDF director Jean Marc Souvira. They can also hack into the company's computer system

---

[71] According to the Central Office for the Repression of Major Financial Crime (OCRGDF), 700 cases or attempts were registered between 2010 and 2014.
[72]*Les Échos Business*, March 16, 2014. Article by Cécile Desjardins.

to collect more data, for example by sending an innocuous e-mail with a virus or Trojan attached. Once installed, the program sucks up the company's documentation and provides the fraudsters with the schedules, direct numbers, emails and all the signatures of the company's employees.

They go so far as to investigate the private lives of company managers. *"Thanks to social networks, Facebook or Twitter, they can find out the names of the children or the secretary's birthday,"* revealed Michèle Bruno, head of the cunning crime repression brigade[73].

They then acquire telephone numbers with the prefix of the country where the company is domiciled. For the fraudsters launch their attacks from abroad—especially from Israel, where the scam specialists operate—but giving the impression that they are in France. *"If the target company is in France, the telephone and fax numbers acquired will begin with the French prefix, in order to instill confidence in the caller who will receive the call[74]."* Experience shows that a call received with the prefix of the country where your company's headquarters is located knocks down the victim's first psychological barrier[75].

This perfect knowledge of the company's structure allows any financial or accounting manager to potentially trust the fraudster. Once in possession of all these elements, the criminals ask to speak to the financial directors of subsidiaries of large French groups, in France or in Europe, calling them by their first name and pretending to be the President of the company. They demand the utmost discretion and claim that they need to make an urgent transfer of funds to carry out a takeover bid[76] or to evacuate part of the treasury to avoid a tax audit.

"Hello Juan, this is the president of the company. I need your help. I have just received an email from the tax authorities urging us to urgently make a bank transfer to regularize our situation, under penalty of imminent tax rectification. I am enclosing the file. I am obviously

---

[73]*Challenges*, May 17, 2012. Article by Thierry Fabre.
[74]*Challenges*, May 17, 2012. Article by Thierry Fabre.
[75]*Le Parisien*, November 17, 2013. Article by Esteban Sellami.
[76]A takeover bid (PTB) for shares or other securities is a commercial transaction in which one or more companies (bidders) make an offer to buy shares from all the shareholders of a company listed on an official market in order to acquire a stake in the voting capital of the company. (NdT).

counting on your utmost discretion". The fraudsters even manage to imitate the president's voice.

If the interlocutor is reluctant, they either use threats or create a personal proximity with their victims by indicating that they will know how to thank them. The goal is always to try to isolate their interlocutor.

The fraudsters then send faxes with the company's headers presenting the forged signatures of the PDG (President and CEO, NDT) and his number 2, or e-mails with the president's forged address (it is possible to do so) in order to validate the transfer order. And the move is done.

The newspaper *Challenges* transcribed some police recordings: *"You must execute this exceptional transfer today. You will receive the documents tomorrow. I'm counting on you, it's very important,"* demanded a fraudster from the accountant of a subsidiary of a large group. *"But sir, I need the documents for an amount like that,"* the employee had replied. The swindler had feigned irritation: *"I just told you that this is an exceptional transfer, do you understand or not? You can do it."* But the accountant had alerted her hierarchical superiors. *"They exert enormous psychological pressure by invoking the urgency of the situation, and often threatening to fire the person,"* explained commissioner Michèle Bruno[77].

Many companies had hesitated to report it, preferring to keep it secret so as not to tarnish their reputation with their customers, but the authorities had nevertheless identified some 360 victims in 2013 alone. Subsidiaries of large groups had been deceived, such as Total, Vinci, LVMH, Accor, Sanofi, Essilor, Vallourec, Coca-Cola, Eurocopter, Hilton, Groupe Zannier, Valrhona, Virgin or Saint-Gobain.

Hundreds of millions of euros had been *"transferred to the accounts of individuals opened in banks in China before ending up in Israel, the rear base of the vast majority of this new class of fraudsters"*, explained the journalist Esteban Sellami, in *Le Parisien*. From September 2013, the fraudsters notably intensified their activities. *"We have noticed a significant increase in complaints for such scams, confirmed a judicial source. Since the beginning of the year, in Paris alone, nearly a hundred cases have been registered[78]."* The matter reached such a point that the Central Directorate of Interior Intelligence had incited its local

---

[77] *Challenges*, May 17, 2012. Article by Thierry Fabre.
[78] *Le Parisien*, November 17, 2013. Article by Esteban Sellami.

delegations to put medium-sized companies, which were also targeted by fraudsters, on notice.

The first case dates back to January 31, 2011. An employee of a company located in Le Havre and specialized in the transport of goods abroad had received a call from a company called Avi. The man on the phone had asked her for a certificate of bank ownership of the company in order to pay an important invoice. A few minutes later, a supposed client of the company from Le Havre called to ask the employee for the personal telephone number of his boss, on the pretext of an emergency. The fraudster had then cancelled the line, probably with some complicity of the telephone operator, to prevent the bank from calling the Pdg for verification. He had then ordered two transfers by e-mail (with his cell phone number attached) in the amount of 200,000 euros to an account in China. Fortunately, the company's banking agency had managed to contact the Pdg who cancelled the transaction. *"One in ten times, the scam works and it is discovered that the money transits through accounts in China, especially Hong Kong, before returning to Israel*[79]*"*, reported an investigator.

But the criminals had taken some spectacular prey. The Seretram production plant, belonging to the *"Géant Vert"* group, for example, had lost nearly 17 million in four days. The shipping company Brittany Ferries had lost one million euros. Also among the victims was the BTP Vinci group, which did not want to *"make any comment"*; or Robertet, one of the world leaders in perfumes based in Grasse, in the Alpes-Maritimes, which had lost some 900,000 euros.

In fifteen months, 180 similar attacks had been recorded by the Central Office for the Repression of Major Financial Crime (OCRGDF). The companies Atreva, Scor, Quick and Nestlé had managed to thwart these attacks, as had Michelin. Large SMEs (small and medium-sized enterprises) had also been attacked, such as Valrhona, a chocolate specialist, or the Trouville casino in Calvados, which had narrowly escaped a 400,000 euro swindle in March.

In April 2011, the fraudsters had even tried to deceive the financial department of the Elysée. After obtaining the bank account number, one of the fraudsters had phoned the bank of the Presidency of the Republic posing as the head of the financial department, and had ordered a transfer of two million euros to an offshore account, which turned out

---

[79] *Le Parisien*, April 21, 2011.

to be in China. Intrigued, the banker had made a few calls to verify, thus thwarting the attempted swindle. According to the weekly *Le Point*, which quoted a report by Agence France-Presse on April 20, 2011, *"this is not the first attempt by these French fraudsters based abroad"*. Which meant, plainly speaking, that these were *"Jewish swindlers based in Israel[80]."*

The company Schneider Toshiba Inverter Europe SAS, based in Pacy-sur-Eure and specialized in the design of industrial variable speed drives, had been the target of the same scam. The fraudsters had posed as a law firm working for the Autorité des marchés financiers (AMF). After convincing an employee in the accounting department that they were operating within the framework of an ultra-confidential takeover bid (IPO), the criminals had told her that she would receive a confirmation e-mail from the Schneider Toshiba Pdg. The victim then received the details of bank accounts located in Cambodia, China, Cyprus, Estonia and Hungary in order to transfer the funds to carry out the alleged takeover bid. The woman had made about ten money transfers between January and February 2014 before becoming aware of the scam. The amount of the damage amounted to more than 7 million euros.

Media Participations in Paris, the comics and comic book giant (Dargaud, Dupuis, etc. — 20 million titles sold each year), almost fell through the same hoops. At the end of January 2012, the headquarters and several subsidiaries were attacked by specialists of the "fraud of false transfers", sometimes referred to by the police as "swindling the president". The financial director of Dargaud Switzerland had received a call from Vincent Montagne, the group's chairman, who had demanded an urgent transfer of 987,000 euros to an HSBC account in Hong Kong, in order to finance a purchase in Asia. The fake Vincent Montagne had strictly forbidden her to inform her boss of the Swiss subsidiary, but the director had contacted her Parisian counterparts, as the amount of the transfer exceeded the maximum authorized limit. The discovery of the identity theft had stopped the operation in extremis.

But the case did not end there: the next day, Vincent Montagne (the real one) had received a call from Commander Girard of the financial

---

[80]There was also a variant: the rental scam. Someone impersonates the landlord who rents the premises to the target company by communicating a change of direct debit, following a supposed transfer. The new direct debit involves an account located abroad to which the rental transfers are to be paid. This is not a small scam, as many companies pay large sums to their landlords.

brigade: *"We know you have been attacked. Make the transfer, that will allow us to catch you in the act."*

Prudently, Vincent Montagne checked with his contacts within the police ... and it turned out that "Commander Girard" did not exist! Then it was the turn of the Société Générale—the bank of Media Participations—to receive calls from the fake Vincent Montagne, who claimed to be calling from the financial brigade and ordered to execute the transfer in order to catch the criminals. The hoax was once again uncovered. In three days, the publisher had received at least 30 telephone attacks! *"The criminals had perfectly planned their operation and acquired a very detailed knowledge of our organization,"* acknowledged Claude Saint Vincent, CEO of Media Participations. *"Their ability to imitate the president's voice and exert psychological pressure on their victims is impressive[81]."*

The secret services—the Central Directorate of Internal Intelligence (DCRI)—had issued a general warning to companies in a circular on "the prevention of fraud through international transfers", detailing the techniques used by fraudsters. So that on March 6, 2012, the divisional commissioner Jean-Marc Souvira, head of the OCRGDF, had discreetly brought together the financial and security directors of some forty major business groups in the conference room of the Medef (French employers' association, NDT) in Paris. *"They were very interested, as many of them had been victims of attacks[82]."*

In a note from the Central Directorate of the judicial police, we read that *"three countries appeared regularly in the scams: Israel, where the criminal groups specialized, France, as the country where the target companies are located, and China as the first destination of the transfers, before reaching Israel".*

In September 2011, three *"Franco-Israelis"* specialized in fake transfers were arrested in Lyon and Cannes, in a palace, during a poker game.

"In spite of everything, many have escaped French justice by taking refuge in Israel, between Tel-Aviv and the seaside resort of Netanya,

---

[81]*Challenges*, May 17, 2012. Article by Thierry Fabre. On identity plasticity, read our long chapter in *Psychoanalysis of Judaism*.
[82]*Challenges*, May 17, 2012. Article by Thierry Fabre

which is very popular with the French[83]", wrote Thierry Fabre in the newspaper *Challenges*.

"Organized gang scams are punishable by 10 years in prison and a 1 million euro fine, but it is difficult to get the perpetrators extradited," said Commissioner Sophie Robert, who had to surrender to the evidence: *"There is currently a form of impunity with this type of scam[84]."*

Apparently, the justice system of the French Republic is generally, and in fact, very lenient towards these fraudsters, particularly those who benefit from complicity within the State of Israel.

The monstrous impudence of Gilbert Chikli

The forerunner of this type of fraud was a certain Gilbert Chikli who had swindled some forty French banks in 2005 by posing as a secret agent. A refugee in Israel, after having been indicted in 2008 by the Parisian judge Sylvie Gagnard, Gilbert Chikli had pulled off one of his most spectacular coups with the Postal Bank[85]. The *Libération* newspaper of October 7 reported the case:

On July 25, just after the deadly attacks in London, a bank branch manager received a call from a man posing as the bank's president, Jean-Paul Bailly: *"The DGSE has asked us to cooperate,"* he told her. *Terrorists are preparing an attack in Paris and are going to withdraw money from your branch. A DGSE agent is going to call you. Do whatever he asks you to do."*

An hour later, *"Jean-Paul from the French services"* telephones the head of the bank branch, gives her a code name, *"Martine"*, demands confidentiality and sends poor Martine on her first mission: *"Your phone line is not secure. You have to get a cell phone that will only be used for our communications. This is a number that you will call to give yours."* Martine runs to buy a cell phone, then leaves her number on Jean-Paul's answering machine. The latter calls her back: *"Whatever happens, you must keep this cell phone on day and night"*.

---

[83]*Challenges*, May 17, 2012. Article by Thierry Fabre
[84]*Les Echos Business*, March 16, 2014. Article by Cécile Desjardins.
[85]We reproduce below our summary of *Psychoanalysis of Judaism* (2006).

According to one of the investigators, Gilbert C[86]. bombards Martine with continuous calls, some forty in two days. He floods her with information about the DGSE's work to thwart an imminent attack. He calls her at all hours, even at night, to such an extent that Martine no longer sleeps. *"If she doesn't answer fast enough, he tells her off. If she hesitates, he beats her. He keeps telling her, "Above all, don't talk to anyone about this." He pushes her to the max. Martine is a wreck."*

Once well conditioned, Martine will obey everything, persuaded that she is *"working for the nation"*. Jean-Paul then orders her, *"Turn on the computer. Tell me the names of the five biggest clients of your branch."* Martine obeys. According to investigations, the fraudster then designates one of the five names at random as the financier of an imminent attack and warns that someone is going to withdraw 500,000 euros from that account that evening. But the branch manager announces that there are only 350,000 euros in the account. Jean-Paul gets pissed off: *"You are really not operational at all!"* Martine cries, empties all the drawers and chests, and finally gets 8,000 euros more. Jean-Paul finally gives in and accepts the 358,000 euros: *"Now, go buy a suitcase. I will call you back."* After buying the suitcase, Martine receives the call from Jean-Paul: *"Before giving the money to the client, we must magnetize the banknotes to trace the entire circuit of terrorist financing and disrupt the entire network. Take a cab..."* He then orders him to get off at a cafeteria on the Place de la Nation: *"Do you see my agents? —No."* Martine sees nothing. *"OK, they are well hidden, they work well. Sit on the terrace."*

A few minutes later, she calls back, *"Go down to the sink and lock yourself in."* Martine goes down to the washroom. He calls her back, *"An officer will knock three times on the bathroom door, hand him the suitcase, go back to the terrace and wait ten minutes for us to return it to you."* Knock knock knock. *"Martine, hand over the suitcase,"* says Shirley, an accomplice of Gilbert C., who ends up taking the loot.

Martine then returns to the terrace of the café and waits... She waits several hours before realizing and admitting the facts as they are. Exhausted, she presented herself to the Judicial Police on July 28th, after three days of *"terrible psychological manipulation"*. The first inquiries of the Judicial Police who traced the telephone number led to *"a number in England redirected to Israel"* and made it possible to abort

---

[86] The newspaper *Libération* had not disclosed the fraudster's surname.

about twenty similar attempts of swindle in August 2005 by warning the bankers in time.

Gilbert C. then invented in September a variant that made him earn much more, getting bankers to make "international transfers" into accounts supposedly used by terrorists. *"With his phenomenal gab," wrote the journalist, "and his way of persuading bankers that they were serving their country in the fight against Al-Qaeda, the "mastermind" Gilbert managed to get millions transferred into the accounts of shell companies created in Hong Kong by his front men. On September 28, a bank disbursed $2.5 million in Switzerland and $2.72 million in Hong Kong. Alerted by a suspicious banker, the Judicial Police blocked the funds. Instead, two transfers totaling 7.25 million euros were transferred on September 29 to accounts in Estonia and immediately deposited by the "Gilbert gang.""*

Gilbert C., 40 years old, and his brother Simon, 38 years old, both born in Paris, live today as refugees in Israel. From his hiding place, Gilbert C. had the nerve to taunt the Judicial Police by telephone: "*I am not going back, I am not going to give up, I am protected by Israel*". After reading the account of this scam, everyone will agree that the word "cheek", commonly used, is now a bit soft to qualify these actions. Unless, of course, it is another form of the famous Jewish humor. In fact, the Jews are fully aware of this monstrous impudence, for they themselves call it by the word *Chutzpah*[87].

But the main victim had not taken it lying down. After the discovery of the scam, she was fired from her job and fell into depression. *"This criminal has no regard for the human damage that his actions have caused*[88]*"*, lamented the lawyer of the unfortunate employee of *La Poste*. For Gilbert Chikli, the whole thing was both a scam and a game. *"I play a scene that gives me a certain pleasure, a certain adrenaline rush,"* he declared in 2010 to the public television channel France 2, which had contacted him.

In January 2008, the press, which had finally revealed his name, informed us that—for the first time—the State of Israel had agreed to extradite one of its citizens. But it seems that the offender had not been in French prisons for long. In the Canal + program, *Special*

---

[87] It is also spelled "*H'utzpah*", and is pronounced like the Spanish J, Jutzpah (NdT).
[88] *Challenges.fr*, May 17, 2012.

Investigation, entitled *CO2, the heist of the century*[89] (March 2013), we see him sunbathing at his luxurious residence in Ashod by his swimming pool. Gilbert Chikli confessed between the lines to being in contact with the CO2 fraudsters and that he sincerely regretted not having been able to participate in the business, given that he was in prison. How long had he been? Answer: less than five years, maybe much less.

He also claimed to have escaped an assassination attempt in April 2012: *"Two guys"* had appeared with *"some kind of machine gun"* and riddled the front of his house with bullets. A grenade had also exploded in front of his house, so his residence was heavily protected. *"To us the mafia, at least to me personally, we are not afraid of it."*

Chikli was behind the attempted swindle of the Elysée Palace in April 2011. After getting hold of the Elysée's bank account number, he had attempted to steal two million euros from the presidential palace together with two accomplices, posing as employees of the financial service. The banker had rightly had the reflex to call the Elysée for verification. The attempt had failed, but the National Agency for vacation checks had fallen into the trap a month earlier, losing one million euros through the same operating method of the fraudsters.

All swindlers are not Jews, and all Jews are not swindlers. But as Jacques Attali (2002) wrote: *"But, among them, as always, things are not done by halves: since they are criminals, it is better to be the first*[90]*."* And, in fact, the biggest scams are almost always perpetrated solely by Jews.

---

[89] Program of Gad Charbit and Jean-Louis Perez. The commissioner Neyret (Case CO2) had taken out for Gilles Bénichou the file of Gilbert Chikli (*Paris-Match* of May 31, 2012).

[90] Jacques Attali, *Los judíos, el mundo y el dinero*, Fondo de cultura económica, 2005, Buenos Aires, p. 410.

4. Diverse and varied scams

The Badache-Apollonia Case

The Apollonia case was a gigantic real estate scam of more than 1 billion euros. The parent company of the scam was a financial and real estate advisory company called Apollonia and domiciled in Aix-en-Provence. It was a family structure run by Jean Badache and his wife Viviane, whose son Benjamin was officially the Chairman.

Since 2003, Apollonia's salesmen have been trying to attract affluent families with good incomes, offering them investments that seemed like a lottery prize: to become "professional furnished apartment renters", buying furnished rooms in holiday homes, studios for students or senior citizens, which allowed for advantageous tax reductions. They guaranteed that the rents would almost completely cover the loans, and that, a few years later, thanks to the inexorable rise in real estate prices, the lucky investors would be able to resell part of the property and enjoy a comfortable retirement thanks to the remaining rents received. *"Your interest,"* said Apollonia's managers, *"is to build a solid retirement for yourselves and an estate for your children."*

The first contact was made by telephone. At the first appointment, the salesman always arrived in a luxury sedan. He would tell the naive victims that the income from the apartment rentals would cover the mortgage payments. *"We give you the documents to get the mortgages, you sign in blank and we do everything. We will fill out the forms and you acquire very well located apartments and it will cost you nothing. You will collect rents every month that will allow you to repay the monthly mortgage payments, as well as co-ownership fees and real estate taxes[91]."*

The victims-to-be were often too busy at their own jobs to verify the documents they recklessly signed. *"Don't worry, we'll take care of everything."* The salesmen, who called themselves "financial advisors",

---

[91] *Le Parisien*, February 7, 2010.

were very careful not to leave their clients any written proof, not even a brochure or a form. Clients would sign a pile of documents, sales contracts, mortgages, leases, various powers of attorney, often incomplete or undated, *"to save time,"* they said. Apollonia's secretaries filled in the missing data, especially the dates, to make it appear that the legal deadlines for reflection and withdrawal were being respected.

On the day of the signing at the notary's office, the last planned action used to take place: *"The Apollonia people were serious, because they even allowed themselves to scold the notary when he was late. After the event, one can't help thinking that it was all planned,"* said one victim.

All investors quickly found themselves over-indebted, with monthly payments far exceeding rental income. In reality, the apartments had been overvalued by 30 to 50%. With an average indebtedness of 2 million euros per client, they were strangled by their mortgages. Some banks seized the fees of a couple of doctors who were forced to resell the apartments. Some saw the wealth they had patiently accumulated throughout their careers swallowed up. A retired dentist had to reopen his practice to repay his debts and borrow from his children to buy back the necessary equipment. The bourgeoisie had relied too much on the word of mouth of Apollonia's magic formula, they could thank their friends for their good advice! In the meantime, Apollonia's swindlers were gorging themselves with commissions on every sale, purchase and apartment management operation, each earning 50 to 100,000 euros per month[92].

A complaint was filed in September 2008 by Jacques Gobert, a lawyer representing 151 families. *"There are nearly 2,000 victims who have each borrowed between 500,000 and 5 million euros to buy tourist or student residences and exploit them under the status of professional lessor of furnished property, sometimes under the Robien regime[93]",* explained Jacques Robert. In total, 300 victims had become civil parties,

---

[92]*Nice matin*, February 24, 2009.
[93]*Le Parisien*, May 9, 2009. [The *Robien* scheme was a French fiscal measure in favor of renting created by the law of July 2, 2003 on urban planning and housing. The effect of the Robien plan (the minister's surname) was to increase new construction, in some medium-sized cities, well above the rental possibilities of the market. This law introduced a regime regulating tax benefits for owners of rented housing meeting certain conditions. This regime came to an end in 2008 and was replaced by the Scellier law (wikipedia)].

in a swindle amounting to about 1.5 billion euros in real estate transactions.

"Apollonia took care of everything, they advised us not to inform our lawyer or our accountant because they supposedly did not know how the matter was going. We had no direct contact with the banks and we didn't have to pay anything: that's what convinced us," said Isabel S., the wife of a doctor who had bought 11 apartments for 2.1 million euros.

"For my part, I have to reimburse 100,000 euros annually to the banks. The rents do not generate more than 45,000 euros for me. Now, I earn 60,000 euros per year. I only have 5,000 euros left to live on with my three dependent children," explained an emergency physician in Marseille.

The investigation had revealed that Apollonia falsified loan applications in order to be accepted. "In *addition, they sold us the goods 40 to 50% above the real value, with mortgages higher than 7%,"* detailed Claude Michel, a former high school director who had to repay 84,000 euros per year and president of the Asdevilm association, which federated all the victims in the case.

Jean-Marc B., a 52-year-old doctor living in Franche-Comté, had been recruited by the network in 2006. He would not have to take care of anything, he had been assured by the Apollonia people. *"They always came to the house and kissed the children, so they could see what kind of relationship they had with us. After two or three visits, they told us, 'There it is, now think it over, but not too much. Don't let this opportunity slip away."* The couple had decided to take the plunge. *"We then had an appointment at a large hotel with the head of Apollonia, Jean Badache. Hair slicked back, gold chain, anecdotes about the luxurious residences, his plane... This was Mr. Jean Badache. In short, he left us with our mouths open. The discussion about the contract barely lasted five minutes*[94]*."*

The doctor had bought ten apartments for 1.8 million euros. The financial set-up meant that repayment would not begin for twenty-four months. Thus, the doctor, who earned between 3,000 and 4,000 euros per month, did not realize it until 2008 when the monthly payments amounted to some 12,000 euros and the rents that were supposed to cover them were only a third of that amount. Bankruptcy was

---

[94]*Libération*, July 25, 2012.

mathematical. *"Up to that point, I didn't know exactly how much the loan was for, nor the exact amount of the rental income. I sound like an idiot, I know. But I had been recommended by friends, word of mouth, one trusts... There were the banks, the notaries, it all seemed to add up ... and I'm not the only one who was fooled."*

Claude Michel, the president of the association of the victims of Apollonia, the Anvi-Asdevilm, had invested 1.4 million euros. A couple from Isère had lost 3.3 million. The highest loss for a victim was 8 million. And on each transaction, Apollonia received between 12 and 15% commission. *Today, we are all over-indebted, registered in the files of the Bank of France,"* said Claude Michel, former director of the institute. *The bailiffs come to our house, seize our assets. The apartments we bought were overvalued by two to six times their true value. Selling them would not cancel our debts[95]."*

The financial institutions also bore their share of responsibility for having worked with Apollonia without carrying out the necessary verifications. *"The banks, such as Crédit Mutuel, are responsible for having granted loans without even making a phone call to the borrower,"* said Jacques Gobert, a lawyer. *"A single phone call from the banks would have uncovered the truth,"* declared Isabel, whose husband had bought 12 homes for 2.1 million euros. *Apollonia made me apply for loans in six different banks. None of them called me back. I didn't even receive the loan offers[96]."* Actions that earned the *Crédit Mutuel* de Marignane agency a full-fledged police search in April. Some victims were *"on the verge of suicide."* A toll-free number for psychological support had been made available to the victims especially for this case. (Alló, Dr. Sapirstein?)

Some notaries had not been very careful about the legality of their actions. Many notarial acts had been drafted and signed in a Parisian hotel, others at the airport in Toulouse, or in a cafeteria in Tarbes or, even worse, in a hospital room in Briançon. However, all notarial acts must be signed in a notary's office during working hours. Three of them were prosecuted and imprisoned. While in custody, a notary had to

---

[95]*Libération*, July 25, 2012.
[96]*Le Moniteur*, February 27, 2009.

respond to an act allegedly signed by him in his office in Aix-en-Provence. However, the client, the doctor, was in Paris that day.

The financial department of the Marseille court had initiated proceedings for "breach of trust and organized fraud" and entrusted them to the judge... Catherine Lévy. The investigations had led to the indictment and imprisonment of five persons in February 2009: Jean and Viviane Badache, and three salesmen, François Mélis, Jean-Luc Puig and Rémy Suchan, who were remanded in custody in Baumettes prison in Marseille. Jean Badache, the boss, was still in custody, while his wife and his collaborators were released on payment of bail amounting to 1.5 million euros.

The investigators followed the trail: after having indicted in February 2009 the head of Apollonia, Jean Badache, six managers and salesmen of the company, employees and secretaries of Apollonia's asset management company, as well as the notaries, they finally tried to prosecute those who had helped to finance the victims.

In February 2011, the sixteenth indictment took place in the person of William Elbaze, head of Cafpi-Defiscalisation for the South of France, who was placed under judicial supervision[97]. As a real estate mortgage broker, he should have been in direct contact with clients, as stipulated by the monetary and financial code, and not simply in collusion with Apollonia.

In July 2012, we were informed of the indictment of five banks, including two subsidiaries of *Crédit mutuel mediterranéen*, for organized fraud, aiding and abetting and concealment.

The victims had not lost everything, as the financial prosecutor's office in Marseille had ordered the total seizure of the convicted persons' assets in order to reimburse them. Justice had blocked the Badache's bank accounts in Switzerland. But when the manager Jean Badache was audited by the financial brigade, he was unable to account for the totality of his assets, as he had so many assets scattered all over the world. The fact is that the Badache family had been successful: a chalet in the elegant Swiss resort of Crans-Montana, estimated at 7 million euros; a Riad in Marrakech, not to mention the family mansion in Cassis where they lived: a luxury villa of 1300 m² habitable equipped with a

---

[97] We remind you that in general it is only necessary to report once a week to the gendarmerie or to the nearest police station.

secret bunker-like room. But Jean and Viviane Badache were innocent, they had to be believed. Their lawyer had warned emphatically: *"We will prove that there was no swindle or breach of trust. Mr. Badache is a good salesman who certainly knew how to play on the greed of his clients*98." Here again is a typical "accusatory inversion".

Money embezzled from charitable associations

Readers of our book on the Mafia (2008) are already familiar with Jacques Crozemarie, the former president of the Association for Cancer Research (ARC) who personally enriched himself with donors' money.

In 2009, the newspaper *Le Parisien* of October 14 reported that 17 non-profit charitable associations were exploiting the generosity and credulity of the Goyim in the same way. The Paris prosecutor's office had launched proceedings against X in March for "aggravated swindling and aggravated breach of trust". Two examining magistrates of the Paris financial court had been appointed to conduct the investigations and to try to clarify the real destination of the millions of euros collected by these associations over the years. The magistrates and the police officers of the BRDA (Brigade de repression de la criminalité astute) were interested in the founders and leaders of these associations, most of them domiciled in the United States. Many of them only had an address in France that corresponded to a company address. Most of them looked like a duplicate of a single model. In the statutes, only the corporate purpose or mission had been modified.

The investigation opened by the public prosecutor of the Republic focused on these associations: Mother Teresa Association for Children (Amte); Association for Research against Diabetes (ARD); Association for Research against Age-related Macular Degeneration (ARDMLA); International Association for Research against Alzheimer's Disease (Airma); European League against Alzheimer's Disease (Lecma); World Aid Mission (MAM); International Medical Mission (MMI); Cancer and Resilience (CER); Breast Cancer Research and Support Fund (FRSCS); *Doctor with a Mission* (Dwam); Operation Lifesaving Childhood (OSE); Action for the Children of the World (AEM); Global Village for Children (VMPE); Bread and Water for Africa (PEA); *Hopegivers France*, renamed Light of Hope; *World Assistance*.

---

[98]*Le Moniteur*, February 27, 2009.

The employees were probably in good faith. Like Jeanette, the French head of the Mother Teresa Association for Children (Amte), who explained that she "*did not manage the checks*[99]" So where did the millions of euros stolen from the simple goyim end up? A myriad of intermediary companies, responsible, for example, for the drafting of mailings to donors, which were also domiciled in the United States, constituted the framework of this international scam. But in April 2014, five years later, the supercops had apparently discovered nothing. Perhaps they had stumbled upon a nest of Sephardim, or else a swarm of Ashkenazis, who had better be left alone to avoid being stung. Who knows?

The heads of real charitable associations may have been legitimately disgusted by this news, as expressed in this passage from an article in the magazine of the association *Infancia-Sol*:

"When one works in a benevolent way 10 hours a day, in a small association to help children who are hungry, to build with difficulty small schools, to help farmers to live from their work, to bring a little justice in this tragically unequal world, and that one reads in the press that large associations, which handle millions of euros, are nothing more than thieves who use the status of association for their personal benefit, one feels that one receives a blow to the head."

There were more reasons to be disgusted. Read, for example, the following: On July 8, 2009, an article in the *Canard Enchaîné* questioned *Help and Action*, an NGO (non-governmental organization) present in 24 countries, essentially in Africa and the Caribbean, and specialized in helping children's education. Apparently, the association had simply lost 600,000 euros on the stock market, due to an *"unfortunate"* investment.

Here's where the donors' money had gone! And this NGO had signed a charter prohibiting this type of practice. *"When you know that, in the poorest countries, such as Haiti, you can transform an abandoned building into a school for a few thousand euros (see our website www.enfants-soleil.org) you understand the extent of the disaster and the discouragement of people of integrity."*

Searching a little more on the internet, we discovered that the president of *Aide et Action* (*Aide et Action*) was a certain Frédéric Naquet, and

---

[99]*Le Parisien*, October 14, 2009

that he had some similarities with Jacques Crozemarie, Albert Bénichou and Francis Choukroun [100]. The association was relocated in Switzerland, while 80% of its donations came from France. In five years, management costs had quadrupled to 8.2 million. The general manager, Claire Calosci, received a monthly salary of 12,000 euros. The article also underlined that the plane tickets paid by the association were for the trips to Dubai and Marrakech of Frédéric Naquet's wife.

"Too many associations and fund-raising organizations have become uncontrollable money-grabbers", the communication director of *Childhood-Sun* was indignant, complaining about the misery of the world: *"Two years ago, 850 million people were suffering from hunger in the world, today there are about one billion, including hundreds of millions of children!"* Dorine Bregman believed that it was more useful to help *"small associations"* like hers... So send your donations to Mrs. Bregman!

Let us recall here the testimony of the very cosmopolitan Guy Sorman[101]: *"The average donor, a widow from Montargis, is unaware that when she donates a hundred francs to a good cause, only a few francs will go to the begging child she saw on the mailbox leaflet or on the poster designed to give her a bad conscience"*. At least half of his money will have gone to pay for the advertising campaign blaming the goyim, and the other half to pay the association's expenses and staff salaries, which are *"on the whole, comparable to those of private companies*[102]*"*.

Bank card number traffic

On August 7, 2010, a 27-year-old man was arrested at Nice airport before boarding a flight to Moscow. He was suspected of being the creator of a network of hacked bank card numbers. Vladislav Anatolievitch Horohorine, alias "BadB", had been the subject of an international arrest warrant issued by the United States since November 2009. The young man, of Ukrainian and Israeli nationality, had organized the hacking of hundreds of thousands of bank data through several websites located in Russia or in Caribbean tax havens:

---

[100] Naquet is a surname that is part of the Sephardic onomastics. Cf. Alfred Naquet, *Planetary Hopes*.
[101] *Jewish Fanaticism* (2007)
[102] Guy Sorman, *Le Bonheur français*, Fayard, 1995, p. 88.

carderplanet.com, opened in 2002 and closed by the US authorities in 2004, then *badb.biz* and *carder.su*, among others. These sites, ironically presented as forums to *"help online e-commerce businesses ... understand their vulnerabilities"*, were in fact real supermarkets for cybercrime. After showing credentials—*carder.su* claimed the sponsorship of two members—the *"carder"* (card forger) collected everything: bank card numbers (so-called *"dumps"*), personal data (last name, place of residence, secret code) and with which to manufacture, forge and recode bank cards. There was also the possibility of contacting "mules", i.e. people willing to risk—against 30 to 50% of the loot—to use the fake bank cards at ATMs. Finally, the network made it possible to launder the money[103].

"For the last 3–4 years, we have been observing a professionalization in this field," noted Damien Bancal, a journalist specializing in cybercrime. *"There are about twenty sites like carder.su in the world, not counting those that are invisible. Some have more than 10,000 members exchanging batches of hundreds of thousands of stolen bank details."*

Vladislav Anatolievitch Horohorine was the world's biggest bank card trafficker, according to *France Soir* newspaper. The United States had ranked him among the five most wanted cybercriminals. U.S. undercover agents had managed to ambush him by posing as potential buyers. He was charged with aggravated identity theft and bank card fraud and counterfeiting, charges that could lead to a 12-year prison sentence and a $500,000 fine in the United States.

Market hucksters

There are some commercial techniques that make it possible to sell expensive, poor quality products to people who have no money and no need for them. In addition to being illegal, these deceptive methods are profoundly dishonest. The swindlers are well aware of this, as they never stay for long in the same region. Peddlers and other huckster merchants usually disappear very quickly, once all the local papanatas have been fleeced. We see them in the markets, or in the warehouses of

---

[103] The biggest money laundering networks are the diamond dealers in New York, Antwerp and Tel-Aviv. Read our book on the Mafia.

the commercial zones of the outskirts, rented for a few months in "precarious leases".

On a website simply titled "market scams", you can read the testimonies of hundreds of victims who complain of having been swindled by unscrupulous hucksters. Let's listen to some of them:

On September 27, 2012, "Alain" posted this message, correctly written: *"Good morning. I would like to tell you what happened to us at the Dignes-les-Bains market on Saturday, July 7, 2012. We were wandering quietly through the market when a woman approached us inviting us to her stall to offer us some free gifts."* At the stall, a man was handing out small gifts of little value, until about ten families were gathered there. There was to be a raffle of two magnificent aluminum frying pans, each priced at 650 euros, as well as glass ceramic cooktops priced at 990 euros. It could be "worth it" to stay. But before the drawing, the scammer asked for the attention of the attendance for five minutes to promote a cookware in aluminum, guaranteed for life, of the brand "La Table des Chefs", made by *"French craftsmen"*, and valued at 2990 euros (which is a bit expensive for pans). *"Persuade people that this is the right price and ask us what the discount would be if by chance there was a commercial offer. Everyone says their percentage and finally the man proposes the battery for 1495 euros, that is a 50% discount, with the frying pan or the plate as a gift. Three families let themselves be duped, including us... We gave three checks, one to be cashed now, and the other two in two months' time".* Back home, Alain has doubts and checks the company's CIF number, which does not exist. The pans had evidently been manufactured in China.

Alain is far from the only one to lament. The messages are often brief, but some give more details. On August 9, 2009, at the flea market in Pau, the scam was the same: *"Several gifts, as useless as worthless... And finally, after an hour of cameleo, the magnificent embroidered tablecloth that has taken four years of hard work appears ... for 4000 euros! But this is a flea market, so the tablecloth goes for only 2000 euros ... what a good deal! Moreover, the good philanthropist included everything with some beautiful stainless pans, a 72-piece cutlery set for 1200 euros, a knife case for 800 euros, a steamer for 450 euros, etc., all for 2000 euros! And the charlatan insisted on the "artisanal" manufacture of the products. Don't believe it, those beautiful shiny pans obviously come from China."*

This was the testimony of Patricia, who wrote on July 11, 2009: *"Three days ago at the Chinaillon market, in the Grand Bornand, we were almost swindled with the same thing: a jug of wine, 6 crystal glasses, a set of kitchenware, a revolutionary mattress; all for 1800 euros. Fortunately, before signing the invoice, we had our doubts and left, but three other couples signed checks to these camel traders. How is it possible that such characters can freely perpetrate their swindles in the markets? It is incompremsibe. And especially the elderly people who do not see anything coming. These people take advantage of people's suffering by making them believe that the super mattress is the miracle solution to their health problems. It's really unfortunate to let these charlatans act."*

The camel dealers always choose their public very well: single women, couples of a certain age ... especially young people are avoided in order to avoid scandals. And those who do not buy anything and publicly show their doubts are invited to leave and treated with contempt.

On July 22, 2009, "JP Henry" wrote: "*I was cheated at the Barcares market when I bought a cookware set for 1200 euros, payable in 6 installments, i.e. 6 checks of 200 euros. I tried to cancel the checks, but my bank confirmed that it was impossible. I sent a registered mail to the address indicated but I doubt it is real. do you have any advice? Thank you.*"

Undoubtedly, not only the Jews today use these sales gimmicks, but from time immemorial these dishonest methods have undoubtedly been the trademark of Jewish merchants. And Christian merchants have always complained about this unfair competition.

In the corporate organizations of yesteryear, under the Ancien Régime, it was forbidden to dissuade or drive away a neighbor's customers. "*Hunting customers*" *was strictly forbidden. It was an 'anti-Christian', immoral action to take away one's neighbor's customers,*" wrote Werner Sombart in his book *The Jews and Economic Life*. The Saxon ordinances on trade of the years 1672, 1682, 1692 stipulated (art. 18.): "*No merchant shall dissuade buyers from his neighbor's store. It is equally forbidden to prevent people, by signs or gestures, from making their purchases where it seems best to them or to direct them towards other merchants, in short, to influence them in any way*[104]." We see perfectly what distinguished Jewish merchants from Christian merchants.

---

[104] Werner Sombart, *Les Juifs et la vie économique*, 1911, Payot, 1923, p. 168.

For centuries, wrote Werner Sombart, the Jewish trade was *"essentially an import trade [105]"*. Here we see them selling low-quality scrap imported from China passing it off as products made in France, encouraging the patriotic sentiment of their victims. Let us look at this instructive example:

The small town of Laguiole, in the Rouergue, is, as everyone knows, one of the capitals of cutlery. Since the beginning of the 19th century, it has been home to a dozen workshops and manufacturers who have forged its reputation throughout the world. The "Laguiole" knives are very characteristic, with a very special design that is unlike any other. However, in 1993, a shrewd and unscrupulous businessman registered the "Laguiole" trademark. Since then, he has marketed not only the knives, but also a whole range of derivative products—from lighters to clothing—mostly imported from Asia. In exchange for royalties, he granted licenses to French and foreign companies, which could then market imported products under the Laguiole name. Gilbert Szajner acknowledged having pocketed between 5 and 10% of the turnover of 22 companies. His markets of choice were Germany, Japan and the United States. In 1997, the Laguiole municipality had been found in favor of Gilbert Szajner and convicted of counterfeiting. But two years later, the court of appeal overturned the decision, arguing that the name Laguiole was a generic way of designating a particular shape of knife. In Laguiole, this *"legal ineptness"* was perceived as a severe blow to the local economy. *"The Chinese can use the name of our village in all legality when we are the ones who live here and have been developing our know-how for decades,"* a merchant was indignant. *"I wanted to launch a new product related to the arts of the table with the Laguiole label and I can not because I would commit an infringement [106]"*, denounced Thierry Moysset, owner of the forge of Laguiole. *"Parasitism"*: *"It's crazy that we the inhabitants of Laguiole are condemned to pay a guy to get rich on the notoriety of our ancestors. Gilbert Szajner has only generated employment in China or Pakistan[107] !"* In the small town of 1300 inhabitants, Gilbert Szajner was nicknamed *"the vampire of Laguiole"*.

In a Jewish journal entitled *L'Écho des Carrières* —this was the name given to the ghettos in the region of the Venaissin County (Avignon,

---

[105] Werner Sombart, *Les Juifs et la vie économique*, 1911, Payot, 1923, p. 183.
[106] *Le Figaro*, September 19, 2012
[107] Read the article in the weekly *Le Point* of April 23, 2014.

Carpentras)—we find a very old testimony about these Jewish merchants. It is an excerpt from the testimony of Thomas Platter, towards the end of the 16th century[108]. Thomas Platter (junior) came from a Protestant family in Basel and had studied in Montpellier. During his stay in the County of Venaissin, under the authority of the papacy of Rome, he had observed the customs of those "Jews of the Pope". They were obliged to wear a yellow hat. The women, for their part, had to adorn it with a yellow silk ribbon. We are in 1596, in the good town of Avignon:

"After lunch at noon, we went to the street of the Jews: it can be closed, if necessary, at its two extremities. The Jews all reside in that vicinity, and are always at any season about five hundred souls. They trade in all kinds of dress and clothing, jewels, drapery and tapestry, armor and arms, linen and bedding, etc. In short, everything that concerns the human body and especially its clothing [...] They sell the old for new. And the fact is that their stores are located on the first floor of the houses, so as far as natural daylight is concerned, it receives rather little from the roof. It is so dark that you can't properly judge their goods. Moreover, when you go out with them into the street, you are still in the dark because the houses are tall, narrow and close together, so that altogether it is difficult to pass through their hands without being swindled or pilfered. It does happen, however, that from time to time one can make a good purchase from them, for these merchants in the Jewish quarter often keep objects found in their stores that have no known owner, or items pawned in exchange for a loan of a few duros made to the depositor, so that later the pawnbroker can sell these objects to you at a good price."

"*It is difficult to pass through their hands without being swindled or pilfered.*" The Jews probably have the fame they deserve. Let us note that today's Jewish merchants have accommodated themselves from the artificial light. Imagine for example that you want to buy a leather jacket, and you make the mistake of going to the Temple market, near the Place de la Republique (Paris). You enter the store, and at first you are frightened when you see the prices on the tags (2000 euros for example). "*Don't worry about the price,*" the shopkeeper assures you. Try it on

---

[108] Testimony translated from Old German into modern French by historian Emmanuel Le Roy Ladurie in his book *Le Voyage de Thomas Platter (1595–1599)*, in *L'Écho des Carrières*, le "Bulletin de l'Association culturelle des Juifs du Pape", (Bulletin of the Cultural Association of the Jews of the Pope), number 27, troisième trimestre 2001.

first, then we'll see. Then you try on the jacket without much enthusiasm... So the jacket fits you wonderfully! Then, pleasantly surprised, the salesman gives you a 40% discount that makes you think you're getting a good deal. You look again in the mirror, and since you are still a little hesitant, the shopkeeper grants you a new discount because he finds you really, really nice. He can't resist and you walk out with a 2000 euro jacket bought for only 800 euros. The day has been profitable! You just don't know that the real value of the garment, manufactured by nobody knows where, does not exceed 200 euros and it is above all the merchant who has made a good deal with his credulity of poor goy.

King Solomon's good business

Many companies have similarly aggressive practices. The furniture sector, for example, is undermined by these parasites. In general, the rogues set up their warehouses on the outskirts of cities or in the middle of the countryside, with very short "precarious leases". This allows their managers to leave as suddenly as they arrived. In August 2007, the Federal Consumers Union (*"UFC Que Choisir"*) of Senlis warned us: *"The method is simple. They are installed for a very short time (precarious lease of 2 or 3 months) in a commercial area. At the end of the period, they disappear, to reappear elsewhere, after having fleeced a maximum of consumers."*

At first, the Sephardic men entice the goy by phone, with an invitation to a raffle and gifts for both of you—it is important that you come as a couple. Once in the store, you see that the prices are astronomical; a 10,000 euro sofa, for example. But the salesman will give you a discount of 60, 70, even 80%, because he is you. Most of the time, a third party intervenes to offer you a new discount, with a proposal of free shipping the same day. In the end, the customer has the impression of closing a golden deal. *"Their published prices are artificially inflated,"* said the Fnaem (National Federation of Furniture and Household Equipment). For 2,000 euros, that sofa now seems like a great deal to you. Of course, you can take it back within seven days, even if the shipment has already been made. In fact, the rules of the door-to-door sales that protect the consumer apply as soon as there was an invitation to the store to take a gift or benefit from an advantage or promotion. To avoid that you think too much about it, you are offered the possibility of immediate delivery and with a request for a credit (which also entitles you to a withdrawal period of seven days). But once the furniture is in your home, it will be difficult to back out, and in the end it will be you who will feel guilty?

On the website of the association *"60 million consumers"*, you could read the summary of a case that had made the news in 2011: *"They lure couples by luring them with gifts before selling them canapés or sofas at prohibitive prices through an insidious commercial strategy"*. It was about the company "Esprit Relax". Mrs. and Mr. Leray, inhabitants of Brittany, had been invited to a raffle, and had taken the bait. Once in the store, they were inundated by the words of a salesman clever enough to make them believe that they were the only winners of a voucher—to be redeemed the same day—for the purchase of a salon. As chance would have it, it was precisely the salon they had their eye on a few minutes earlier. In the end, the couple signed for the purchase of a 2,500 euro sofa, with a 12% usurious credit! After a few days of reflection, the Leray couple wanted to retract their decision, but "Spirit relax" had apparently made *"threats"*. *Relax*, but not very *cool* in the end! Contacted by *60 million consumers*, the company had not deigned to respond.

A website from the Besançon region (*besac.com*) reported another case dating back to November 2004. The sign *"Leather plus leather"* had appeared weeks earlier on top of a hangar in the town of Champagney. Soon the business practices of the store specializing in leather salons were the talk of the region. *"It looked like an anthill, the salesmen were active from one side to the other. Some talking on cell phones, others passing by with order notes in hand, animated discussions between two salesmen while another engaged in negotiations with a couple of prospective customers. In front of the store, a rental truck is ready to load a leather salon. For a Wednesday afternoon, the atmosphere is quite lively in this furniture store lost in the middle of the countryside... So far, nothing too abnormal, apart from the eagerness and apparent nervousness of the employees."*

There was no advertising for this store in the local newspapers. However, customers flocked to the store every weekend. In fact, *"Cuero más cuero"* only made contact by telephone, with promotional gifts to attract the souls of the pitcher: a coffee maker for the lady or a drill for the gentleman. Once the couple was on the spot, they were attended by a first salesman, then a second. The astronomical prices could be a deterrent (more than 14,000 euros for a 2 and 3-seater leather lounge couch). Fortunately, the suckers had won the raffle. *"According to your gift number, you are still entitled to a discount of x hundred euros."* They could also offer to buy their old salon for a substantial sum. In the end, the goy had the impression of benefiting from a vertiginous reduction, even if he was about to be fleeced by paying his salon some 5000 euros. Certainly, it was twice less than the starting price, but at least twice more than the real value of the goods. The labeling, the quality of the hides, everything seemed to be in conformity when visiting the store. But this type of practice, which is on the borderline of legality, is the work of dishonest people.

The Repression of Frauds qualifies these procedures as "misleading advertising", because the price claimed is never the advertised price and because the discounts are purely fictitious. In 2010, the administration in charge of consumer affairs and fraud repression (DGCCRF) had found anomalies in 126 of the 261 furniture stores inspected, and had opened 52 contentious proceedings. According to one expert, the techniques for erasing the trail were everywhere identical: *"Telephone and mail bombardment, change of manager and company tax identification number..."* The National Federation of the Furnishing attacked in justice it also these swindlers, because it considered that its brand image as organization of the respectable tradesmen was discredited[109]. But the prosecutors do not always pursue the owners, so that most of them are never bothered and can continue to move from one province to another.

Although at least one had been hunted down: *"After the strong condemnation of King Salon in 2007, there was a remarkable reflux of the phenomenon,"* explained the Federation's director, Jean-Charles Vogley. *"But since 2009, there has been a resurgence of these outlets that rarely stay more than two months in the same place."* The founder of King Salon was a certain Daniel Cohen, who owned twenty stores. At the beginning of 2007, he was sentenced by the Bordeaux correctional court to six months' suspended imprisonment (against eight months unconditional, as requested by the prosecution). A ridiculous sentence, considering the damage he had caused. The store managers were sentenced to simple fines of 2,000 euros, and 20,000 euros for the companies. *From a formal point of view, there was an infringement,"* commented Pierre Sirgue, the lawyer for two managers. *But we thought there would be some tolerance because these practices are common to all furnishing professionals."* Let's rather say that this

---

[109] It acted, after all, like the trade guilds of yesteryear, before the French Revolution, which did not accept Jews.

practice is common to "some" furnishing professionals; not all! In any case, as far as "King Salon" was concerned, no anti-Semite would have been fooled: it was obvious that "King Salon" was hiding the mythical "King Salomon". French justice was under the spell of that great righteous king!

There are also, thanks to the Internet, much simpler techniques to swindle, provided that you have a good base of withdrawal: for example, a small country in the Middle East that never extradites its criminals and swindlers. It is enough to offer furniture for sale, and not to deliver it, as simple as that. The company *Usine Déco*, for example, apparently wanted to impose itself on the online furnishing and decoration market: from the sofa to the lighting fixtures, through the bedding. Created in 2011, *Usinedeco.com* had concluded 25,000 sales in 2012, for a turnover of 10 million euros. But from the beginning, customers began to complain, and on July 18, 2013, the company *Usine Déco* was declared in judicial liquidation. On the Internet, however, the complaining voices of hundreds of victims are still being heard:

"I ordered a canapé on April 3. They charged me the next day... I waited until April 15 to call them. After 20 attempts, I manage to talk to them and they inform me that the carrier will call me within a week for delivery. Since then, I have had no further news and it is impossible to contact them, either by phone or email."

Here is another testimony: *"I ordered a bathroom cabinet for 641 euros in October 2012. The delivery never took place, always postponed. I cancelled the order. I was told "we will refund you in 30 days", and since then nothing, and we are in June 2013."*

"Welcome to the club of the swindled! On April 21, 2013, I ordered a canapé whose amount with shipping costs came to 336.99 euros. I was immediately charged on my card. The delivery was supposed to take place between May 9 and 16, 2013, but since then nothing. I phone non-stop. When I manage to talk to them, they always tell me the same thing: "Don't worry, we will take care of your order and get back to you". And of course no news. I send messages, no response. I can't take it anymore. This morning I called them on the phone and, to my luck, the answer is: "I'm sorry, but we are having computer problems". For once I managed to get them on the phone, tough luck, the computer crashes, they really take us for assholes!"

"Hi. Like many of you I am having problems with Usine Déco, as they still have not delivered the sofa I ordered from them at the beginning of February. It was supposed to be delivered to me between the 15th and 22nd of February, but I have still received nothing except an incredible number of excuses, each one more bogus than the other. It started with "we have a computer glitch and the delivery date you were told was not correct". Then. "We are out of stock and your sofa will not arrive until March 1 ″ . Then: "Your order will be in our warehouse on March 21". Then: "Ma'am, your order is ready and a carrier will contact you". Despite one call per week (in which I spend an hour fighting on the phone before contacting them), the situation has not changed much, except that the fault lies with the carrier who has logistical problems! Unlucky for them, a consultant mistakenly gave me the name of the carrier, which I called ... and it turns out that the carrier has no logistical problems!"

The scammer in chief was one Guy-David Gharbi, whom we actually saw in a promotional video boasting about the merits of the company with a very self-confident air. On the Internet, this individual also provoked some virile reactions from his clients. The message of this Cyril Liotta, for example, was anything but ambiguous. We have kept his blunt spelling as is: *"Hello everyone. Like all of you I'm well fucked up. I've gone up to Paris to fuck that bitch Guy-David Gharbi, the director. And what do I find at the address of Usine déco: a fucking clinic! A fake address! If anyone knows where I can find Gharbi couscous[110] let me know, I have to fuck that bastard in the ass. If I go to jail, I'm counting on you my brothers and sisters."* The least we can say is that Guy-David Gharbi did not leave his customers indifferent!

The counterfeiters

Jews have always played an important role in the forgery of identity documents, which is perfectly logical, no matter how little one knows the Jewish spirit and the plasticity of Jewish identity[111]. In Eastern Europe, before World War II, they lived apart from the rest of the

---

[110] A brand of couscous marketed in France.
[111] We strongly recommend our readers to read our *Psychoanalysis of Judaism*, especially the chapter on the plasticity of Jewish identity.

population, relating only among themselves, outside the borders separating Poland, Russia, Austria-Hungary and Romania.

This identity was quite transparent in a novel by the famous novelist Stefan Zweig entitled *Mendel, he of the books*, published in 1929. The scene takes place during the First World War. His character, Buchmendel, was on his way to the military censorship office where his identity card was demanded: "*I couldn't quite understand. Hell, what, if he had his papers, his documents. And where. He only had a peddler's card. The commander raised more and more the wrinkles on his forehead. He had to clarify once and for all the question of his nationality. And what had his father been, Austrian or Russian? Jakob Mendel calmly answered that he was, of course, Russian. And him? Oh, he had smuggled himself across the Russian border thirty-three years ago to avoid military service. Since then he had been living in Vienna. The commandant grew increasingly impatient. When had he obtained Austrian citizenship, Mendel asked. He had never bothered about such things, so he was still a Russian? And Mendel, who had been bored to death by these questions for a long time, answered indifferently: "Actually, yes,*[112]*"*.

Another prominent Jewish writer of that time, Joseph Roth, provided a valuable testimony (among many others) about this Jewish identity that mocks the borders and the identity of the Goyim: "*It is not surprising the lack of piety of the Jews towards their names. With a lightness that is surprising, Jews change their names, the name of their parents, the sound of which, for a European spirit, always has at least a sentimental value. For the Jews, the name has no value, because it is simply not their name. The Jews, the Oriental Jews, have no name. They carry forced pseudonyms*[113]. *Their real name is the one by which on Sabbath and holidays they are called in the Torah: their proper Jewish name and that of their father. The surnames, however, from Goldenberg to Hescheles, are imposed names. Governments have ordered Jews to accept names. Are they their own? If someone is called Nachman and*

---

[112] *Europe* Magazine, June 1995, p. 48. In *The Mirror of Judaism*, 2009. Stefan Zweig, *Mendel, el de los libros*, Acantilado 33, 2009, p. 23.

[113] In his great study on the Jews of the shtetls—those Eastern European villages inhabited by Jews—Mark Zborowski gave this explanation: "*The obligation to bear a patronymic surname appeared with the edict of tolerance promulgated by Josephus II in 1787, in the regions of Habsburg obedience, after the partition of Poland. It was progressively imposed in all other regions throughout the 19th century.*" (Marc Zborowski, *Olam*, 1952, Plon, p. 422, in *Psychoanalysis of Judaism*).

transforms his first name into the European Norbert, is not Norbert the disguise, the pseudonym? Is it something more than mimicry? Does the chameleon feel pity for the colors he is continually forced to change to? In the United States, the Jew writes Greenboom instead of Grünbaum. He is not conducive to the changed vowels[114]."

It is thus easier to understand why Jews from these regions, who would later disperse throughout Western Europe and the United States, often changed their identities without any qualms during their pilgrimages[115]. Identity forgery was therefore a common activity within the community.

Adolfo Kaminsky, born in Argentina in 1925 to Russian Jewish parents, was one of the great counterfeiters, a king of forgeries. His family had settled in Paris in 1932. In 1944, he had enlisted in the Resistance, specializing in the industrial manufacture of false identity documents for his fellows. After the victory of the Jews, he was hired by the French secret services, but resigned at the beginning of the Indochina war, *"for refusing to collaborate with the colonial war"*. On the other hand, he was totally in favor of the colonial war waged by the Zionists against

---

[114] Joseph Roth, *Judíos errantes,* Acantilado 164, Barcelona, 2008, p. 109. [Joseph Roth went on to explain that Jews who wanted to cross borders used to give false data to obtain their identity documents, since such data had the advantage of being more credible for customs officers and the police. Joseph Roth put the matter in a somewhat convoluted and misrepresentative way: *"Such names cause difficulties for the police. The police don't like difficulties, and if only it were only the names! However, the dates of birth don't fit either... How did he get across the border? Without a passport? With a false one? Besides, it turns out that he is not called what he is called, and although he presents himself under so many names, which, in itself, implies that they are false, they are also probably false from an objective point of view. The man who appears on the papers, on the registration card, does not share the same identity as the man who has just arrived. What can be done? Should he be locked up? In that case, the one who is locked up is not the real one. Should he be expelled? In such a case, the one expelled is an impostor. But, if he is sent back to his point of origin to bring new documents as it should be, with indubitable names, the one sent back is not, in any case, only the authentic one, but the impostor is eventually converted into an authentic one. It is thus returned once, twice, three times, until the Jew realizes that he has nothing left but to provide false data in order to pass as authentic... The police have made the Oriental Jew come up with the excellent idea of concealing his authentic and true-though muddled-personal circumstances... Everyone is astonished at the ability of Jews to provide false data, but no one is astonished at the clumsy demands of the police."* In Joseph Roth, *Judíos errantes,* Acantilado 164, Barcelona, 2008, p. 74, 75. Note the Talmudic-inspired *pilpul of* this argument (see note 418 of *Psychoanalysis of Judaism,* 2022). (NdT)]

[115] Obviously, this is a partial explanation: many more elements allow us to understand the Jewish identity.

the Palestinian people. From 1946 to 1948, he put his skills at the service of Jewish emigration to Palestine. At the end of the 1950s, he committed himself in favor of the Algerian FLN against the French by integrating the Curiel network (an Egyptian Jew). From 1963, he helped the liberation movements in South American countries (Brazil, Argentina, Venezuela, Salvador, Nicaragua, Colombia, etc.) and Africa (Guinea-Bissau, Angola, South Africa). He also worked for the Spanish anti-Francoists and the Greek Marxists in their struggle against the "dictatorship of the colonels". In 1968, he agreed to fabricate false identity papers for Daniel Cohn Bendit so that he could speak at a public meeting in France. The government of General de Gaulle, who, at a press conference in November 1967, had described the Israeli Jews as an *"elite, self-confident and domineering people"*, had to be overthrown at all costs: this was unforgivable[116].

The manufacture of counterfeit banknotes is another of their specialties[117]. In 2006, a film was released that dealt with the subject, entitled *The Counterfeiters* (*Die Fälscher*). The film was directed by an Austrian filmmaker, Stefan Ruzowitzky, who was inspired by a book by a German Jew named Adolf Burger, commercially titled *The Devil's Workshop*. The young Adolf Burger, a trained typographer, had begun his career as a forger in 1939, in a clandestine Communist Party printing house. For three years, he had printed false baptismal certificates to avoid the deportation of his fellow Slovaks (*"We are good Catholics! We have done nothing wrong!"*). Arrested in 1942 in Bratislava, he was deported to Germany.

In the film, the hero, Salomon "Sally" Sorowitsch, arrested by the Gestapo, is interned in the Mauthausen camp. Thanks to his know-how, Sally is transferred to the Sachsenhausen camp, some thirty kilometers north of Berlin, where he is taken in by Commissar Herzog, who runs a secret operation. The Nazis want him to collaborate in "Operation Bernhard", whose objective is to destabilize the Allied economy by printing millions of counterfeit pounds sterling and dollars. This enterprise is entrusted to 140 Jewish counterfeiting specialists. With the support of Jewish experts, Sorowitsch is tasked with printing foreign

---

[116] Very famous declarations of General De Gaulle. On this phrase of the general read *The Jewish Fanaticism* and *The Eschatological War*.

[117] At the beginning of August 2014, we read that a network of counterfeiters had been dismantled in the United States. 77 million in 100 dollar bills had been manufactured. A dozen people had been arrested, including four Israelis.

currencies on a large scale. *"This is how I got involved in the most secret Nazi operation, the SS counterfeiting workshop, in blockhaus 18 and 19. There were about 140 of us, Jews only, who should all have been liquidated, reduced to ashes, but in the end it turned out otherwise."*

For two years, these Jews would manufacture bank bills, false documents and stamps. British pounds sterling first (131 million), English, American, Swiss passports, etc. *"Against the Soviets, we were making NKVD cards, and documents from all over the world for Nazi spies."* The operation was so secret that apparently the Sachsenhausen camp chief himself was unaware of the workshop's existence. When the printers went out to wash up, the whole camp was locked, no prisoner had the right to look out of the window. Surely a prisoner who was too curious would have been executed immediately: the Nazi SS with their skull badges would have forced the other prisoners to kill him, butcher him and feed on his flesh.

Later, the evil Nazis wanted to manufacture counterfeit dollars. But to manufacture dollars, the technique was different. *"The only act of sabotage we were able to carry out was to delay the manufacture of the necessary gelatin by several weeks. But we couldn't delay it for long because we were threatened with death. The first two hundred or so bills we made were perfect ... but it was too late for them, the Russians were already 150 km from Berlin."*

Back in Prague after her release, Sally Sorowitsch recounted to Czechoslovak police the details of the largest banknote counterfeiting operation in history. *"The British forbade this to be discussed at the Nuremberg trial. The British economy would have gone bankrupt if this case had come to light after the war. People never knew until today that so many British pounds sterling had been counterfeited. Now that the film is coming out in theaters, people are going to understand that the Nazis were not only murderers, but also counterfeiters. It was my goal to reveal that, and I have succeeded."* So, the "Nazis" were counterfeiters. It can even be said that it was "in their blood," for centuries, perhaps millennia. The title of the book, *The Devil's Workshop*, was in any case very appropriate, considering that it was again a characteristic accusatory inversion.

In 1829, a socialist philosopher like Charles Fourier (not at all Christian) had already noted: *"The Jews who arrogate to themselves the title of*

God's people have been the true people of hell, a vile scoundrel in whose annals crime appears again and again in all its crudity and ugliness[118]."

Since ancient times, Jews have been accused of being counterfeiters of money, which is perfectly natural from their point of view, since they remain in all the countries of the world without being or feeling citizens of any country (except the State of Israel since 1948), and feel no obligation or loyalty to the country in which they live[119]. Charles Fourier had noted that, in London, in England, the Jews, already numerous and influential, were eager to subvert traditional society and engaged in all kinds of rapine: London, he wrote, then had *"3000 Jews who distributed false currency, whipped the servants to rob their masters, the children to rob their fathers[120]."* And he insisted a little further on in his text, *"The Jewish nation believes any treachery praiseworthy as long as it tries to deceive those who do not practice their religion. It does not flaunt its principles, but we know them quite well[121]."* According to him, they had to be *"scattered among the villages, intermingled with the Christians, placed far from the frontiers, sea coasts and places of traffic and smuggling, forbid them usurious professions, the functions of privateers, brokers and other jobs of rapine or legal cunning, etc. These are the conditions that social security would demand for the admission of a sect essentially hostile to other nations and vitiated by a long proscription... Is it necessary to attract more chamarileros, agiotistas, usurers, brokers, smugglers and distributors of false currency that already abound everywhere? It would be to swamp the country with parasites and miscreants whose number is already too great[122]."*

In the middle of the 17th century, William Prynne, a very popular English publicist, had spoken out strongly against Cromwell's readmission of the Jews into the country: *"The Jews known formerly in*

---

[118] Charles Fourier, *Égarement de la raison démontré par les ridicules des sciences incertaines*, 1806, chapitre 1.
[119] In our previous books, we have shown, through numerous testimonies, that their "patriotism" is always followed in the same book, sometimes a few pages apart, by cosmopolitan declarations and their faith in the mission of a "chosen people". When these quotations are put together, the effect is often quite comical.
[120] Charles Fourier, *Le nouveau Monde industriel et sociétaire*, 1829, Préface, Article 3.
[121] Charles Fourier, *Le nouveau Monde industriel et sociétaire*, 1829, Section VI, Chapitre XLVIII
[122] Charles *Fourier, Éducation postérieure, Garanties à exiger*, Manuscrits publiés par *La Phalange*, revue de la science sociale.

England, as they still are in other countries, for filing, clipping and counterfeiting coin, practicing usury and extortion in the most miserable manner, for being the greatest cheats, swindlers and impostors in the world as regards their goods and all their produce without exception, were on account of all this excluded, and should remain so, and never be readmitted among us under the provisions of all our legislation[123]."

In the Middle Ages, Jews were accused of adulterating currency. We say here "the Jews", and not "some Jews", since this activity was apparently a monopoly. When the coins were minted with grooves, they adopted the acid reduction technique. They also used to use other techniques to deceive the goyim. This was a testimony from North Africa in 1902: *"The Israelite jewelers of the time used yellow arsenic to give the brass the color of gold, and white arsenic to disguise the alloy of copper and silver. This fraud was so frequent that in the city of Algiers alone more than 3000 kilograms of this substance were used every year. The government of Louis-Philippe was impressed by this and thought of prescribing measures to make this dishonest industry impossible[124]."*

In 1847, in his *Letter on Kiev*, the great novelist Honoré de Balzac recounted what he had seen in Central and Eastern Europe: "(…) when a Jew appears in a family who has no spirit of rapine, who is incapable of washing ducats in acid, of cutting rubles, of cheating Christians, and who lives in a life of poverty.) *when a Jew appears in a family, lacking the spirit of rapine, incapable of washing ducats in acid, cutting rubles, cheating Christians, and who lives in idleness, the family feeds him, gives him money, he is considered a genius; it is the opposite of civilized countries, where the man of genius passes for an imbecile in the eyes of the bourgeois; but then the saint of the Jewish family must continually read the Bible, fast and pray, like a fakir[125]."*

---

[123] William Prynne, *A Short Demurrer*, in Daniel Tollet, *Textes judéophobes et judéophiles dans l'Europe chrétienne à l'époque moderne*, Presses Universitaires de France, 2000, p. 170.
[124] Paul Eudel, *L'Orfèvrerie Algérienne et Tunisienne*, 1902.
[125] Read the full passage in *The Jewish Mafia*.

Memory fraud

We will not mention here the testimonies of the great witnesses of the Shoah[126] such as Elie Wiesel, Simon Wiesenthal, Samuel Pisar, Marek Halter, etc. In our *Mirror of Judaism* (2009), we have amply demonstrated their propensity to fabulation.

Jews—it must be said and repeated—accounted for a tiny fraction of the casualties of World War II, which caused 50 million deaths—Europeans for the most part. And among the Jews who died, many were soldiers or partisans who died not as Jews, but as combatants. Numerous Jewish civilians also perished: perhaps as many, if not more, than the number of children, old people and women burned alive in a single night in the bombing of Dresden in 1944. Moreover, one could speak at length about all those political commissars of the Red Army, mostly Jews, who exhorted the Russians to die in order to defend Isr ...—excuse me—the great and holy Russia. Are they to be considered as "Jews exterminated by the Nazis" or as soldiers killed in action? There are also all those counted as "exterminated" dead because they were no longer in Poland in 1945, but who appeared alive in Moscow or New York in the 1950s, etc. Numerous books have been written on the subject. We will not make a macabre account here, since the only thing that interests us in the present work is to understand how some Jews managed to enrich themselves with this subject.

In the *Jewish Mafia*, we saw that the wrongdoers had not hesitated to swindle their own fellow human beings: Israel Perry, an Israeli lawyer, had thus recovered the compensation for concentration camp survivors agreed upon by the German State. In 1983, the Jewish state and the Federal Republic of Germany had in fact reached an agreement under which all former deportees of Israeli nationality could receive compensation of up to 100,000 Marks, as well as a German pension and social benefits. Israel Perry had then specialized in representing and mediating for the former deportees in order to claim their rights from Germany. To this end, he had them sign powers of attorney that the former deportees did not fully understand. In twenty years, the intermediary had processed thousands of files in this way and embezzled some 320 million DM (about 150 million euros). When clients complained that their applications were not progressing, Israel

---

[126] *Shoah* (calamity, destruction) is the Hebrew term for the Holocaust. In France, this word is often used.

Perry invoked *"German ill will"* and the slowness of international diplomacy. The "German pension scam" had been a huge scandal in Israel. In February 2008, Israel Perry finally appeared in court. The swindler was sentenced to 12 years in prison.

We also saw the case of the "Hungarian" mafioso Semion Mogilevitch, who had enriched himself in the 1980s by offering his services to Jews who wished to leave the USSR to settle in Israel, selling their property and sending them their money. There was also the case of Ignaz Bubis, the president of the Jewish community in Germany, who had diverted funds received from the German government to invest them in Eros Centers. Mickey Cohen, who, after World War II, organized charity galas in Los Angeles for the Israeli army and lost the money in poker games. Or Didier Meimoun, a Tunisian Jew from Paris who came from Brussels in the 1990s and invested his "clients'" money, guaranteeing them rates of return of 12 to 17.5%. At the beginning of 2001, those who had trusted him for years learned of his sudden disappearance. They had to surrender to the evidence: the swindler had eclipsed 50 million stolen from hundreds of members of his own community[127].

Nevertheless, the goyim represent the vast majority of the swindled. We saw in *The Jewish Mafia* how the World Jewish Congress, under the presidency of Edgar Bronfman, had undertaken a fruitful extortion of funds: the recovery of Jewish assets "spoliated" during the war. Indeed, an investigation had established that there were still 775 inactive accounts in Swiss banks totaling some 32 million dollars. An international campaign, carried by almost all the Western media, literally turned to slander and libel: the Swiss as a whole were denounced for profiting from *"blood money"*; they had committed *"unprecedented theft"*; dishonesty was *"the foundation of the Swiss mentality"*; their *"greed"* was unparalleled; they had *"profited from genocide"*; they were guilty of "the *greatest theft in the entire history of mankind*". International pressure was such that in February 1997, Switzerland agreed to set up a special fund of 200 million dollars for the victims of the Shoah. This sum was in no way an acknowledgement of debt, but was to be seen as a gesture of appeasement and goodwill on the part of the Swiss. However, the World Jewish Congress, far from declaring itself satisfied, stepped up its pressure. Jewish financiers now called for an economic blockade of Switzerland. Some states and important municipalities in the United States withdrew their funds

---

[127] Read *The Jewish Mafia,* chapter *Swindling Your Community.*

invested in Switzerland. In June 1998, the Swiss banks raised their offer to $600 million, but Abraham Foxman, president of the ADL (Anti Defamation League, the leading "anti-racist" league), declared that it was *"an insult to the memory of the victims"*. In mid-August, the Swiss finally gave in and agreed to pay 1250 million dollars (1.25 billion dollars). All the Jewish associations elbowed their way in to claim their share of the spoils.

Of course, the amounts extorted from Switzerland were a pittance compared to what Germany had been paying annually to the State of Israel and above all to Jewish individuals for decades. In 1976, Nahum Goldman, the founder of the World Jewish Congress, wrote in his biography: *"In reality, Germany has paid sixty billion marks to date and will pay a total of eighty billion. That is, twelve or fourteen times more than we had estimated at the time... One could not reproach the Germans for having been stingy and for not having kept their promises128."* And since 1976, the flow of German money has not stopped flowing into Israel's vaults. The truth is that the German Federal Republic was a real cash cow. On May 3, 2007, on the English-language website of the German newspaper *Spiegel Online International*, an article noted that—according to the German Finance Ministry spokesman—the German government had already paid out some 64 billion euros to Holocaust survivors.

Since the survivors of the "death camps" (*"600,000 survivors"*, according to Nahum Goldman) had been largely compensated by successive German governments, their children in turn began to claim their share of the cake. Thus, in 2007, some Jewish associations asked Germany to compensate the second generation of victims, claiming that the Jews had suffered deep psychological trauma. The idea of these descendants of survivors was that the dreadful drama their parents had lived through (the gas chambers, the crematorium ovens working day and night, the babies thrown alive into the fire, the giant barbecues, the dogs biting genitalia, the Jews transformed into soap and lampshades, the "geysers of blood", the "blood geysers", the "blood geysers", and the "blood geysers") was not a problem for them, the "blood geysers,"

---

[128] Nahum Goldmann, *Le Paradoxe juif, Conversations en français avec Léon Abramowicz*, Paris, Stock, 1976, p. 146-164. Goldmann speaks of 600,000 survivors of the "death camps": "In 1945, there were almost six hundred thousand Jews, survivors of the German concentration camps, that no country wanted to take in". (*Le Paradoxe juif*, p. 237).

and other unnamed atrocities 129) had caused considerable psychological damage, and that it was therefore only fair that Germany should pay for the indispensable *"psychological or even psychiatric treatments"* for 40,000 *"mentally and psychologically affected"* second-generation survivors. But the fat, good-natured German had realized that she was being taken advantage of. In May, the German government made it known that it had no intention of paying these expenses, which did not fall *"within the principles of international treaties on reparations"*, and cut off the Fisher Fund, the instigator of this brilliant idea. In July of the same year, we read on the English page of *Ynetnews* that attorney Gideon Fisher, the creator of the Fisher Fund, had decided to bring the case to justice: *"The undeniable proof that the defendant [Germany] intended to destroy the Jewish people, was that it had even planned to harm the second generation of survivors of the Jewish people knowing that if the final solution was not fully successful, the emotional damage caused to the second generation would be so severe and substantial that it would irreparably affect the Jewish race itself and destroy it completely. These deliberate actions have caused and continue to cause the plaintiffs severe psychological and emotional damage, for which they should be compensated."*

The problem is that we can see these psychological disorders in Jews long before the Second World War, as we have shown in our books. And that is precisely the reason why Sigmund Freud, who came from a Hasidic Jewish family, had developed psychoanalysis at the end of the 19th century: in order to treat and cure his fellow Jews, who obviously represented almost all of his clientele. Thus, it was not the "shoah" that disturbed these poor Jews. It is perfectly legitimate, on the other hand, to observe to what extent these sick people with an overflowing imagination—the hysterical phenomenon studied by Freud—can indulge and wallow in morbidity and mentally embellish an imaginary shoah on the basis of an already sufficiently painful history[130].

In any case, the Fisher Fund's claim came to nothing, as we heard nothing more about it.

---

[129] Read *The Mirror of Judaism* (Hervé Ryssen, *Le Miroir du judaïsme*, Baskerville, 2009, p. 173-218).
[130] On this subject, it seems essential to read our *Psychoanalysis of Judaism* (2006), and its extension in the third parts of our *Jewish Fanaticism* (2007) and *The Mirror of Judaism* (2009).

But the claims of the Jewish "memory" associations increased within the framework of the "Claims Conference", the "Conference for Jewish Material Claims Against Germany", an organization created in 1951 and in charge of studying and defending the compensation claims of the victims of Nazism. In June 2008, we learned that the "Claims" had secured a juicy $320 million supplement to be *"distributed to Holocaust survivors."*

In March 2009, Germany's monthly payments to *"needy survivors from Eastern Europe"* increased by 35% in non-EU countries and by 11% in EU member countries, announced the Claims Conference organization after negotiations with the German Ministry of Finance. The increase amounted to 60 million euros over ten years.

On December 20, 2009, we read on the website of the Israeli daily *Haaretz* that the State of Israel was once again demanding money from Germany as compensation for the "Holocaust". The author of the article, Moti Bassok, reported that Finance Minister Yuval Steiniz was demanding between 450 million and 1 billion euros from Germany to compensate the 30,000 Israeli survivors subjected to forced labor in the ghettos. The Israeli authorities estimated that—according to a law on ghetto workers voted in 2002 by the German parliament—each of the 30,000 survivors of forced labor still alive was entitled to a back pay of 15,000 euros. This time it was the jackpot: in January 2010, it was agreed that Germany would pay 500 million euros to Jewish forced laborers as an old-age pension.

In March 2010, the Claims Conference meeting in Berlin negotiated an additional 91 million euros to guarantee an increase in home care services and pension payments to enable survivors to live in dignity. This was an increase of 25 million euros over 2009. In addition, a new additional pension had been obtained: 36 million for about 1300 survivors in Western Europe.

In December 2010, another news from Germany confirmed that aid to survivors would double in 2011 to 110 million euros. The money would be used to finance essential social services for Jewish survivors around the world: home care, food, medicine and basic necessities. There were still 520,000 "Shoah survivors" in the world, half of whom lived in Israel.

Also in December 2010, the German railroad company had announced a donation of five million euros to Nazi victims for projects in Eastern Europe. Deutsche Bahn had already donated several million euros to the victims of Nazism since the foundation "Remembrance, Responsibility and Future" was set up in 2000.

Other updates: April 2011: The Claims Conference announced that the German government had given the go-ahead for a 15% increase in funding for Holocaust survivors, from 110 million euros in 2011 to 126.7 million euros in 2012. In total, Germany was to allocate 513 million euros to this organization between 2011 and 2014 to help Holocaust survivors.

November 2011: After a new negotiation between the German government and the Claims Conference, it was agreed that Jews who had worked in the ghettos would receive, at one time, 2000 euros, independently of the monthly compensation they already received. *"We want to make sure that all survivors who qualify for this new measure can benefit from it in compensation for the suffering of having worked under the Nazi boot,"* Rabbi Julius Berman, the chairman of the Claims, had declared. Until then, only Jews who had worked in the ghettos located in the territories annexed by the Third Reich were eligible for compensation. The German government was to re-examine 56,000 claim files that had been rejected. While I'm winning, I'm still playing!

Seventy years after the fact, some still find a way to make money out of the whole story. In February 2014, SNCF (France's railway company, NDT) saw a contract threatened in the United States for its role in the "Shoah". French trains had indeed been used to deport Jews. A lawyer specializing in this type of extortion, Stuart Eizenstat, began negotiating *"eventual indemnities for the families of American Holocaust victims transported by SNCF in 1942."* The negotiations were kept secret, so it was not known how many victims were involved. *"SNCF's persistent refusal to accept responsibility for its role in the Holocaust continues to be an insult to the victims,"* a U.S. senator believed. It should be noted in passing that there was never any question of compensating the sons and daughters of the 70,000 French civilians (men, women and children) killed by Anglo-American bombs between 1942 and 1945.

On November 11, 2011, members of the memory mafia were found guilty of a new scam. After eleven months of investigation, seventeen people were arrested in New York accused of having swindled the victims of the "*shoahnanás*"[131]. Of the seventeen people arrested, six were members of the Claims Conference. These six individuals, who were supposed to review and approve applications from alleged victims, had actually validated more than 5,500 fraudulent applications. These individuals "*came mostly from the Russian Jewish community in the Little Odessa neighborhood of Brighton Beach,*" a New York City suburb. In return, these employees kept a portion of the money for themselves and their accomplices.

The system was well established: newspaper advertisements in the Russian-speaking Jewish community offered applicants help in filling out their applications in exchange for a commission. An accomplice would prepare false marriage, schooling or birth certificates—Russian or Ukrainian—in order to fit the compensation criteria, all based on a thorough knowledge of the history of the "Holocaust." "*Despite the sometimes gross falsifications, the applications were quickly validated. And, by the way, the corrupt employees pocketed a good percentage... They described the hell of the labor camps and ghettos. Others told how, as children, they had fled from the Nazis under bombs to hide until liberation... But their stories, full of realistic details, were false*[132]." In fact, a good portion of those 5500 "survivors" were not even born in 1945.

The scam amounted to some $42.5 million. Some 4957 people had received a one-time payment of $3600 between 2000 and 2009, for a total amount of $18 million, claiming to have been forced to leave their hometown because of the Nazis. A second fund had benefited 658 people, who had received monthly payments of $411 (for a total amount of $24.5 million), after claiming to have lived in the ghettos for at least 18 months, or in the labor camps for at least six months. At the top of the system was a certain Semen Domnitser, who had been in charge of these two funds since 1999 and validated the files transmitted to the German government, which paid the Germans on their behalf. 900,000 tons of bombs dropped on their heads during the war had made the Germans cooperate without complaint!

This case was not the first. Even back then, immediately after the war, small-time swindlers were already trying to squeeze the most out of the

---

[131] "*Shoahnanás*": pun and title of a satirical song by the French-Cameroonian humorist Dieudonné (NdT).
[132]*France Soir*, November 11, 2010.

defeated country. Philipp Auerbach, for example. He was born in Hamburg, then settled in Belgium in 1934 with his wife and children. He had become an important head of the chemical industry and had supported the communists during the Spanish civil war by supplying them with gasoline and chemical products. Arrested in 1940 by the Germans, he remained in several concentration camps, in Buchenwald and Auschwitz, without being "exterminated" at all. According to the *Jewish Virtual Library* website, he testified after the war that in Auschwitz he had been forced to make soap from human remains. But since the end of the 1980s, no one dares to talk about this ridiculous fable anymore.

All in all, Auerbach was an Auschwitz survivor," like many others. On September 15, 1946, he was appointed "Bavarian State Commissioner *for* Racial, Religious and Political Persecution" *(Staatskommissar für rassich, religiös und politish Verfolgte)* in Munich, whose field of competence was reparations for victims of the Nazi regime. It dealt with legal advice, re-housing, reintegration into the economy and ... financial compensation. Philipp Auerbach created deported Jews out of thin air in order to receive the compensation money. He was charged with corruption, attempted extortion, breach of trust, swindling, false declaration under oath, usurpation of academic title, violation of monetary law. Sentenced to two and a half years in prison and a fine of DM 2700, he ended up committing suicide in his cell[133].

Oscar Friedman's revenge

Oscar Friedmann was a Jew of Polish origin, whose father, born in Galitzia in southern Poland, had emigrated to Antwerp. Oscar was born in that great city in 1908. In 1975, he published in Calmann-Lévy editions his autobiographical book entitled *A Second of Happiness*. Oscar Friedmann presented in it the vision of the world instilled in him by his father in his childhood:

"For me, there were on the one hand the Jews like my father, his friends, the shames, the chiddelech, the einiklech, the schlichim; on the other side, the non-Jews like the maids, the nannies, the street sweepers, the chimney sweep, the shabbat goy—the one who comes to the house to light or put out the fire on Shabbat since it is forbidden to us on that

---

[133] Jews represent the most suicidal population in the world, and by far.

day—the police officers, the drunks who hang out in the streets and whom we call shaigets (crooks) ... and in general all non-Jews are inferior people. I am the son of Schmuel Friedmann, I am a son of King[134]."

"When I was fourteen, as usual, my father took me to a rabbi. Apart from the Talmud and the poskim (laws), they teach us above all a fanatical hatred for everything that does not belong to our self-enclosed world. One must hate the non-religious Jews, the Zionists (even if they are religious, like the Mizrachim, for one must not "ascend" to Eretz-Israel before the coming of the Messiah), even hate the Hasidim who are not of our clan[135]."

When the war broke out in 1914, his family was not the least bit concerned: "To tell the truth, this war does not interest us. We feel neither German, nor Austrian, nor Polish. At least 'we'—the older ones in the family. My younger siblings and I, on the other hand, are German superpratiots—weren't we educated in a German school[136]?"

And yet, two pages further on, we can see once again that the Jew, as usual, is ready to say anything to deceive the reader: "On November 2, 1917, the Jews burst into a fabulous joy. Everyone dances, everyone becomes anti-German, everyone goes over to the Allied side, even the most fierce anti-Zionists. I don't understand much, except that the British have given a country to the Jews: it is the Balfour declaration... the prehistory of the State of Israel[137]."

Oscar Friedmann then began his career as a swindler:

---

[134] Oscar Friedmann, *Une Seconde de bonheur*, Calmann-Lévy, 1975, p. 30.
[135] Oscar Friedmann, *Une Seconde de bonheur*, Calmann-Lévy, 1975, p. 40.
[136] Oscar Friedmann, *Une Seconde de bonheur*, Calmann-Lévy, 1975, p. 33.
[137] Explanation: Jews only reason in terms of priority enemy. And the priority enemy of the Jews, in 1914, was Tsarist Russia, where they had no right of citizenship and did not exercise absolute dominion over power, despite their financial might. After the fall of the Tsar in March 1917, a Kerensky decree of April 2 had granted them equal rights. Jews all over the world no longer had anything to expect from Germany, and the cosmopolitan financiers changed their coats. Two days later, as if by chance, the U.S. Senate finally voted to go to war against Germany and Austria-Hungary. The Germans called this U-turn by the Jews the "stab in the back". In November (according to the Gregorian calendar), the Bolshevik revolution installed the Marxist Jews in power in Russia.

"*Forced to go back to work, I quickly found a new job: selling oriental perfumes by weight. The system is very simple and advantageous. I approach a woman on the street:*

—Madam, may I? Your handkerchief... I will perfume it free of charge.

As long as I hold it in my hand, I know it won't go away.

—What do you prefer? Heliotrope, Jasmine, Cyprus, Rose, Carnation?

While I make her smell all the perfumes advertised one by one, I take advantage of the opportunity to encircle her as much as possible: not only for pleasure, but to finish her off.

—It will be three francs a gram. The jar comes free, I tell him as I refill the jar:

—Here are ten grams.

The victim, who no longer knows where he stands, believes that a full bottle costs three francs and indeed finds it cheap: when he opens his purse, I quickly help myself:

—Ten grams, thirty francs. Thank you very much, madam. Stunned, the woman generally does not dare to say anything. If by any chance she protests, I reassure her immediately:

—Maybe it's too much? Don't worry, I'm only going to give you five grams.

And she leaves without protest, glad to have saved fifteen francs[138]."

In the 1930s, he was involved in the organization of rigged wrestling matches (*catch*): "*After ten minutes of fierce combat in the ring, Max Krauser throws Zbitsko over the ropes and the two continue the fight in the hall. Some cronies scattered here and there intervene and are knocked out. The crowd erupts, convinced that they are real spectators, and the police must intervene to bring the fighters back into the ring. The room is already in frenzy when the supreme mess occurs, a stunt inspired by the last Popeye movie: Zbitsko lifts Max Krauser and throws him to the floor, which collapses: two boards had been previously sawed, and during the whole fight the wrestlers had avoided stepping on that corner of the ring. Wrestlers and referees have disappeared into the pit. The announcer announces the draw, which makes it possible to organize*

---

[138] Oscar Friedmann, *Une Seconde de bonheur*, Calmann-Lévy, 1975, p. 65.

a rematch ... the success of which is assured. The catch is obviously not the paragon of sports wrestling, but it amuses me a lot for its circus side and for the reactions of the public, which is still unaware that there is too much money at stake for the show not to be carefully rigged[139]*."*

In 1940, Oscar Friedmann was imprisoned in a camp in Austria. Suddenly, the man became extremely patriotic: *"The Jews proclaim themselves one hundred percent French*[140]*."*

In 1945, he was apparently in top form, and a British colonel entrusted him with the important mission of occupying a nearby village: *"I take the lead of a patrol of Corsicans and Russians. We installed ourselves in the town hall without difficulty... All arms are to be surrendered immediately. All those who keep them will be shot on the spot."* And after discovering a cache of weapons, Friedmann decided to apply a firm hand: *"Five minutes later, the people are there, crying, begging me. I then turn to the women and children around me: 'You have before you a gruel Jude (a horrible Jew) according to your Dr. Goebbels. Do not be afraid, the Jew is here to protect you. On the other hand, these men have hidden weapons; we have warned them, we have given them a chance. They have stubbornly denied it. Let them die now like men, without weeping..."* The mayor, the carpenter, the milkman, the teacher, etc., everyone was put to the sword. *"Thereupon, justice is done."*

Later, back in Antwerp, Oscar Friedmann gave free rein to his personal justice, in parallel with his trafficking: *"Revenge, arresting collaborators, uncovering the kapos, trafficking... I strike like a savage, using all the low blows I learned when I was practicing wrestling".*

He then became a diamond broker and amassed a lot of money: *"As a nouveau riche, I spent a lot of money.* Thank God, this story eventually ended well: *"Since I didn't want to have children, I bought nine dogs, each one more beautiful*[141]*."* For once in his life, he had acted humanely.

Let us give the floor to the French socialist Charles Fourier, who wrote these lines at the beginning of the 19th century, after the Jews were admitted into the national community following the French Revolution: *"They will correct themselves, say the philosophers. Not at all: they will pervert your customs without changing their own. By the way, at what*

---

[139] Oscar Friedmann, *Une Seconde de bonheur*, Calmann-Lévy, 1975, p. 80.
[140] Oscar Friedmann, *Une Seconde de bonheur*, Calmann-Lévy, 1975, p. 107.
[141] Oscar Friedmann, *Une Seconde de bonheur*, Calmann-Lévy, 1975, p. 199, 201, 202.

time will they correct themselves? in a century's time? In the meantime, we shall suffer them; of this we are already tired; will they be corrected in ten years' time? Then let them spend ten years in the countries where they dwell! If a leper or a plague-stricken person were entrusted to you in your house and you were told that he would be cured in ten days, you would reply: let him spend the ten days in his home; then we will visit him and check him before admitting him. Now, are not the Jews with their mercantile customs the leprosy and the perdition of the social body? Wait then to ascertan their healing before welcoming them among you, or else give up speaking of good customs. If time were to correct them, they would not already have been corrected in London, where they were admitted long ago, and where they run the streets, encouraging the children of families to steal, etc. They leave the Jews in France for a century; they will organize their sect in every town, dealing only with their fellows; they will become in France what they are in Poland, and will end by subtracting the commercial industry from the nationals who have hitherto exercised it very well without the Jews. So it is in Germany, where honest merchants are driven out of business because they cannot compete with the Jews. Wherever they shine, it is only at the expense of the nationals. Look at Genoa and Livorno, ports whose situation is equally favorable and whose trade is similar. If the Jews were not admitted in Livorno, this port would be full of Tuscan merchants instead of being populated by Jews... In short, the Jews, in politics, are a parasitic sect that tends to invade the commerce of the States at the expense of the nationals, without identifying itself with the fate of the homeland. Far from correcting themselves in France, they are more than likely to propagate their infamous morals, for they are already bitterly complained of in Lorraine and in Franche-Comté, where they have been introduced in great numbers since the Revolution. They practice in the villages a thousand tricks and scoundrelships which were unknown to these still quite Frankish peoples[142]."

The Talmud and the Jewish mentality

The Talmud is the holiest book of the Jews. This book, which contains the teachings of the rabbis of the first centuries of our era, has more authority for the Jews than the Torah itself (the Bible, the Old Testament

---

[142] Charles Fourier, *Publications des manuscrits de Charles Fourier*, 1835-1856, *Du commerce et des commeçants*, Librairie Phalanstérienne.

of the Christians). It transcribes or summarizes the stormy discussions that took place in the various academies of Palestine and Babylon. A teacher enunciated a problem, his disciple proposed a solution, which was answered in turn by the disciple's disciple, and the next generation solved it in this way. Several generations of teachers and students continued again and again with the same debate, which the Talmud reported in a brief passage or in a simple paragraph[143].

The simplest things were the subject of discussion and quibbling. The rabbis sought mysteries in the clearest or most insignificant phrases of the Torah, indulging in the most extravagant conjectures. They went so far as to argue that every passage in the Bible had potentially sixty or even six hundred thousand explanations.

An Enlightenment Jewish philosopher of the 18th century, Solomon Maimon, who resided in Poland, amusingly mocked some Talmudic lucubrations: "*For example, how many white hairs can the red-haired cow have so that it is still considered red-haired?*" or "*Is it permitted to kill a louse or a flea on the Sabbath?*" But it is true that Solomon Maimon was somewhat at odds with his own community.

Bernard Lazare, an anarchist socialist and supporter of Dreyfus[144], left a rather illuminating book on the subject. Bernard Lazare published in 1894 a book that was intended as a response to Edouard Drumont's *The Jewish France* whose success had been resounding. The following passage gives an insight into what this Jewish "Law" can be and its universal character in Judaism: "*But the Jew had something better than his god: he had his Thora—his law—and it is she who preserved it. This law, not only did he not lose it when he lost the ancestral territory, but on the contrary it reinforced his authority: he developed it and increased his power and also his virtue. When Jerusalem was destroyed, it was the law that became the bond of Israel: it lived for its law and by its law. Now: this law was meticulous and formalistic, it was the most perfect manifestation of the ritual religion in which the Jewish religion had become under the influence of the doctors, an influence that can be opposed to the spiritualism of the prophets whose tradition Jesus*

---

[143] Elie Wiesel, *Célébrations talmudiques*, Seuil, 1991, p. 275.
[144] The Dreyfus case had as its origin a judicial sentence of allegedly anti-Semitic court, on a background of espionage and anti-Semitism, in which the accused was Captain Alfred Dreyfus of German shepherd Jewish origin, and which, for twelve years, from 1894 to 1906, shocked the French society of the time, marking a milestone in the history of anti-Semitism. (NdT)

continued. These rites that foresaw every act of life and that the Talmudists complicated to infinity, these rites molded the brain of the Jew and, everywhere—in all countries—they molded it in the same way. The Jews, though dispersed, thought in the same way in Seville and in New York, in Ancona and in Regensburg, in Troye and in Prague. They had about beings and things the same feelings and the same ideas. They looked through the same lenses. They judged according to similar principles from which they could not deviate, because there were no serious and minor obligations in the law: all had an identical value because all emanated from God. All those whom the Jews drew to themselves were imprisoned in this terrible gear that crushed minds and molded them in a uniform way[145]."

This was also what Mark Zborowski wrote in his great anthropological study of Eastern European Jewry: "*A page of Talmud looks the same as it did a hundred years ago, and it looks the same in Vilna and in Shanghai. All over the world, pupils meditate on the same Torah, the same Talmud, the same Rachi commentary. The children chant with their flute-like voice the same text that opens the Michnah... Wherever his steps lead him, and as little as it is in a traditional community, the scholar of the shtetl will find the same studies, the same debates carried on with ardor and zeal.*"

If Jews react so strongly when one of their own is denounced as a swindler, it is because they know that the image of the entire community is tarnished. We find this same uniformity and atavism in the writings of Jewish intellectuals of today as of old. "*In the teachings of traditional Judaism, the barriers of time are blurred and confused,*" wrote Zborowski. *The habit of referring to ancient texts to govern the present and to modern texts to elucidate the past has forged between past and present an indestructible chain to which each scholar adds a link... Such silent disdain for Western divisions of time and space affirms that the unity of tradition is more solid than breaks in physical and temporal continuity[146].*" This is precisely what some called "the eternal Jew" *(Der ewige Jude).*

---

[145] Bernard Lazare, *Anti-Semitism, its history and causes, (1894).* Editions La Bastille, Digital Edition, 2011 p. 120, 121.
[146] Mark Zborowski, *Olam*, 1952, Plon, 1992, p. 107, 108.

The Talmud contains everything and its opposite[147]. Some rabbis preach tolerance, while others condemn it; some approve of usury, but others reject it, etc. But the truth is that the whole work contains many very offensive and insulting passages against non-Jews, and especially against Christians. In the first half of the 13th century, Nicolas Donin had been the first to denounce the horrors contained in the Talmud. And he knew it first hand, since he himself was a former Jew who had left the sect. Then, in the 16th century, Christian Hebraizing scholars continued to study the Talmud and confirmed what everyone suspected. Here are some precepts taken from this "holy book":

Christians are idolaters, do not associate with them (Hilkhoth Maakhaloth); Christians are impure because they eat impure food (Shabbath, 145b); Jewish women are defiled by the mere encounter with Christians (Yore Dea, 198); Jews are human, Christians are not, they are beasts (Keritot, 6b); Christians are created to serve Jews (Midrash Talpiyot, 225); Christians are no more to be pitied than pigs when they are sick to their guts (Orach Chayim, 57, 6a); the seed of the goyim is like that of beasts (Yevamot, 98a); dead Christian slaves are to be replaced like cattle (Yore Dea, 377); Jews are to be called men, not Christians (Yevamot, 61a); striking a Jew is like slapping God in the face (Sanhedrin, 58b); a Jew is always considered good, despite the sins he may commit. It is always the shell that is soiled, never its bottom (Chagigah, 15b); wine must be thrown away if it has been touched by a Christian (Avodah Zarah, 72a, b); the vessel purchased from a Christian must be thrown away or purified (Yore Dea. 120, 1); etc.

And as for how to trade with Christians, the sages of the Talmud say the following: the property of a Christian or a gentile is in vain, it belongs to the first Jew who claims it (Baba Batra, 54b); if a Christian mistakenly returns too much money, it must be kept (Choschen Ham, 183); Jews may keep a Christian's belongings without worrying about it (Choschen Ham, 226); it is permitted to perjure and cheat Christians in court (Baba Kamma, 113a, b); Jews who cheat a Christian must share the benefit equally (Choschen Ham, 183); usury is permitted with Christians and apostates (Iore Dea, 159); etc.

---

[147] The Gemara is the part of the Talmud that collects the endless discussions and commentaries of the rabbis. The rabbis practice *Midrash* (commentary, explanation, interpolation). See the long note on *Midrash* in *Psychoanalysis of Judaism*.

Furthermore, they may lie, if it is in the interest of one of their own and the community. Jews may swear falsely by using phrases with double meanings, or by any subterfuge (Schabbouth Hag., 6d and Kol Nidré).

It is permitted to indirectly kill a Christian, for example, if someone who does not believe in the Torah falls into a well, the ladder must be removed (Choschen Ham, 425). And many more quotes that might not seem credible to neophytes, as they are really insulting to the goyim.

Nicolas Donin had assembled several excerpts from the Talmud, followed by thirty-five counts as the basis of accusation.

As a result of his work, on June 9, 1239, Pope Gregory IX had sent a letter to all the bishops of France, England, Castile, Aragon and Portugal ordering them to confiscate all copies of the Talmud and hand them over to the Dominican and Franciscan monks. The sovereigns of those countries were to assist the bishops, while the priors of the Dominicans and Franciscans were charged with opening proceedings against the Talmud and burning all copies.

Our European ancestors had understood that the profound nature of Judaism was nourished by the precepts contained in that book. King Saint-Louis, concerned about this, had ordered a trial, which took place on June 12, 1240 at the Palais de Justice in Paris, under the presidency of his mother Blanche of Castile. After much debate, it was decided to destroy the book, and on June 6, 1242, twenty-four carts containing 1200 copies of the Talmud were burned in the Place de Grève. Thereafter, throughout Europe, numerous Popes continued to warn Christians against the horrors written in the pages of the Talmud[148].

---

[148]Read more in detail in Hervé Ryssen, *History of Antisemitism*, Baskerville, 2010.

PART TWO
THE SHARKS OF FINANCE

The great sorcerers and manitus of international finance are not all Jews; far from it. But members of this community have always exercised great influence in this activity. When new frauds come to light, one can be almost certain that some child of the "chosen people" will appear, again making the front page of the media news[149].

1. Pyramid fraud

The pyramid scheme is the great timeless classic of financial fraud, commonly called "Ponzi scheme", after the name of the swindler who wreaked havoc in Boston in 1921. Journalists often repeat this expression to avoid talking about "Goldstein's pyramid" or the "Cohen scheme". But since December 2008, this type of fraud will be associated, and for a long time, with the name of Bernard Madoff, who broke all records in this field. This fraud consists for an ambitious financier in collecting money from his clients by promising them higher than normal interest rates. When a client asks to get his money back at the agreed interest rate, in whole or in part, the investor gives him the money deposited by other clients who entered more recently.

---

[149] At the end of 2022 Sam Bankman-Fried, the latest financial genius from the Jewish community implicated in the multi-billion dollar fraud of the cryptocurrency exchange platform FTX, was in the news. His connections to the funding of the US Democratic party and Ukraine's embattled government give an idea of the magnitude of the scandal. In contrast to the seriousness of the matter, the presentation of the scam and the cartoonish and ridiculous figure of the outlandish character and his collaborators almost seemed like a humorous anti-Semitic parody. (NdT)

Let us imagine that A succeeds in convincing the individual or company B to give him 100 euros, promising to return 150 euros after one year. The following year, A returns to B the 100 euros plus the interest that has been subtracted from the contributions of the new investors, C and D. Since B is satisfied with this investment, he decides to invest again a much larger sum and, naturally, through word of mouth, persuades all his friends to enter into this good business. This scheme is reproduced as long as new investors deposit their money and there are more people entering the system than leaving.

At the beginning, customers flock to the scam, attracted by the financial promises, especially when the first investors are satisfied and give the investment a great deal of publicity. But sooner or later, the scammer fails to attract enough new investors to remunerate the old ones. The initiators and early arrivals have more than recouped their initial investment, while the latecomers lose everything.

Bernard Madoff, the absolute champion

Bernard Madoff was a well-known financier on Wall Street. Coming out of nowhere, he had established himself as one of the most important figures in the business world. In the early 1990s, he had managed to become the chairman of Nasdaq, the stock market for high-tech stocks in New York. But his fame was forged above all with his investment fund, Bernard Madoff Investment Securities (BMIS). He guaranteed his clients a reasonable return of 6 or 7% per annum, when the market was offering only 5%. He gave the impression of being very skilful, as he never reduced the returns distributed to his clients, regardless of the fluctuations of the stock market. Considered a prudent investor, everyone trusted him. His investments were considered as safe as U.S. Treasury bonds.

Bernard Madoff was also heavily involved in numerous charitable and cultural organizations, for which he was revered by the Jewish community and even dubbed by Wall Street brokers the "Jewish Treasury Bond." With the help of word of mouth, investors rushed to deliver their money into the hands of the prodigious businessman.

His empire was really a family business. He ran the house with his brother Peter, the number 2 in the partnership. After finishing his studies, his two sons, Mark and Andrew, did not hesitate for a moment and went straight into the family business. But Bernard Madoff loved working alone. His brokerage firm occupied the entire 17th floor of the

Lipstick Building, that lipstick-shaped building on New York's Third Avenue. It was his sanctuary; no one penetrated there and controlled his activities. Those who wondered how it was possible to generate such interest for so long, with such regularity, and wondered what the financier's secret could be, Madoff smilingly replied: *"Don't ask, don't tell"*. A fund manager who had wanted to audit the firm was told: *"Only Madoff's brother-in-law is authorized to audit the accounts, in order to keep Madoff's strategy secret and prevent it from being copied"*.

"Bernie" Madoff had a reserved appearance. He made no attempt whatsoever to impress his surroundings or to show off in an ostentatious manner. He was a discreet man. Most of the time, he simply refused to meet potential investors. Madoff did not solicit potential investors; on the contrary, it was up to them to insist that they enter this supposedly very closed club and deposit their money. He exerted a kind of magnetic attraction, as if investing in his funds was a priceless privilege. The simple fact of having an appointment with the businessman could take several months, even years, so that when the investor finally succeeded, he would show up for the appointment with only one clear objective: to be accepted as a client, without reservation. At first, Madoff insisted that new investors deposit little money, so that they would not be suspicious. In this way, he managed to instill confidence so that they would later invest much larger sums.

These new investors were absolutely necessary to the proper functioning of his company. In fact, their money was remunerating former clients who wished to recover the principal plus interest, and not the lucrative investments that Madoff was supposed to be making. Attracting new investors was therefore indispensable, even if it had to be done in a mundane way. His wife Ruth remembered all these dinners, golf games, galas, all these relationships that had to be maintained all the time. Meanwhile, "Bernie" followed his teams of *Macher* (a Yiddish word for a character who has contacts)—his prospectors—who told in influential circles how their money was so well invested with Madoff. When the duped person asked, the *Macher* would invariably reply, *"You can't approach him directly without being introduced. But maybe he can do something for you."*

After having targeted the richest people in New York, Madoff had done the same in Florida starting in 1996. He spent most of his time in Palm Beach, the millionaire's paradise that welcomes big business owners, best-selling writers, famous sports figures and wealthy philanthropists. He was a regular at the very select Palm Beach Country Club, one of its

300 exclusive members—all from the Jewish community. Everyone had blind trust in this great philanthropist who showered Jewish charities. Madoff was one of their own.

But with the collapse of the financial markets at the end of 2008, following the bankruptcy of Lehman Brothers in September, many clients preferred to withdraw their funds for fear of losing their money, so that in December Madoff had to face refunds of 7 billion dollars. The whole pyramid collapsed. On December 10, Madoff gathered his children, who apparently (but no one has to believe the swindler's version) were unaware of the fraud, to announce the catastrophe to them. They alerted the authorities. On December 12, 2008, Bernard Madoff, 70 years old, was arrested at his Manhattan home by the federal police.

Of the twenty-one billion dollars that had been delivered over twenty years, there was nothing left. Counting the accrued interest that remained unpaid, the investors had lost no less than $65 billion (49.1 billion euros). It was the biggest pyramid scheme in the history of mankind. And this gigantic fraud, which had lasted twenty years, had been perpetrated by a man revered as a Wall Street celebrity.

A financial shoah

The consequences of the scam had an impact on thousands of investors and savers around the world. Some savers had given their money directly to Bernard Madoff's company, while others had placed their money indirectly through investment funds working with the financier.

French banks were relatively unaffected. Natixis had lost about $450 million and BNP Paribas another $300 million. The British bank HSBC, the world's third largest bank in terms of capitalization, recognized losses of almost $1 billion, while the Swiss bank UCB reported losses of $850 million. The Spanish bank Santander was hit hard with 2.33 billion euros, especially the clients of its Optimal fund[150].

While most of the swindled investors had gone through bank intermediaries, the Palm Beach investors, on the other hand, were often people very close to Madoff. Palm Beach Country Club members were in a state of shock; they had a sense of having been betrayed by a friend.

---

[150] https://www.elmundo.es/mundodinero/2008/12/14/economia/1229282291.html (15/12/2008). (NdT).

"The community is in a state of shock. No one imagined that someone like him could do that to his friends," explained Carlos Carraca, an island resident. *"Many families were ruined, some lost everything, millions."*

Some celebrities had also suffered losses in the scam. A foundation of filmmaker Steven Spielberg had deposited a significant part of its resources in the hands of the former Nasdaq chairman. American real estate and media mogul Mort Zuckerman—owner of the *New York Daily* and *US News & World Report*—had not been spared either. As for the Elie Wiesel Foundation for Humanity, which had presented its annual award to President Nicolas Sarkozy in September, it issued the following statement: *"It is with deep sorrow and sadness that we inform you that we have been, along with many others, victims of one of the biggest financial frauds in history. The Foundation held some $15.2 million managed by Bernard Madoff's investment fund, i.e. almost all of its assets."*

Jewish charitable organizations had also been hard hit. According to Gary Tobin, president of the San Francisco Community Research Institute, donations made to various American Jewish associations for charitable purposes amounted to 5 billion dollars a year (20% of which went to Israeli organizations). The newspaper *Le Monde* of December 28, 2008, which took up this information, pointed out that, in relation to this enormous amount of money, "the *part managed by Madoff was not known, but it must have been considerable*". "This is a *catastrophic event for the Jewish community*[151]," commented Rob Eshman, editor-in-chief of the weekly *Jewish Journal*, published in Los Angeles. In Boston, the Lappin Foundation, which financed trips for Jewish youth to Israel, had to lay off its entire staff and announce its closure. As for the Chais Family Foundation, which donated around $12.5 million each year to Jewish good works, it too had closed its doors and laid off its staff. *"The entire fund has been invested through Bernard Madoff's intermediary and, consequently, the fund has been completely lost"*, its president Avraham Infeld had declared. Thus, President Vladimir Putin, to whom the leaders of the elected community attributed the *"greatest plundering of Jewish interests since the 1930s*[152]*"*, had just found a serious competitor.

---

[151] *Le Monde*, December 28, 2008.
[152] Read the first part of *The Jewish Mafia*.

Between negligence and complicity

Some victims had formed an association. *"Where's my money, that's all I want to know today!"* cried Phillys Moltchatsky, a 62-year-old woman shaking with rage. *"It's Parkinson's disease,"* she confessed in shame. *It's gotten worse because of Madoff, I've lost 1.7 million[153]."* The sexagenarian was part of a group of three hundred victims who attacked in justice for negligence the SEC (Securities and Exchange Commission), the gendarme of the New York stock exchange. In June 2009, the joint complaint had been dismissed in the first instance. In fact, no one had ever won a lawsuit against the SEC.

Helen Chaitman, 67, had to go back to work after losing everything to Madoff. *"Fortunately,"* she was a bank fraud lawyer. She devoted all her energy, along with the other victims, to proving the SEC's negligence. *"The SEC had conducted seven investigations of Madoff in eleven years, involving twenty-seven people. Not only did it let him operate his Ponzi scheme for twenty years, it officially approved it[154],"* he said in a slow voice that poorly disguised his anger.

In reality, the pyramid scheme created by the American financier could have been unveiled in 1992, sixteen years earlier, as revealed in a September 2009 400-page report written by David Kotz, the SEC's inspector general[155]. According to David Kotz, the SEC had missed numerous red flags. Between June 1992 and December 2002, no fewer than six complaints from individuals or financial decision-makers had come to the SEC, but the investigations had been cursory. *"Despite three examinations and two inspections, no thorough and competent inspection had ever really been carried out,"* he acknowledged. The inspector general blamed it all on *"the relative inexperience"* and lack of training of the staff in charge of examining these transactions.

Faced with this embarrassing narrative, SEC Chairwoman Mary Schapiro had to make her *mea culpa*. *"It is a failure that we continue to regret,"* she said, acknowledging all the missed opportunities to unmask Bernard Madoff. She had also added that, since then, the agency that oversees the stock markets had made numerous changes in order to better detect financial infractions.

---

[153] *Le Figaro*, June 29, 2009.
[154] *Le Figaro*, June 29, 2009.
[155] *Le Figaro*, September 3, 2009.

The goyim could, however, see things differently. Republican Senator Charles Grassley, for example, for his part, considered the dysfunctionalities brought to light by the Kotz report to be *"further evidence of the culture of deference in use at the SEC vis-à-vis Wall Street elites."* One could legitimately ask questions about the SEC's deputy director at the time when Madoff was at the height of his glory, one Eric Swanson, married to Shana Madoff, a niece of Bernard Madoff. But for David Kotz, the inspector general, nothing could prove the slightest collusion with the swindler. And we had to believe him.

The U.S. courts had appointed a liquidator, Irving Picard[156], who was entrusted with the task of recovering the victims' money. Irving Picard relentlessly pursued all the accomplices and alleged beneficiaries of the swindle. He first accused certain banks which, according to him, had encouraged or at least had not dissuaded their clients from placing their money in the Madoff funds, knowing the risks and collecting their commissions in the process. According to the investigators, the intermediaries could not have been unaware of the fraud, since the returns were unrealistic. Above all, their withdrawals were too large to be honest: $12 billion had been withdrawn from the Madoff fund in 2008, $6 billion three months before the debacle[157].

In December 2010, Irving Picard claimed no less than $9 billion from the British bank HSBC, which was initially thought to have been a victim of the scam. But according to the official, HSBC had *"created, promoted and nurtured an international network of a dozen provider funds domiciled in Europe, the Caribbean and Central America."* The bank strongly denied this.

Irving Picard also accused the US bank JP Morgan, the main bank of the Bernard Madoff Investissement Securities (BMIS) fund, of complicity and demanded 6.4 billion dollars. The bank had deliberately ignored several red flags indicating that the money came from fraudulent operations. *"JP Morgan had consciously turned a blind eye to the fraud, even after being warned several times against Madoff."*

---

[156] Irving H. Picard (b. 1941) is a partner in the law firm BakerHostetler. He is best known for recovering funds from the Madoff investment scandal. Irving Picard is Jewish.
[157] *Le Figaro*, June 29, 2009.

The bank had responded that this accusation was *"irresponsible and exaggerated."*

Irving Picard also claimed $555 million from Swiss bank UBS, accused of having recovered the amounts stolen by Madoff from investors in two of its funds. UBS defended itself against such accusations, arguing that *"they were not liable to those investors for the unfortunate consequences of the Madoff scandal."* An appeal had been filed against the banks Natixis and Citigroup, from which the liquidator was claiming respectively $400 million and $425 million. The other banks targeted were the Belgian Fortis (BNP Paribas group), the Dutch ABN Amro, the Spanish Banco Bilbao Vizcaya Argentaria, the Japanese Nomura and the American Merrill Lynch.

Irving Picard had also initiated proceedings against members of Madoff's family, starting with his brother Peter and his sons Mark and Andrew, thus recovering some 80 million. He accused the three men of not having detected the scam and not having suspected the origin of the money that financed their lifestyle. The complaint accused the eldest son, Mark Madoff, in particular, of having misspent $66 million (49.8 million euros) to acquire real estate assets consisting of prestigious properties in New York, Connecticut and Nantucket. In December 2010, Mark Madoff, 46, was discovered dead at his home in New York. He had hanged himself in his apartment in the Soho neighborhood of Manhattan.

Bernard Madoff had been tried quickly, a few months after the scandal. On March 12, 2009, he decided to plead guilty, which allowed him to avoid a trial before a jury but also an investigation that would have undoubtedly lifted the veil on several mysteries. On June 29, 2009, the former Wall Street glory was sentenced to 150 years in prison, the maximum foreseen by law. The judge had thus ensured that he would end his life behind bars. Madoff did not appeal the sentence.

From the back of his cell in Butner, North Carolina, Bernard Madoff refused, however, to be the scapegoat. In an interview with the *Financial Times* at the end of March 2011 and published on April 9, Madoff singled out JP Morgan: *"I'm not a banker, but I know that billions of dollars going in and out of a bank account should raise red flags... There are people inside the bank who knew."* These accusations had provoked widespread outrage. JP Morgan responded tersely that Madoff's statements were *"false."*

In his previous interview, in February 2011, he had already made similar accusations. He also accused regulators of incompetence, first and foremost the SEC (Securities and Exchange Commission): *"In 50 years, I've had probably 50 SEC controls, and my company has always been considered a model"*.

The alleged victims were actually their accomplices

Over time, and as the investigation progressed, it became increasingly clear that the large Madoff account holders who had presented themselves as victims had previously been major beneficiaries of the scam. Some investors who had held funds in the Madoff accounts, hoping for one last windfall, were indeed "victims" in December 2008. But this was without taking into account the gains made in previous years. This was what was denounced by a *New York Times* columnist, Joe Nocera, who had titled his article, *"Of course Bernie had accomplices: his victims*[158] *!"*

In an interview granted to the *Politico* news agency, and published in the Israeli daily *The Times of Israel* on March 21, 2014, Bernard Madoff had confessed that Jewish charities had made more money than they had lost, in fact probably much more: *"Religion has nothing to do with it,"* Madoff pointed out, adding: *"I don't think I have betrayed Jews, I have betrayed people. I have betrayed people who trusted me—some were from the Jewish community. I have made more money for Jews and their charities than I have lost."*

Irving Picard calculated the number of individuals or companies that had made money by withdrawing their bet in time thanks to Madoff in 2000; about a thousand were accused of having taken undue advantage of the system or of having participated as accomplices of the swindler. *"The people who made money did so at the expense of those who lost it all*[159]*"*, he had declared. And he was determined to make them give in. To do so, he had threatened to invoke the *"claw back"*, a legal procedure that allows the reclaiming of unduly withdrawn capital. Irving Picard and New York State Attorney General Preet Bharara believed that those who claimed to have been swindled—very wealthy investors, bankers,

---

[158] *Le Monde,* December 21, 2010.
[159] *Les Échos,* July 28, 2010.

large foundations, etc. who had previously enjoyed indecent returns—should return what they had received.

The receiver had seriously admonished them: either you return your profits to the last penny, or else we file a complaint and a court will decide. He had especially adopted this attitude with all those who had had a good enough nose or an informed enough ear to withdraw the money shortly before the fall. It bears repeating: $12 billion had been withdrawn from BMIS in the ten months before the collapse, half of it in the last three months. Irving Picard had simply denied victim status to those who had withdrawn more money than they had deposited in the Madoff fund. Only the real losers would be compensated.

In the interview given to the *Financial Times* at the end of March 2011, Madoff confusingly indicted his four main "clients" — Jeffry Picower, Stanley Chais, Norman Levy and Carl Shapiro. *"They knew something was wrong. They were complicit,"* he claimed. Of his four former top clients who had helped him stock the fund with fresh money—all members of the Jewish community—three had passed away. But their heirs, and especially their lawyers, had jumped into the fray to expose the lies of the former Wall Street "star". Old Carl Shapiro, the last one still alive, claimed that Madoff was a liar. *"His latest statements are no more credible than all the other lies uttered for decades[160]."*

In her 2011 book on the rise and fall of Bernard Madoff, the famous American journalist, Diane Henriques, who worked at the *New York Times* until 2011, underlined the key role played by the four *"wealthy Jewish businessmen"* in Madoff's career, betting on him in the late 1970s [161]. Other names circulated: Robert Jaffe (Carl Shapiro's grandson), Noel Levine, Ezra Merkin in New York, all high-level Jewish financiers. But all claimed innocence, claiming they had lost a lot of money. No doubt they had lost a lot in December 2008, but how much had they made in the previous years? Investigators were trying to establish their level of responsibility, unraveling their guilty obfuscation and active complicity.

For its part, the SEC, which had let the gigantic swindle pass, had filed its first action in June 2009 against the Cohmad (Cohn-Madoff) fund which leased offices to the swindler, right across the street from its own.

---

[160] *Le Point*, April 11, 2011.
[161] Read the article *The jewish Roots of Madoff's Crime*, on the website of the Jewish newspaper *The Jewish Daily Forwards*, May 10, 2011.

Cohmad Securities was founded in 1985 by Bernard Madoff and Maurice Cohn, a friend of Madoff and former neighbor. Its main activity consisted in directing investors to Madoff funds in exchange for commissions on the amounts invested. Cohmad's vice president was Robert Jaffre, married to Ellen Shapiro, Carl Shapiro's daughter. Robert Jaffe, who worked in Palm Beach, had brought 150 accounts totaling $1 billion into the Madoff investment fund.

The elder Carl Shapiro had built his fortune in textile manufacturing and was very close to Madoff, whom he considered a bit like his son. But in December 2008, when the Madoff house collapsed, he lost, by all accounts, some $545 million; a loss that could chill any friendship. Two years later, however, following investigations by Irving Picard, we learned that Carl Shapiro had actually made a killing. He had invested hundreds of millions with Madoff, and had regularly reaped the rewards of his investments over the previous years, probably with the complicity of his old friend. But at the ripe old age of 97, he claimed to know nothing about the scam. In December 2010, Carl Shapiro nevertheless agreed to repay 625 million dollars, just at the time when the American justice was about to seize his JP Morgan account. We then learned that the Shapiro Foundation, *"The Carl and Ruth Shapiro Family Foundation"*, used to make generous donations to the *"Beth Israel Deaconess Medical Center"*, but that because of the scandal, he said, he could no longer be so generous. The Jewish associations were going to sink into the most horrible misery, no doubt about it!

Norman Levy, a real estate tycoon, was also an old friend of Madoff. He also said of Madoff that he was his *"adopted son"*. It was he who introduced the swindler to major investors. His offices were located just below those of Madoff's company, on the lower floor. New York investigators claimed that there had been billions of back and forth of checks between Madoff and him. And he also had a foundation, the *Betty and Norman F. Levy Foundation*, which had apparently lost a lot of money in December 2008. But Norman Levy did not have to mourn these losses much, as he had passed away in 2005, at the age of 93. Before his death, Levy had named Madoff as executor of his estate, and he had transferred $250 million to his investment fund.

Stanley Chais, a successful businessman and respected philanthropist, served as Madoff's Hollywood hook. He also persuaded the unwary to invest. In May 2009, Irving Picard had taken legal action against him, accusing him of having been an accomplice since his investments with Madoff were paid back at an average of 40%, sometimes even 300%, i.e. profits equivalent to more than $1 billion since 1995. When the Madoff empire collapsed in 2008, Chais's audited accounts showed that his clients had invested more than $900 million in the fraudster's fund. In June, the SEC in turn filed a complaint against the controversial businessman who eventually died in 2010 at the age of 84 from a blood disease. His foundation, the *"Chais Family Fondation"*, which donated a lot of money to dozens of Jewish and Israeli associations as well as to the Hebrew University of Jerusalem, had closed in December 2008, leaving thousands of Jewish children destitute.

One of the major beneficiaries of the scam was Jeffry Picower, another "philanthropist", "defiscalization" specialist and professional investor operating in Palm Beach, Florida, within the most distinguished circles. Jeffry Picower had been in close relationship with "Bernie" for thirty years, and held some twenty accounts at BMIS. A lawyer and accountant by training, he had made his fortune in real estate and juicy investments. Together with Madoff, he had made such extravagant profits that in 2008 he had entered the Forbes Top 400 of the richest men in the United States; in 371st position. The liquidator Irving Picard had found that the profitability of some of his accounts with Madoff sometimes reached 100 to 500% per year—even 1000% in one of them! —An example: on April 18, 2006, Jeffry Picower had deposited 125 million in an account. Eight months later, the interest had earned him 81 million. Just before the collapse of the Madoff pyramid, he had withdrawn no less than 500 million dollars, so it was obvious that he knew about the scam. Jeffry Picower had amassed billions. On October 25, 2009, eleven months after the collapse of the Madoff fund, his wife found him dead in his pool in Palm Beach, Florida. Heart attack, the autopsy concluded. He was 67 years old. After his death, ABC television hinted that Picower had been the mastermind of the scam: *"Many investors believed he was the mastermind of the massive Madoff scam."* Indeed, during the three decades that the scam lasted Picower had accumulated more profits than Bernie himself.

Irving Picard claimed exactly $7.2 billion from Picower's widow, although he had to struggle for a long year to reach a settlement. In December 2010, the woman finally agreed to repay this enormous sum of money in exchange for a promise from the liquidator and New York State Attorney General Preet Bharara to waive all legal proceedings and to admit that her husband was not voluntarily involved in the pyramid scheme[162]. It was the largest sum ever settled by a private individual after a lawsuit, but honor was safe. After that, Barbara Picower had then stated that she was *"absolutely convinced that her husband was not an accomplice of Madoff."* Her lawyer gave the following explanation, *"It's not out of guilt. My client believes in the principle that anyone who profits from fraud should restore the sum to its rightful owners. It is a moral principle."* And, as everyone knows, in Judaism, you don't mess with moral principles!

Jewish charities had not lost everything either, as they had tried to make us believe at the beginning. Several associations declared as loss-making at the beginning of the scandal were in fact among the beneficiary clients targeted by Irving Picard: *"The America Israel Cultural Foundation"* owed about $5.32 million; *"The American Committee for Shaare Zedek Medical Center"* owed $7 million; *"The United Congregations Mesorah"*, a religious association, owed about $16 million; *"Hadassah"*, the Zionist women's organization, had announced in December 2010 that it was prepared to repay $45 million, etc. All these associations had benefited greatly from the donations of "philanthropists" or had knowingly invested in the Madoff fund.

"Last but not least, banker Sonja Kohn was among the biggest beneficiaries of the scam. She was the founding president and main shareholder of the small Austrian bank Medici (which employed only 16 people). Sonja Kohn owned 75%; the rest belonged to Bank Austria, a subsidiary of UniCredit, the largest Italian bank, which gave Medici some credibility. In December 2008, Sonja Kohn, 60, had claimed to be one of Madoff's main victims, losing $2.1 billion. In January 2009, she had sent an email to Bloomberg's newsroom introducing herself as *"a victim"* of this story and denying having been *"a friend of Bernard Madoff"*.

In April, interrogated for six hours by a Vienna prosecutor, audited by two SEC agents and Austrian investigators, she had once again defended her innocence: *"I am not guilty. I am the mother of five children and 24 grandchildren*[163]*."*

But in December 2010, Irving Picard's 160-page report seriously questioned her version. She was accused of having invested 9.1 billion

---

[162] *Le Monde*, December 21, 2010
[163]*Newsweek*, February 20, 2011. *"Summary of the meeting obtained by Newsweek and translated from German."*

dollars over 23 years in the Madoff fund, i.e. almost half of the 19.6 billion dollars (14.8 billion euros) that had gone up in smoke. It was also known that in November 2008, just before the scandal broke, Sonja Kohn had recovered $536 million from the fund.

In reality, she collected money from her clients on Madoff's behalf, and secretly cashed out in return. *"Madoff found in Sonja Kohn a criminal soul mate, whose greed and dishonest inventiveness matched his own*[164]*"*, Irving Picard had stated. Six members of Sonja Kohn's family were also in the crosshairs. *"No Ponzi scheme can last without a steady flow of fresh capital, and Ms. Kohn's firm was responsible for providing that steady flow of money for Madoff,"* explained Irving Picard.

Before Bernard Madoff's confession in December 2008, Medici Bank had begun to diversify its sources of income in order to distance itself from its main partner, who then accounted for 90% of its financial activities. But without success; that had not been enough and the bank was intervened and placed under judicial control in January 2009, and was disqualified in May of the same year.

Sonja Kohn, born in Blau, had grown up in the small Jewish community of the Austrian capital before marrying a banker, Erwin Kohn. In 1984, she founded the Medici Bank in Vienna. A year later, she was settling about forty miles north of New York, in an Orthodox Jewish community in Monsey. She wore a wig on top of her shaved head, as required by her religious tradition. In 1985, Sonja Kohn was introduced to Bernard Madoff by a manager of Cohmad Securities, and then moved back to Vienna in 1990 to find rich European investors. She had thus become Madoff's European right-hand man in Europe. She also had a villa in the Nahlaot neighborhood of Jerusalem, where she traveled several times a year to see her son, Rabbi Avraham Zeev Kahana, the director of the Talmudic school *The Gates of Halacha*. She financed the school. In more than 20 years, this Austrian bank had given its American accomplice 9.1 billion dollars, without ever informing its clients of the final destination of the funds.

Irving Picard's report mentioned that she and her husband had planned to move to Switzerland in the months preceding the collapse of the

---

[164] *Le Figaro*, December 11, 2010. Apart from this small article in the *Figaro*, and another in *France24.com*, no article has appeared in the French press about this Jewish banker, which is quite symptomatic of the control of our media.

Madoff pyramid. Indeed, Sonja Kohn had been spending a lot of time there for several years, especially in the vicinity of a hunting ground for billionaires[165]. It was in Switzerland that she began to frequent some of those famous "Russian" oligarchs who had plundered Russia in the 1990s, after the fall of the Soviet empire. The banker had placed part of her savings in the Madoff fund, so much so that, apparently, some of them wanted to take her skin off her back. Be that as it may, this is what she had claimed to disappear with her husband at the beginning of 2009[166]. In December 2010, Sonja Kohn was still a refugee of unknown whereabouts. A Jewish newspaper, *The Jewish Daily Forward*, headlined, *"But where is Sonja Kohn hiding?"* The author of the article, Debra Nussbaum Cohen, legitimately wondered if she was not hiding in the Orthodox Jewish community in Jerusalem, in Bnei Brak[167].

Compensate victims

In December 2010, good news finally reached the ears of the victims: the Geneva-based bank UBP had decided to reimburse nearly 500 million dollars to the *Trustee*, the U.S. authority that administered the bankruptcy of the funds controlled by Bernard Madoff[168]. This was the first international settlement of such magnitude. Pursued for more than $2 billion, the bank, founded by Edgar de Picciotto, was still run by his family of origin from Lebanon's small Jewish community.

To date, Irving Picard had recovered $9600 million from banks, private foundations and numerous "charitable" associations, out of the twenty billion lost, so that many real victims of Bernard Madoff received the first compensation payments at the beginning of 2011. The liquidator had only taken into account the amounts invested without interest. In September 2012, Irving Picard had announced the sending of compensation checks to 1230 victims, for a total amount of

---

[165] There is in Davos an important Hasidic Jewish community, with their kaftans and their schtreimels, those characteristic fur hats. [On Hasidic (esoteric and Kabbalistic) Judaism, read *Psychoanalysis of Judaism*.
[166] No information has been available since then.
[167] *The Jewish Daily Forward*, December 16, 2010.
[168] Trustee (or trust administrator) is a legal term that can refer, in its broadest sense, to any person who has ownership, authority, or position of trust or responsibility for the assets of another person. A trustee may be a person who is allowed to do tasks without profiting from them.

$2500 million. The amount of the checks ranged from $1784 to $526.8 million, the average payment being $2 million.

In December 2013, it was announced the creation of a compensation fund for victims of the Madoff fraud (*Madoff Victim Fund*) of about 2350 million dollars, reserved for victims who had not been reimbursed for their initial investment, with indirect investors having a certain priority over direct investors. This initiative was intended to partially compensate the thousands of registered victims. On May 14, 2014, the fund (MVF) set up by the Department of Justice to register claims had received 51,700 complaints from 119 countries. This was three times more than the number of complaints registered during the judicial procedure. About 58% of the complaints came from the United States. At the beginning of 2014, the US bank JP Morgan Chase from which Bernard Madoff's account was operated for two decades, finally agreed to pay 2.6 billion dollars to this fund. This agreement allowed the first US bank to escape criminal prosecution. JP Morgan was not accused of having committed fraud, but of having turned a blind eye to the scam. However, it was quite clear that the bank's management was aware of the scam. In 2011, in a jailhouse interview, Madoff himself said, *"There are people in the bank who knew what I was doing."* Jamie Dimon, the chairman of JP Morgan[169], had preferred not to warn the US regulators and to continue his very lucrative relations with the swindler. But while Madoff had been sentenced to 150 years in prison, Jamie Dimon was free.

The death of the goy

In France, many had been fooled: retired businessmen, wealthy senior executives, show business stars, heirs to old industrial dynasties, etc. When the Madoff scandal broke, their names were rumored in the elegant offices of reputable Parisian lawyers. A great Cognac family name was said to have lost 280 million euros in the scam. There was also talk of the Racamiers (heirs to the Vuitton fortune), the Guerrand-Hermès family, the heirs to part of the Bouygues family, the husband of a former movie star, etc. Nobody wanted to confirm the rumors. Thousands of anonymous savers had been caught in the trap after investing with their eyes closed in sicavs and investment funds, which in turn invested in funds related to Madoff. Some had invested tens of

---

[169] Jamie Dimon was the descendant of a "Greek" banker.

thousands of euros, others hundreds of millions. Forty-five Parisian financial institutions (BNP Paribas, Natixis, Meeschaert, Aforge, La Compagnie Financière Edmond de Rothschild, etc.) had steered their investors, directly or indirectly, towards Madoff products, sometimes even without knowing it.

The Madoff system was based above all on relationships of trust and friendship. Bernard de la Villehuchet, the brother of investor Thierry de la Villehuchet, gave some explanations: *"Word of mouth worked at full capacity. Everyone wanted to get into Madoff, which offered returns of 6 to 7% when the stock market was plummeting."* The success had become so great, especially since the financial crisis of September 2008 (the *subprime* crisis), that the entire jet set and businessmen dreamed of investing in this miracle fund whose access was presented as a privilege. Joining Madoff was like joining a "hyper-select" club: you had to be co-opted, and the membership card cost several million euros. A Parisian lawyer told the following anecdote: *"One of my clients was told: 'I can't get you into Madoff. With 5 million euros, they won't accept you. You need more*[170]*"*.

The man who had sounded out French investors came from an old aristocratic family. He was Thierry Magon de La Villehuchet (René-Thierry Magon de La Villehuchet). He was a Breton from Saint-Malo, with a reputation for integrity. Settled in New York, where, curiously enough, he had become friends with Madoff over the years, becoming one of his most important intermediaries. As president of an investment company, he attracted the crowned heads and great European fortunes for the king of Wall Street. With his partner Patrick Littaye, he had played a key role in seducing the European crème de la crème. Of the 3 billion dollars that his company had invested for its clients, 2.25 billion had gone to the Madoff fund. As it turned out, when the scandal broke in December 2008, the man had not been informed of anything, as he had not had time to withdraw his clients' money. On December 23, Christmas Eve, Thierry de La Villehuchet committed suicide at the age of 65 by slitting his wrists in his Madison Avenue office.

"He was the most honest man in the world, a true medieval gentleman," recalled Marie-Monique Steckel, director of the Alliance française in

---

[170] *Le Figaro*, February 20, 2009.

New York and a lifelong friend[171]. He was rather the goy in all his splendor. Everyone can draw their own conclusions. If he had been a good Catholic, he would not have frequented these Phoenician environments.

Seven centuries ago, the great Italian theologian St. Thomas Aquinas (1225–1274) had expressly warned us in his *Summa Theologica*: "*Do not frequent them except in case of necessity, and if, in fact, you are firm in the faith. Avoid familiar dealings with them if your faith is wavering and nothing obliges you to see them[172].*"

The little Madoffs

Bernard Madoff is by far the biggest pyramid fraud swindler. But in reality, "Madoff pyramid" scams are quite frequent, judging by the number of scandals that have broken out in recent years, and we note that Jews are not the only ones in the fray. A certain Allen Stanford, for example, arrested in 2009 in the United States, had collected money from thousands of investors, some 7 billion dollars: a 110-year prison sentence for him in March 2012. In April 2010, Thomas Petters was sentenced to 50 years in prison for a $3.6 billion pyramid scheme. The others were smaller fish[173].

In 2007, Sergei Mavrodi, nicknamed the "Russian Madoff" (probably Jewish), was convicted in Moscow for a small swindle of 4.3 million dollars. In France, for example, there was the case of Sylviane Hamon, a 49-year-old former bank employee in the Tours region. Since her dismissal, she claimed to work on behalf of a credit company and promised extraordinary returns (up to 30%) thanks to her contacts in the banking world. He offered his services to friends, neighbors and even

---

[171] *Le Figaro*, June 30, 2009.
[172] St. Thomas Aquinas, *Summa Theologica*, II-IIa, c. 10, art. 10: "*If it is indeed a question of Christians who are firm in the faith, so much so that from their communication with infidels one can hope rather for their conversion than for their departure from the faith, they should not be forbidden to communicate with infidels who have never received the faith, that is, with pagans and Jews, especially when necessity presses. If, on the other hand, it is a question of simple and weak faithful in the faith, whose perversion may be feared as probable, they should be forbidden to deal with the infidels; above all, they should be forbidden to have excessive familiarity and unnecessary communication with them.*" (NdT).
[173] See the U.S. website *ponzitracker.com* (Ponzi Hunter!).

members of his in-laws. This is how she had stolen nearly three million euros from dozens of victims. She was arrested in December 2011.

In January 2014, we also had a "Madoff de l'Indre". The swindle of Roland Bernard—an insurer—amounted to seven million euros. He had cheated about sixty people. These little Madoffs were perhaps people with good intentions at the beginning, but they were quickly caught in a gear from which they did not know how to get out, rather than in a headlong rush.

Scott Rothstein and his billionaire

In November 2009, an FBI memo reported that noted Florida business lawyer and real estate star Scott Rothstein had been arrested. The 47-year-old had set up a Madoff pyramid scheme. Certainly, compared to Madoff's gigantic scam, his was very small. But still, according to the *Wall Street Journal*, it amounted to a billion dollars, putting him well up in the *hit parade* of the biggest swindlers in history. It was five times more, for example, than the huge Sentier scandal that had made headlines in France in the late 1990s[174].

Rothstein, who ran a firm of 70 lawyers and 150 employees (Rothstein Rosenfeld & Adler), had launched into financial investments in 2005, offering double-digit returns. He was also quite original in that he also offered to sell his "clients" shares in lawsuits brought against U.S. companies allegedly accused of sexual harassment or tax fraud, for example.

The case broke out in October 2009, when investors complained about not being paid. A single fund, Banyon Investments, located in Florida, claimed to have invested 775 million at a loss. Banyon even had to declare bankruptcy, losing the fortunes of its own clients in the process.

In June 2010, Rothstein was sentenced to 50 years in prison by the Fort Lauderdale court in North Miami. This very pious Jew was to have all the time to pray to Yaweh, the god of swindlers[175]. *"I have a deep faith*

---

[174] On the Sentier case, read *The Jewish Mafia*.
[175] According to the Talmud, the holy book of Judaism, defrauding the goyim is permitted, and even considered a mitzvah (commandment), a "blessing", when it is for the benefit of the community. See our *History of Antisemitism*, 2010.

in Judaism, from which I draw my strength," he declared. "Putting on tefillin is a way for me to connect with God[176]."

Rothstein had been a major benefactor of the Las Olas Boulevard synagogue, affiliated with the Chabad-Lubavitch Hasidic movement. The local Jews had even placed a plaque with his name on the façade of the building.

All of his assets had been confiscated: his eighteen properties in the United States (in Florida and Manhattan), his private jet, his $5 million yacht, his garage of sports cars, including his white Lamborghini and Ferrari Spider, as well as hundreds of valuable jewels. The total amounted to some $100 million[177].

With all that money, this observant Jew did what all Jewish billionaires do: he financially supported the Republican Party. Although he might as well have financed the Democratic party. In fact some fund both.

Bruce Friedman, a Californian Madoff

On September 13, 2010, French authorities, requested by the FBI, arrested Bruce Fred Friedman in front of his hotel in Cannes. The 60-year-old man, who lived in Southern California, had fled the United States in the midst of proceedings against him for a fraud estimated at hundreds of millions of dollars. Between 2004 and 2009, Friedman had organized a "Madoff-like" scheme, offering his clients to invest their money in rental properties. But he pocketed the millions and lived the high life, accumulating property and luxury cars. At the end of December 2011, Friedman was still in prison in Cannes without being extradited. His hundreds of victims were still demanding the 228 million that had disappeared.

His former clients held a grudge: *"I want to see him in the worst jail in the world, for the rest of his days,"* said Patricia Hank, who had invested $300,000 of her pension. *"I'd like him to stand trial here in Los Angeles, to stare him in the eye and tell him what I think of him."* But in March

---

[176] A book has been dedicated to him: *The Scott Rothstein story*, 2013. Typhilim are phylacteries, small leather wrappings or boxes containing Scripture passages that pious Jews wrap around their left arm and forehead to pray.
[177] *La Tribune de Genève*, January 8, 2010.

2012, we would learn that the con man, awaiting extradition, had passed away.

Eliyahu Weinstein scammed his community

In August 2010, a news story reported that the Orthodox Jewish community in New Jersey, next to New York, had been the victim of a $200 million scam. Eliyahu Weinstein, 35, had used his contacts within the Lakewood Jewish community to gain the trust of potential investors. Weinstein promised prospective victims juicy profits by investing with him in the purchase and sale of residences.

"It is always shocking to see someone steal from others to finance their lavish lifestyle, but it is especially infuriating to see this person exploit his own community," said Paul Fishman, New Jersey's attorney general. The defendant had amassed an impressive collection of jewelry and luxury watches valued at more than $200 million.

Tzvi Erez, the little "Canadian" Madoff

In the same genre, we have the case of Tzvi Erez. In January 2010, there was talk of a "Canadian Madoff". But it was once again—and this is horrible to say—a member of the "chosen people". Tzvi Erez, 42, was a prominent member of Toronto's Jewish community and ran a small printing company. In 2007, he had begun a more lucrative activity that involved draining the savings of his community members. He claimed that he negotiated large contracts for blue-chip clients, demanding cash advances. In return, he guaranteed annual interest of 30%. Thus, between January 2007 and February 2009, Erez had reaped $27 million.

Nevin Shapiro relaxes in Miami

In April 2010, an American businessman, Nevin K. Shapiro, was prosecuted by the SEC, the New York stock exchange regulator, for a $900 million pyramid scheme[178]. Nevin Shapiro, founder of Capitol Investments, was accused of having sold financial securities to investors since 2005 that, according to him, were risk-free and allowed

---

[178] *Le Monde,* April 21, 2010.

an annual rate of return of 26%. The SEC also accused the businessman of having embezzled 38 million dollars contributed by investors for his personal benefit, in particular by buying a 5 million dollar house in Miami, a million dollar yacht and several luxury cars. A very wealthy and big fan of the University of Miami Hurricanes, he regularly provided the team's players with prostitution services, trips, evenings and dinners in trendy restaurants and nightclubs.

Philip Barry and the porn business

In September 2009, the SEC announced that it had reported a New York fund manager for a $40 million pyramid scheme. Philip Barry had promised 800 investors high returns with safe investments. He boasted of having a strategy that allowed *"returns of at least 21% per year"*. Only these safe investments were not made in the financial markets, but were invested in real estate and in his pornography mail-order business: Barry Publications.

Barry Tannenbaum: A South African Madoff

A man named Howard L., an accountant by profession, had given 90,000 euros to a friend of his, Barry Tannenbaum, who had guaranteed to be able to make his money work for him. *"I don't deny that the profit he guaranteed me was very high, but I had no reason to worry, he was a good friend, a good guy with a good reputation."* He later confessed to feeling *"very disappointed."* When his bank called him on May 29, 2009, he understood everything. *"They couldn't cash the check sent by his friend."*

Howard L. was one of the victims of South African businessman Barry Tannenbaum, who was *"the author of the biggest scam in the country's history[179]"*. Revealed by the local press, the scam amounted to between 10 and 15 billion rand (between 900 and 1.3 billion euros). Approximately 400 people had fallen into the network in South Africa, but also in the United States, Australia and Europe.

Barry Tannenbaum, who was the founding son of a large domestic pharmaceutical company, imported pharmaceutical compounds from abroad for resale to local generic drug manufacturers, mainly

---

[179] *Le Monde*, June 19, 2009.

antiretrovirals for AIDS patients. Instead of borrowing from banks, the 43-year-old turned to private investors, promising interest payments of 15–20% after three months. At maturity, the lender could choose to either recoup his profit or reinvest it. It was in fact a Ponzi scheme (which should now be renamed "Madoff"), the principle of which is to undress one saint to clothe another. Tannenbaum's company was real, but he had falsified the orders of pharmaceutical companies in order to inflate them. In this way, he reassured investors about the viability of the project when payment delays occurred. The bubble had finally burst when most of the lenders, affected by the crisis, had preferred to withdraw their investments.

Ezri Namvar, the Madoff of the West Coast

In December 2008, a news item informed us that the Iranian Jewish community in Los Angeles had a high-flying swindler in its midst. More than $500 million had disappeared without a trace, according to a court report. At the center of the scandal was one Ezri Namvar, an Iranian Jewish immigrant, banker and real estate agent, who had shorn hundreds of families of their savings with a "Madoff-like" scheme. His company *"Namco Financial Exchange"* was intended to facilitate tax evasion operations for real estate sellers. Described by his detractors as "the Bernie Madoff of the West Coast", Ezri Namvar, 60, was sentenced in October 2011 to seven years in prison[180]. Numerous duped investors were (apparently) Jews from the Iranian community living in and around Beverly Hills.

Two Madoffs commit suicide

In January 2009, Arthur Nadel, a 75-year-old Sarasota, Florida resident, was missing with some $350 million he was responsible for. His disappearance had been reported to police by his wife, according to the *Sarasota Herald Tribune* newspaper. *"I feel cheated, dejected, I don't know who to trust anymore,"* said one of his clients, who estimated his loss at $730,000. Before disappearing, M. Nadel had left a letter in which he explained that he was going to commit suicide, although perhaps his intention was to make believe a fake suicide[181].

---

[180] *Los Angeles Business Journal*, October 11, 2011.
[181] *LePoint.fr*, January 18, 2009.

In the same line of events, we had Samuel Israel, who had tried to make believe his suicide in 2008. He had abandoned his vehicle on the Hudson River Bridge, some forty kilometers from New York. He had left a note, but the cops didn't give him much credit, as they never found his body. Samuel Israel had been sentenced to twenty years in prison by the federal court in the case of a 450 million dollar scam stolen from the savers of an investment fund.

Seymour Jacobson: a Swiss who loved Belgium

In September 2008, a first complaint was filed in Switzerland with the Basel Public Prosecutor's Office against the *Compagnie d'Escompte financier* (CFE). Belgians, Swiss and French—but especially Belgians—regretted having invested almost 2 billion euros over ten years. It was "one *of the biggest international financial swindles of the last ten years*[182]." CFE was the company of Seymour Jacobson, a 71-year-old financier whose daughter, Delphine Jacobson, had married writer Paul-Loup Sulitzer in 1993. In 2008, Seymour Jacobson and his children, members of the board of directors, had decided without the necessary majority to transfer the headquarters of the Swiss company to Belize, a British tax haven in Central America, south of Mexico. The funds were transferred to a company called *Argentom Trust*, which was subsequently liquidated. The savers lost everything.

Claire Arfi, a "Madoff in a skirt".

Claire Arfi, dressed in Dior and Gucci, was the CEO of a wealth management company, *Etna Finance*. Life was smiling at her. She drove luxury cars, lived with her husband and children in a magnificent Parisian apartment, had three people at her service and frequented the elite of Parisian financial circles.

Her husband, Ricaldo Zavala, had been implicated and then released in the Pechiney case, a notorious insider trading crime committed during the purchase of the Triangle company by the French group in 1988. Convicted in that state scandal, businessman Samir Traboulsi continued to dine at his home regularly. Ricaldo Zavala was a stunted spendthrift. He could be seen behind the wheel of his blue Bentley, white leather

---

[182] *RTL info,* September 4, 2008.

interior seats, or his 4×4 Mercedes. *"He spoke seven languages, going from Hebrew to Romanian, German to Italian and French[183]."* He had with his wife a 350-square-meter apartment on the Trocadero, decorated with sculptures by Botero and Niki de Saint-Phalle. Director of a brokerage company with a well-stocked contacts book, Ricaldo Zavala defined himself as a business facilitator, and pocketed commissions in passing, of course. Every summer, he rented two suites at the Beach Hotel in Monaco, with a private store on the beach. An American national, born in Switzerland, Zavala had a taste for travel: Monaco, Israel, the West Indies…

Within the Etna Finance group, Claire Arfi, recruited in 1999, took care of her clients' portfolios with complete independence and provided them with regular progress reports. She made her first mistakes in 2000. After the attacks of September 11, 2001, which shocked the United States and sent the stock market tumbling, all of the intrepid portfolio manager's investments were dangerously shaky. But Claire Arfi carefully concealed the situation and continued to promise her investors fantastic returns. It was a textbook flight forward.

To clients worried about their assets, she would reply in essence, *"Contrary to those who lost everything on 9/11, I bet the other way around, so we've made money!"* Some clients, delighted by her particularly genial manager, handed her more savings to invest. But they didn't know that to plug the holes, Claire Arfi was taking from some accounts to pay the others.

Claire Arfi had started speculating in the high-risk markets, buying and selling on the same day. *"We trusted her, we were friends or acquaintances; she said she had created a specific mathematical model. But it was pure appearance. In reality she was gambling like at the casino,"* said one of the victims, a company director.

Some customers stopped receiving statements. In 2002, one customer was stunned when he learned that his bank had received a signed letter from him "requesting *that statements no longer be sent to his home address but directly to Etna. I didn't sign that letter, so who signed in my place?"*

At the same time, her husband's *broker* was caught by the law. Charged on January 17, 2002, he was asked to pay a bail of 1.2 million euros

---

[183] *Le Point*, March 14, 2003.

(later reduced to 300,000 euros). He was asked to explain his stock exchange practices: with his small group of *brokers*, they rigged the prices of bonds with intermediaries: they bought the most expensive securities for their clients and were paid by hand. Zavala was charged with "organized fraud and aggravated breach of trust". According to the investigation carried out by the Financial Brigade, 281 operations concluded by the *brokerage* gang between 1993 and 1997 were highly suspicious and involved a damage of 35 million euros.

While Zavala was in legal trouble, Claire Arfi had continued throughout 2002 to manage her client portfolio. Until the moment when, in September, two clients claimed their assets (about 4 million euros), and discovered to their astonishment that their accounts were empty. Then another investor came forward, also complaining that he was not receiving any statements from his account. This was the general alarm bell. The head of Etna Finance, Eric Parent, ordered an internal investigation. In January 2013, the examining magistrate Françoise Desset was trying to shed light on a hole of 15 to 23 million euros. Claire Arfi, the general manager then disappeared for several weeks. She had fled, completely terrified.

Several dozen wealthy clients, all friends of Claire Arfi, had been ruined. The president of a high-tech consulting firm had lost five million. Important company presidents, distribution businessmen, as well as one of the owners of the Carat group had lost their entire fortune.

Claire Arfi had returned to Paris in November, but had cancelled her landline. She used a foreign cell phone and consulted lawyers to try to negotiate. In the meantime, Etna Finance had declared the claim to its insurer and filed a complaint for "breach of trust, forgery and use of false documents" as well as check embezzlement. In February 2003, Etna Finance, ordered to repay the amounts lost, went bankrupt.

Claire Arfi, for her part, was not tried until April 2010. Aged 49, she was sentenced to four years in prison, two unconditional. But she had appealed. Angry with her former friends, she had moved to another apartment bought by Ricaldo Zavala on Victor Hugo Avenue. In total, the double "indelicacy" of the Bonnie and Clyde of the finance industry had resulted in 50 to 60 million euros. In March 2012, we were informed that Michèle Elmaleh, alias "Claire Arfi", had been sentenced on appeal to three years' imprisonment, an unconditional one which she would probably not even serve. She had been presented by the prosecutor as *"an unscrupulous seductress, calculating and manipulative."* Definitely, French justice is very lenient with swindlers.

Fast, easy and effective cash

A massive fraud occurred in Colombia. This was a textbook case! Listen to the story: created in September 2007 in Pasto, in the south of Colombia, the DRFE company had attracted its first clients by offering investments in a fund with very high profitability. The entry of new clients allowed the company to pay the accrued interest to the first clients. All happy, they had rushed to tell their friends and family about their experience, many of whom had deposited all their savings. The constant flow of new savers had greatly fed the base of the pyramid. Within a year, DRFE had thus attracted more than two million clients, mostly poor people. In November 2008, the company announced in a brief statement that it had been forced to reduce interest rates to 70%, instead of the 100 to 150% offered at the beginning, because of the *"global economic crisis"*. But the rumor of the DRFE director's flight abroad had caused a wave of panic among savers who rushed to the agencies. In front of the offices, the most educated could read an unusual sign—although those who could not read could also quickly decipher the message, which read: *"Since you are stupid and believe in magic, you will have to work hard to get your money back[184]."* The owners of the company openly scoffed at the suckers they had duped. It is worth mentioning that the name of the company, DRFE, simply meant in Spanish: "Dinero, Rápido, Fácil y Efectivo."

Two million Colombians, mostly from the working classes, had lost all their savings. Some had pawned their houses, cars, in the hope of a quick profit. The boldest had taken on debts in other banks. Faced with the extent of the catastrophe, President Alvaro Uribe decreed a state of emergency, allowing him to legislate by decree for thirty days, which could be extended. The head of state apologized to the population for having taken so long to react and announced stiffer penalties for those responsible for the fraud and promised to return the money to the stolen savers. Carlos Suarez, the young businessman who owned DRFE, has been wanted by Interpol ever since. In February 2009, the man handed himself in at the Colombian embassy in Sao Paulo in Brazil[185].

---

[184] *Le Figaro*, November 21, 2008. [*Pyramid crisis in Colombia*, wikipedia source (NdT).
[185] The Colombian pyramid crisis was another particularly exemplary case, although the communal origin of the offender is neither certain nor confirmed. However, readers of *The Jewish Mafia* (chapter on slavery and the sugar industry) know that many Jews had

2. The great stock market frauds

In August 2013, six Americans were arrested and charged for their involvement in an international stock fraud ring estimated at $140 million. They were accused of having inflated the prices of billions of shares that were worth only a few cents and of having distributed them to investors in more than 35 countries, in North America, Europe and Asia. We find this type of fraud reported in a number of high-profile cases.

Sadly, Abraham Hochman has passed away

On January 21, 2009, six men between 56 and 76 years of age were arrested in Madrid and Barcelona in connection with a stock fraud on the London Stock Exchange, but later released on bail. Five Spaniards and one Argentinian were accused of having provided false reports to the British stock exchange. One of them, Mariusz Rybak, had created an investment company in Spain, *Langbar International*, domiciled in Bermuda and managed from Monte Carlo. Langbar's share price on the London Stock Exchange was artificially inflated by the publication of false documents and false advertisements in the trade press. The company had allegedly won more than $600 million in contracts in Argentina in construction waste management. Again, Langbar had announced that it was going to invest in a gold mine that would undoubtedly be *"one of the most important in the world"*. Langbar claimed to have cash reserves of US$633 million, deposited in Banco do Brasil. This had convinced some prestigious firms such as Gartmore and Merrill Lynch to invest in the business.

False contracts and certificates of deposit were exchanged between Langbar and its main shareholder, *Lambert Investment Financial*. This financial company, also domiciled in Bermuda, had been created by an individual named Abraham Arad Hochman, 53, a former agent of the

---

fled the Spanish and Portuguese Inquisition in the 17th century and had taken refuge in the Caribbean and South America. They used to change their surnames very often and declared themselves to be good Catholics and went to mass on Sundays.

Mossad—the Israeli secret services—who managed from Barcelona the money of about 2,000 wealthy Jews from Latin America and Israel.

The British justice system had opened proceedings in November 2005 after the Langbar company published a statement in which it announced that it could not *"establish or confirm the existence"* of about 370 million pounds (about 632.7 million dollars) in its Dutch and Brazilian bank accounts. *The Guardian* reported that Abraham Hochman died of cardiac arrest on June 24, 2011, and that the British judiciary had closed the case.

But was he really dead? The journalist added that many, upon hearing the news, *would "pop the champagne cork that weekend somewhere in Europe."* Unless it was in Israel...

Michael Milken and junk bonds

The Michael Milken case is not really a stock market fraud, but it provides an insight into the financial madness of the 1980s—the era of the *"golden boys"*—which saw the birth of such hardened criminals as Jordan Belfort, brought to the silver screen in Martin Scorsese's film, *The Wolf of Wall Street*.

In the 1980s, Michael Milken had become the undisputed king of world finance. He was the object of true devotion, praised by the press and all the media because he had succeeded in convincing investors to invest money in medium-sized companies with a new financial instrument: *junk bonds* ("high-yield bonds" or "junk bonds"). Thanks to *junk bonds* and the persuasive talents of Michael Milken, alias *junk bonds king*, these companies were able to access financing directly from the capital markets and no longer through the banks, as previously only large, solvent companies had been able to raise capital on the market. The investment entailed a certain amount of risk, so the interest rates for investors were much higher than the average186.

---

[186] In finance, a high yield bond or junk bond is a fixed income security that has a high risk of default and in return has to pay a higher interest rate. Generally, it is issued by a little known or poorly recommended entity. They are speculative grade bonds, bonds with a low credit rating that are classified below the so-called investment grade. These bonds have a high risk of default or other adverse credit events, but usually pay a more lucrative coupon than better quality bonds to make them attractive to investors. (wikipedia. NdT).

In 1977, Michael Milken was working as an investment officer at Drexel Burnham Lambert Bank, a second-tier firm at the time headed by one Dennis Levine. Because of his close relationships with industry, Milken's bank often had access to inside information, so when he traded *junk bonds*, he had first-hand information about the companies. While it is illegal to trade stocks on the basis of inside information (this is called "insider trading" or "insider trading", as we will see below), there is no such law for junk bonds[187]. Milken was essentially saying to his lenders: *"Make a huge portfolio of junk bonds and it doesn't matter if a few go bad—the higher income of the winners more than offsets the losses of the losers. Drexel was prepared to play the companies, Milken explained to institutional investors. Join us. Invest in the future of North America, in the small companies that will make us great*[188]*."*

The *junk bond* market was a resounding success: *"From virtually zero in 1970, new junk bond issuance grew from $839 million in 1981 to $8.5 billion in 1985 and $12 billion in 1987. By then, junk bonds constituted 25 percent of the [industrial] corporate bond market. Between 1980 and 1987, ... $53 billion in junk bonds entered the market*[189]*."* Many corporations, in all sectors, had issued *junk bonds*. New liquidities were now available, flooding companies with fresh money. If the borrowing company generated enough profit to repay, the bonds went up, and when it lost money, the bonds went down in anticipation of a default.

In 1985, after attracting tens of millions of dollars in his new speculative market, Michael Milken had so much money that he didn't know where to invest it. He could not find enough interesting companies, despite their weak growth, to absorb all those liquidities. With his colleagues at Drexel Bank, he came up with a solution: they were going to use *junk bonds* to finance takeover bids for undervalued companies by offering their assets as collateral to bond buyers. This was like mortgaging the companies.

Thanks to his business sense, his good contacts and the trust he enjoyed with investors, Milken was able to raise phenomenal sums of money.

---

[187] A bond is a transferable security that constitutes a debt security representing a loan. The bond is transferable and can therefore be listed on the stock exchange.
[188] Michael Lewis, *The Liar's Poker*, (1989), Booket (Grupo Planeta), Barcelona, 2019, p. 332–333.
[189] Michael Lewis, *The Liar's Poker*, (1989), Booket (Grupo Planeta), Barcelona, 2019, p. 336.

Thanks to him, predatory investment firms began to launch hostile takeover bids for uncompetitive companies. Buying a company with borrowed funds then became common practice. This mechanism became known as LBO: *leveraged buy-out* (thanks to borrowed funds)[190]. The LBOs financed by Milken and Drexel Bank were extremely aggressive, fast and profitable. The investors (*"raiders*[191]*"*) took the majority of the shares, and once they got rid of troublesome managers, they cut employee wages and benefits, split colossal bonuses and plundered what was left by dismantling the company and reselling it in pieces[192].

Through *junk bonds*, company owners, even backed by the board of directors, saw themselves on an ejection seat. Because owning the debt of a distressed company means actually taking control of it. In fact, if the company defaults on the interest due, the bondholder can demand its seizure and liquidation. *"And how can that be, if I own forty percent of the shares? We hold one hundred million dollars of its bonds, and if it defaults on a single payment, we are left with the company*[193]*,"* explained Milken.

Drexel Bank made an immense fortune during this golden period of the stock market. It was the era of *golden boys* like Ronald Perelman (America's twelfth-sixth fortune in 2012), Carl Icahn (fortune estimated at 20 billion)—two Jewish billionaires. *"Milken made the dreams come true for all the renowned corporate sharks—Ronald Perelman, Boone Pickens, Carl Icahn, Marvin Davis, Irwin Jacobs, Sir James Goldsmith, Nelson Peltz, Samuel Heyman, Saul Steinberg and Asher Edelman*[194]*."* Then there was Carl Lindner, Victor Posner, Meshuam Riklis, Laurence

---

[190] A *leveraged buyout is the* acquisition of a company in which the funds used to finance the transaction are mostly debt instruments. This type of transaction is usually carried out by private equity funds.

[191] From English, invader, thief, robber, plunderer, pirate (NdT).

[192] It is highly recommended to watch Oliver Stone's film *Wall Street* (1987), based in part on Michael Milken's biography. Michael Douglas plays the main character (Gordon Gekko), although nothing is revealed about the Jewishness of the financial shark—or of the actor himself! The Jew does not exist; he is an invention of the anti-Semites, as Jean-Paul Sartre would say.

[193] Michael Lewis, *The Liar's Poker*, (1989), Booket (Grupo Planeta), Barcelona, 2019, p. 332.

[194] Michael Lewis, *The Liar's Poker*, (1989), Booket (Grupo Planeta), Barcelona, 2019, p. 337.

Tisch, etc. All of these individuals are part of the cult. All had borrowed from Milken to buy and dismantle companies[195].

But the *"raiders"* soon realized that it was not even necessary to buy a company in order to dismantle and resell it: it was enough to simply threaten it so that the managers—eager to get rid of the *raiders*—would buy back the *raider*'s shares at the price of gold. Thus was born the "blackmail of the takeover bid".

These practices led to an epidemic of "insider crime" or "insider trading". Ivan Boesky, a Drexel Burnham stockbroker, had woven a network of insiders whom he bribed handsomely. When he had access to interesting inside information about a company, Boesky would immediately raise funds through Milken, buy shares and resell them to *raiders* once the purchase was launched. He enriched himself indecently in this way.

This prosperous era lasted until the 1987 crisis—the U.S. Savings Banks crisis. At the beginning of the decade, the 3,000 Saving and Loan Associations had about $1.3 billion in assets, or 30% of the total assets held by depository financial institutions. Traditionally, they borrowed and lent on a long-term basis at a moderate interest rate to the middle and lower classes who wanted to invest in real estate to buy a home. The federal government allocated funds to the Cajas at preferential interest rates and guaranteed savers' money deposits, but their investments were subject to restrictions. Everything changed radically in the 1980s, with the rise in the price of money, which destabilized the "Saving and Loan". How to remunerate deposits at 15% while continuing to receive only 10% for long-term loans already granted? To get out of this situation, President Reagan's administration (right-wing liberal) embarked on a program to deregulate the sector. Thus, in 1981, the US Congress decided to authorize savings banks to speculate. From now on, a single shareholder could control a savings bank, with the right to create an unlimited number of subsidiaries in multiple sectors of activity. This had whetted the appetite of predators.

---

[195] *"Milken is Jewish, and Drexel, when he joined, was, in his view, an old-line investment bank run by young white, Protestant men with an anti-Semitic streak."* Michael Lewis, *The Liar's Poker*, (1989), Booket (Grupo Planeta), Barcelona, 2019, p. 326

Milken had recruited swindlers, business owners such as Charles Keating (a Catholic), David Paul and Ivan Boesky, to acquire the Savings Banks under State control: they bought from Drexel large amounts of bonds and served Milken as "captive companies" with which the bank "beat" the accounts (made quick and repeated transactions). These two techniques maximized Drexel's income from commissions. Michael Milken and his friends had thus financed Charles Keating for the purchase of Lincoln Savings; Keating did not have to put a single cent out of his pocket. Even Drexel had overfinanced him: the deal required $51 million, but Drexel had issued more than $125 million in junk bonds of American Continental Corp (ACC), the holding company used by Keating to make the purchase. Investors had answered the call.

Milken could get his captive companies to buy all the junk bonds that the market refused to buy. *Junk bonds* were thus overvalued. And it mattered little that this made Lincoln Saving or Cen Trust even more solvent, since their bankruptcy was certain. In the event of default, federal insurance absorbed the losses because the deposits were guaranteed by the state. This is how Michael Milken indirectly sold his *junk bonds* to the US taxpayer. We know from Ivan Boesky and Charles Keating how Milken had launched the idea. He boasted that a deregulated savings bank, under the institutional umbrella of the state, would make them *"merchant princes[196]"*.

Lincoln Saving had in turn been initiated into the "takeover bid racket". The Savings Bank had bought a large amount of Gulf Broadcasting shares above the market price. This investment was imprudent and reckless for a Savings Bank that had very little capital, since this transaction could have made Lincoln insolvent if the stock price had fallen, even slightly. Gulf Broadcasting had finally repurchased Lincoln's shares at the price of gold.

Savings banks went into debt up to their eyebrows in search of speculative investments and stock market funds to finance them. Tom Spiegel's Columbia Savings and Loan had become Drexel's largest client, increasing its assets from $370 million to $10 billion, partly

---

[196] William Black, *Une Fraude presque parfaite, Le pillage des caisses d'épargne américaines par leurs dirigeants*, Éditions Charles Léopold Mayer, 2012, p. 128. (*The Best Way to Rob a Bank is to Own One: How Corporate Executives and Politicians Looted the S&L Industry*).

invested in *junk bons*. A Charles Knapp had inflated the assets of a California savings bank from $1.7 billion to tens of billions of dollars.

Benjamin Stein, author of the book *License to steal*, wrote: *"The Drexel machine sucked the blood out of captive Savings Banks like a vampire, draining savers' funds dry[197]."*

The liquidities of the financial markets then represented 80% of the new deposits of the savings banks. Managers had financed colossal real estate projects, encouraged by a favorable tax regime. A frenzied maelstrom of purely speculative investments ensued. The savings banks plunged into dubious loans for hotels, shopping centers and restaurants. Large unoccupied office towers appeared like mushrooms in the big cities.

When the favorable tax regime for real estate investment disappeared with the Tax Reform Act of 1986, the bubble deflated. At the beginning of 1985, 515 savings banks were insolvent, one-sixth of the sector's assets; but the debacle would have been worse if the government had taken longer to act. All in all, it was one of the biggest financial scandals in the history of the United States.

In Texas and California the bankruptcies were the most resounding and costly. In fact, deregulation in those two states had been the most permissive, as anyone could purchase a savings bank and invest in almost anything[198].

Junk bonds were not the main cause: in fact, the losses of the savings banks due to *junk bonds* were estimated at 10 billion dollars, but the losses due to the real estate market amounted to 300 billion. Savings banks had not had more than 10% junk bonds on their balance sheets, in general much less, since 90% of this volume was in fact held by a dozen or so savings banks that had gone bankrupt[199]. The savings bank sector was not a major buyer of junk bonds, but it was the most important group of Milken's "captive" savings banks that had played a crucial role in the overvaluation of *junk bonds*.

---

[197] Jean-François Gayraud, *La grande Fraude*, Odile Jacob, 2011, p. 173.
[198] According to William Black, *"there were more than 300 savings banks controlled by fraudsters."* (p. 121). *"Together, California and Texas encompassed more than half of the fraudulent Savings Banks and accumulated more than half of the total losses."*
[199] William Black, *Une Fraude presque parfaite, Le pillage des caisses d'épargne américaines par leurs dirigeants*, Éditions Charles Léopold Mayer, 2012, p. 128.

In 1989, Michael Milken was indicted on 98 counts, including insider trading, racketeering, extortion and tax fraud. Milken pleaded guilty to six counts and was sentenced to ten years in prison. The harshness of the sentence was due to the link established with the looting of the savings banks[200].

In March 1992, after an agreement with the authorities, Milken and his family had agreed to pay another 500 million dollars in addition to the 400 million dollars he had already paid to the SEC (Securities and Exchange Commission). In the meantime, Drexel bank had gone bankrupt ... and Milken had already been released from prison, where he had only stayed for 22 months, that is, less than two years.

This scandal marked the end of the first major financial crisis of the great era of deregulation. The frenzy of junk bonds, leveraged buyouts and IPO racketeering that characterized the 1980s marked *"a milestone in the metamorphosis of Wall Street from tradition-ridden exclusive club to illegal casino, drunk on cash and cocaine*[201]*."*

Jordan Belfort: a Leonardo DiCaprio with a kippah

Jordan Ross Belfort grew up in the New York City borough of Queens. Like many of his peers, he was driven by the greed and irrepressible desire to "make money" so often seen in his community. At the beginning of May 1987, at the age of 23, Belfort had joined the prestigious L.F. Rothschild bank on the lowest rung of the ladder (as an entry-level "broker", i.e. a simple executor of client orders) and discovered the frenetic world of Wall Street. But five months later, on October 19, the day he started his first day as a confirmed broker, the stock market crashed. That day went down in history as the famous

---

[200] The *Savings and Loan Associations* debacle ended with the sentencing to unconditional prison terms of more than 800 Savings Bank officers (directors and senior management). The longest was Woody Lemons, the president of the Vernon Saving and Loan Association, who was sentenced to 30 years in prison. Charles Keating, president of Lincoln Savings, was convicted of fraud, racketeering and extortion. Sentenced to 10 years in prison, he was released after 4 1/2 years due to a procedural flaw. When his trial was retried, he decided to plead guilty, which allowed him to be sentenced to 4 years in prison, a sentence he had already served. William Black, *Une Fraude presque parfaite*, p. 443
[201] Charles Ferguson, *Inside Job, the financial crisis...* Ediciones Deusto, Barcelona, 2012, p. 58.

"Black Monday". The Dow Jones index of the New York Stock Exchange had fallen by 22%, bankrupting L.F. Rothschild[202].

The young Jordan Belfort then took a job on the outskirts of the city and discovered a small market where brokers without computers earned a few dollars by selling shares of small companies outside the official stock market. He immediately stunned his new co-workers with his ease on the phone. The commission being 50% and not 1%, Belfort amassed $7,000 in his first month. Some time later, his yellow Jaguar attracted the attention of his neighbor, Danny Porush, who resigned from his job to follow him in his new projects.

Jordan Belfort then started his own company, which he set up in a garage with some of Danny Porush's friends. In 1989, he named it Stratton Oakmont, which within a few years became one of the largest brokerages on the East Coast. Thanks to his determination and insolence, Belfort had managed to attract hundreds of young brokers from all over the country. Belfort had become the "Wolf of Wall Street[203]". At its peak, the Stratton Oakmont firm employed about a thousand young brokers, and those over thirty were counted on the fingers of one hand. They all repeated in a loop the argument Belfort himself had invented to sell investors ultra-speculative stocks at $1 or $2. He shrieked like a madman on the phone, with the sole objective of never being hung up on until he had convinced the client.

Stratton Oakmont bought shares at low prices of unlisted companies on the OTC market and then resold them in its own trading room[204].

---

[202] Contrary to Martin Scorsese, the director of the movie *The Wolf of Wall Street* based on Belfort's book, one is not obliged to believe all the coincidences and extraordinary stories told by the con man. When one has read the testimonies of Elie Wiesel or Simon Wiesenthal, one has learned to decipher the statements of these fabulators.

[203] Actually, no one ever called him that. It is the nickname he gave himself in his book.

[204] An *over-the-counter* (OTC) market is an unorganized parallel market where stocks, bonds and other financial instruments such as credit derivatives are traded. In the United States, OTC trading is conducted through brokers using services such as the *OTC Bulletin Board* (OTCBB) and *Pink Sheets*. The OTC market is monitored by the NASD (National Association of Securities Dealers). Since it is not traded on any major exchange and little research is done, these trades are considered risky. Since trading in that market is very infrequent, the difference between bid and ask prices is very large. Stratton Oakmont, Inc. was an *over-the-counter* (OTC) securities brokerage house based on Long Island. Stratton Oakmont organized *pump-and-dump* schemes in that parallel stock market, a form of small-cap stock fraud that involves artificially inflating the price of one's own stock through false and misleading positive statements to *"pump"* it to investors in order to sell that stock, purchased at a low price, at a higher price. Once

You had to, Belfort wrote in his book, *"identify start-up companies with potential for growth and so desperate for money that they were willing to sell me a substantial portion of their stock in exchange for my financing them ... the process of buying stakes in private companies and then selling a portion of my original investment (and getting my money back) was what had made Stratton like a stock printing press. And, as I used the power of the trading floor to bring my own companies to market, my net income went up and up. On Wall Street, that process is known as financial engineering[205]."* He was artificially driving up the share price of the companies he introduced to the stock market, after having personally bought large quantities of shares himself, but also through shell companies or proxies domiciled in tax havens. He was thus circumventing the law which obliged an investor who bought more than 5% of the shares of a company to disclose his intentions. Once the company he had introduced on the stock exchange, and after the share had risen substantially, he would resell his own shares, causing the share price to fall and the other investors to be ruined.

In his 2007 book *The Wolf of Wall Street*, Jordan Belfort wrote: *"A typical Stratton issue consisted of two million units being offered at four dollars each, which, in itself, wasn't too spectacular. But with a soccer field full of young Strattonites smiling, phoning and gouging people's eyes out, the demand soon became spectacularly greater than the supply ... for every unit given at the initial public offering price, it had to buy ten times the amount received when the issue began trading in the secondary market[206]."*

Belfort also gave some explanations about what he called his "mousetraps," which were his shell companies: *"Of the two million that was released to the market, half would go into my mousetrap accounts. I would buy them from them at about five or six dollars a share and deposit them in my company's account. Then, I would use the power of the trading room, the immense purchases that would be generated by*

---

the scheme's operators *"dump"* their overvalued shares, the price drops and investors lose their money. Stratton Oakmont also tried to maintain the price of a stock by refusing to accept or process sell orders for it.

[205] Jordan Belfort, *The Wolf of Wall Street* (2007), Booket (Grupo Planeta), Barcelona, 2015, pp. 88, 77–78.

[206] Jordan Belfort, *The Wolf of Wall Street* (2007), Booket (Grupo Planeta), Barcelona, 2015, p. 116.

that encounter to drive the price up to twenty dollars a unit, which would assure us a profit of fourteen to fifteen million on the papers[207]."

In this way, Belfort managed to amass a considerable fortune in a short period of time. At the beginning of 1993, he was at the height of his glory. He had just broken his own profit record by taking the Steve Madden shoe manufacturer public, of which he had acquired 80% of the shares. The deal had earned him $12.5 million in three minutes. *"Hence, in order to control Steve, I had to have the ability to manage the price of his stock once it went public. Since Stratton would be his principal trader, virtually all buying and selling would take place within the four walls of our trading room, giving me the opportunity to drive the price of the stock up and down as I saw fit. So if Steve didn't behave as he should, I could drive his stock price down to mere pennies. In fact, that was the sword of Damocles hanging over Stratton Oakmont's investment banking clients. And I was employing it to make sure that they remained loyal to the Stratton cause, which meant that they would issue shares to me at below market value, so that I, drawing on the power of my trading room, could sell them and make immense profits[208]."*

His main mousetrap was one Elliot Lavigne, president of Perry Ellis, one of the largest clothing manufacturers in the United States: *"In addition to being a first-rate gambling and drug addict, Elliot was also a sex obsessed and compulsive adulterer. He stole millions of dollars a year from Perry Ellis. He had secret agreements with his overseas factories, which charged the company an extra dollar or two for each garment they made. Elliot received a percentage of that overbilling. It was in the millions. When I made him earn with my securities issues, he would give me my share using the cash he received from his factories abroad. It was a perfect exchange that left no trace… He had paid me more than five million dollars in cash, which was safe in safety deposit boxes in different banks in the United States. I still wasn't sure how I would go about transferring all that money to Switzerland, but I had some ideas[209]."*

---

[207] Jordan Belfort, *The Wolf of Wall Street* (2007), Booket (Grupo Planeta), Barcelona, 2015, p. 121.
[208] Jordan Belfort, *The Wolf of Wall Street* (2007), Booket (Grupo Planeta), Barcelona, 2015, p. 94.
[209] Jordan Belfort, *The Wolf of Wall Street* (2007), Booket (Grupo Planeta), Barcelona, 2015, p.179-180.

Intoxicated by this rapid rise that had made him an immensely rich man, Belfort indulged in all sorts of follies: house with twenty-four rooms, helicopter rides—which he piloted himself—luxury cars (white Lamborghini, Aston Martin, chauffeur-driven limousines), trips with his 37-meter long yacht *Nadine*; but also luxury prostitutes and drugs, lots of drugs, all kinds of drugs: Mandrax, Xanax, Valium, Qualuuds (Methaqualone), MDMA, Marijuana, Cocaine, etc.

The movie *The Wolf of Wall Street*, released in November 2013 in the United States and directed by the celebrated Martin Scorsese, adapted Belfort's biography quite faithfully. Most of Leonardo DiCaprio's entries (in the role of Belfort) come from the book, as do most of the sometimes hard-to-believe vicissitudes: the helicopter landing on his property while fully stoned; the rocky wreck of his yacht in a storm off the Italian coast, and so on. But Scorsese's film is above all a vulgar succession of scenes of tasteless debauchery. Cocaine is snorted on the buttocks of a prostitute, for example. For almost three hours, scenes of sex and drug addiction alternate with the ostentation of the "hero's" wealth. Vulgarity appears at every corner; the word *"fuck"* is uttered 569 times[210].

Certainly, we had been warned from the beginning. Indeed, at the beginning of the film, we see young Jordan listening to the wise advice of a chief broker of the Rothschild house. Mark Hanna (played by the excellent Matthew McConaughey) revealed to him the golden rule of Wall Street: *"Put the clients' money in your pocket. We don't create anything, we don't build anything; we don't know if the stock market will go up or not. We always have to reinvest our clients' profits... And we get rich while we're at it!*[211]*"* Mark Hanna also encouraged the young Jordan to take cocaine to improve his performance: *"That's what Wall Street is all about. But I'm telling you, cocaine helps you get through this job! This stockbroker thing is crazy. I mean, don't get me wrong, the money and all that is great, but you're not creating anything, you're not building anything. So, after a while it gets monotonous... The truth is, we're just dishonest salesmen*[212]*."*

---

[210] Martin Scorsese was also inspired by the film *Boiler Room*, by Ben Younger (USA, 2000).
[211] Jordan Belfort, *Le Loup de Wall Street*, Le Livre de Poche, 2017, p. 23 [passage included due to translation discrepancies with the Booket version].
[212] Jordan Belfort, *The Wolf of Wall Street* (2007), Booket (Grupo Planeta), Barcelona, 2015, pp. 22–23.

The only aspect that does not appear—neither in the book nor in the film—are the thousands of victims of the swindler and his henchmen. Another element that is conspicuous by its absence is the Jewishness of the protagonists, which filmmaker Martin Scorses refrained from showing to the viewers. Indeed, the lead actor, Leonardo DiCaprio is a goy with a Nordic face. Certainly, Belfort himself does not have specifically Jewish features and looks more like any European individual, although his morals are far removed from the morals of a Catholic Christian or a Muslim, and his financial practices and obscene materialism are not part of the traditional customs of European populations. Once again, then, the goy must bear all the vilenesses of the Hebrew, especially his passion for profit, his insatiable thirst for material goods, so characteristic of the Jewish spirit and which Jordan Belfort brings out in many passages of his biography. We learn that he earned, at the height of his glory, a million dollars a week. He exhibits his wealth to the reader repeatedly: his *"spectacular black crocodile-skin cowboy boots ... had cost two thousand four hundred dollars and he adored them"* and how he *"sported a slim, sober eighteen thousand dollar Bulgari gold watch"* (page 52); his *"limousine, a ninety-six thousand dollar bordello on wheels"* (page 63), his purchase of *"a green Aston Martin Virage for two hundred and fifty thousand dollars"* (page 297) and *"the brand new pearl white Ferrari Testarossa with twelve cylinders and four hundred and fifty horsepower"* (page 450). Or the $3,000 bottles of wine, the $10,000 restaurant bills; *"We clinked glasses and drank five hundred dollars worth of wine in less than a second"* (page 255), his *"twelve thousand dollar white silk bedspread"* (page 342), the *"shopping bags containing one hundred and fifty thousand dollars worth of women's clothing"* and his wife's watch, a *"brand new forty thousand dollar Cartier constellated with diamonds"* (page 452). When his son was born at *"Long Island Jewish Hospital, less than two miles from Stratton Oakmont,"* Belfort tells how he walked *"around the maternity unit handing out gold watches"* (page 440).

In a speech to his stockbrokers (which we see at the end of the film), he publicly mentioned the beginnings of one of Stratton's early collaborators, "Carrie": *"When we think of Carrie, we imagine her as she is today: a beautiful woman who drives a brand new Mercedes, lives in the best neighborhood on Long Island, wears three thousand dollar Chanel suits and six thousand dollar Dolce & Gabana dresses, who spends her winter vacations in the Bahamas and her summer vacations in the Hamptons ... and you all know that Carrie is one of the highest paid executives on Long Island, on track to make over a million and a half this year!"* (page 334). All the runners applauded this speech frantically. In another scene, we see Belfort exhorting his men to take money from the clients. The young brokers react furiously, triumphantly, clenching their fists and shouting hysterically.

We are here light years away from the soul of the Latin, Celtic, Germanic or Slavic man, although it must be recognized that the Jewish spirit[213], by contagion, has managed to deeply impregnate the spirit of many Europeans, especially among Anglo-Saxon Protestants. In his book, Belfort mentioned the recruitment of his brokers: *"Most of my first hundred Strattonites came from the bosom of those ghettos of the Jewish upper middle class ... the wildest Jews of Long Island who inhabited the neighborhoods of Jericho and Syosset[214]."*

Here is how Belfort described in his book his friend and main collaborator Danny Porush, played in the film by the character called "Donnie Azoff": *"Danny Porush was a Jew of the ultra-wild variety. He was of medium height and build, about five feet eight and seventy-five pounds, and had no identifying features that would give him away as a member of the Tribe. Not even his steel blue eyes, which generated about as much heat as an iceberg, had anything Judaic[215]."*

All of Belfort's other accomplices were Jewish, especially Danny Porush's friends who were present at the creation of the Stratton Oakmont partnership. There was "Brad", a criminal sports doping products dealer, Nicky Koskoff, Kenny Greene, Chester and Robbie Feinberg. Andy Greene, a childhood friend of Belfort's was the company's lawyer. He is very recognizable in the film because of his wig. *"Choza and I had known each other since grade school. Back then, he had the most spectacular blond hair imaginable, soft as corn silk beards. But by the time his seventeenth birthday came around, that wonderful head of hair was already a distant memory[216]."* Belfort described him as *"a vulgar Jew in his fifties, with a few manes and a*

---

[213] We believe it can be summed up as "buy low and sell high". (NdT)
[214] Jordan Belfort, *The Wolf of Wall Street* (2007), Booket (Grupo Planeta), Barcelona, 2015, p. 138.
[215] Jordan Belfort, *The Wolf of Wall Street* (2007), Booket (Grupo Planeta), Barcelona, 2015, p. 80. *"He also explained to me that he had married his first cousin, Nancy"* p. 81. On consanguinity within the Jewish community, read *Psychoanalysis of Judaism*.
[216] We see here Belfort's tendency to exaggerate.

prodigious potbelly," remarking further *"his egg-shaped Jewish skull*[217]*."*

Todd Garret was another old acquaintance, a kid from the neighborhood where Jordan Belfort had grown up. Todd had entered the drug business early. *"He was in his early twenties and making hundreds of thousands of dollars a year. He spent summers in the south of France and on the Italian Riviera, and winters on the glorious beaches of Rio de Janeiro*[218]*."* He was *"the biggest qualuuds dealer in the United States."* In the film we see him with a Hebrew letter on his long necklace, with his wife of Slovenian origin and Swiss citizen, both arriving at the Geneva airport with hundreds of thousands of dollars attached to their bodies.

The only non-Jew in the gang was of Chinese origin: *"Victor Chang was Chinese by birth and an adopted Jew, having grown up among the wildest Jews on Long Island*[219]*."* In his book, Belfort expresses much contempt and hostility toward him. But in reality, all of these Jews harbored a deep contempt for all Goyim in general. Belfort gives vent to his feelings of hatred for the WASPs (White Anglo-Saxon Protestants) throughout his biography: *"blue-blooded WASPs and overpriced horses"*; *"Personally I detest both"* (pages 31–32); *"Sir Max, a refined gentleman of impeccable manners and an accent that reeked of British aristocracy"* (page 109); *"their idiot sons and daughters"* (page 223); *"the WASP sons of bitches"* (page 252); Thurston Howell III *"was a stupid WASP. In typical WASP fashion, he had married a female of his species ... an atrocious blonde as dumb as he was"* (page 337); *"an old WASP son-of-a-bitch with an IQ of sixty-five and an incontinence problem"* (page 338). Now imagine a novelist writing a book for the general public with these expressions: *"He was a Jew bastard who reeked of swindling and international high finance".*

It looked like the Jews were finally going to get their revenge: *"Brookville Country Club was not the only one that restricted Jews from entering. No, no and no! All the clubs in the area were off limits to Jews and anyone who wasn't a blue-blooded WASP son of a bitch... However,*

---

[217] Jordan Belfort, *The Wolf of Wall Street* (2007), Booket (Grupo Planeta), Barcelona, 2015, pp. 86–87.
[218] Jordan Belfort, *The Wolf of Wall Street* (2007), Booket (Grupo Planeta), Barcelona, 2015, p. 243.
[219] Jordan Belfort, *The Wolf of Wall Street* (2007), Booket (Grupo Planeta), Barcelona, 2015, p. 138.

as time went on I realized that the WASP's time had passed, that they were a dying breed, like the dodo or the spotted owl. And while it was true that they still had their little golf clubs and hunting grounds as last bastions of resistance to the encroaching shtetl hordes, these were nothing more than 20th century Little Big Horns, about to fall under the savage Jews who, like me, had made their fortune on Wall Street[220]*."*

But Jordan Belfort would not be a true Jew if he did not try in one way or another to guilt-trip his Goyim readers. Listen to him complain about anti-Semitism and the suffering endured by the poor Jews when *"Hitler had ravaged Europe and exterminated six million Jews in the gas chambers*[221]*"*: one must remember that *"those Swiss sons of bitches"* had kept the money that the exterminated Jews had in their bank accounts. *"To this day, billions and billions of dollars remain unclaimed... All that Jewish money had been lost forever, absorbed by the Swiss banking system... I looked out the window, seeing nothing but the ghosts of a few million murdered Jews. They were still looking for their money*[222]*."*

In short, his main motivation, professionally speaking, could be summed up in this simple question: "How to get the most money out of the pockets of those stupid WASPs? In fact, he himself unveiled his mentality, taking his case as a general one: "After all, *everybody ripping everybody off is the nature of 20th century capitalism, and the one who ripped off the most people was ultimately the one who won the game. In that sense, I was the undefeated world champion*[223]*."*

With morals like his, Jordan Belfort could at least have understood one of the many causes of anti-Semitism. But it is true that this criminal never mentions in his book his countless victims who do not seem to matter to him in the least.

---

[220] Jordan Belfort, *The Wolf of Wall Street* (2007), Booket (Grupo Planeta), Barcelona, 2015, p. 64. The Shtetls were the small villages and towns inhabited by Jews in Eastern Europe before World War II. Jordan Belfort indeed had high aspirations and role models to emulate: *"My office was at the far end of the business lounge and as I made my way through that hectic human sea, I felt like Moses in cowboy boots. The corridors were opening up for me as I went along."* p. 69–70.

[221] Jordan Belfort, *The Wolf of Wall Street* (2007), Booket (Grupo Planeta), Barcelona, 2015, p. 177.

[222] Jordan Belfort, *The Wolf of Wall Street* (2007), Booket (Grupo Planeta), Barcelona, 2015, pp. 177–178.

[223] Jordan Belfort, *The Wolf of Wall Street* (2007), Booket (Grupo Planeta), Barcelona, 2015, p. 49.

To stimulate his combativeness and will to win, Belfort needed drugs, lots and lots of drugs. He took an average of eighteen qualuuds (methaqualone) pills every day, his *"drug of choice[224]"*, in addition to his copious doses of cocaine as an accompaniment.

However, it was not because of his drug use that Jordan Belfort was initially prosecuted. In 1992, the SEC (the gendarme of Wall Street) had filed a first complaint against Stratton Oakmont, "*accusing(ing) him of stock manipulation and employing high-pressure sales tactics[225].*"

The FBI began to take a direct interest in him. Feeling spied on, afflicted with paranoia, Belfort gave himself up to the consumption of any product that could bring him some kind of serenity: morphine "*against pain*", Soma pills "*to relax my muscles*", Xanax "*for anxiety*", Prozac "for *depression*", Paxil "for *panic attacks*", Zofran "for *nausea*", Valium "*to relax my nerves*" ... and "*half a liter of single malt Macallan scotch, to get me through everything else[226].*"

But to no avail. In 1994, he had to leave the Stratton presidency; after which he was arrested and forced to post a ten million dollar bail. He could only get out of it by selling his assets and agreeing to cooperate with the FBI. In 1996, Stratton was intervened and closed down by the regulatory agencies, for "*stock manipulation and violation of business practices.*

---

[224] So much a favorite that Belfort was ecstatic about a particularly stimulating brand: "*The geniuses at Lemmon Pharmacochemistry marketed their qualuuds under the brand name Lemmon 714... They were legendary, not only for their potency but for their ability to transform Catholic school virgins into fellatio queens. Hence their nickname "leg openers". —I want them all! —I barked.*" The Wolf of Wall Street, p. 341–342. (NdT).

[225] Jordan Belfort, *The Wolf of Wall Street* (2007), Booket (Grupo Planeta), Barcelona, 2015, p. 274. [As we have already seen, the main tactic of Belfort's scam was the *Pump and dump* ("inflate and dump"). A form of stock fraud that involves the holder of a stock, knowing its low future potential. The broker uses disinformation campaigns to overvalue the asset or his influence in the media to attract new investors to artificially raise its price. Belfort's trading room, with its brokers, created the artificial demand to drive up the stock price. Once the leader of the *"pump and dump"* scheme succeeds in inflating the price of his shares far above their rational value, he sells his shares en masse, the price falls, readjusting to the real price or even falling below it while investors lose their money. Stocks that fall victim to this scheme are known as *chop stocks*. This tactic is very well exposed in the movie *Boiler Room*, by Ben Younger (USA, 2000), inspired by the Stratton Oakmont case].

[226] Jordan Belfort, *The Wolf of Wall Street* (2007), Booket (Grupo Planeta), Barcelona, 2015, p. 465.

Belfort was not sentenced until 2003: four years in prison for stock fraud and money laundering. According to Judge John Gleeson of the Federal District Court in Brooklyn, Belfort had to repay $110 million to the 3,000 investors who had been cheated and robbed. Upon his release from prison, he would have to pay 50% of his monthly income into a compensation fund for all his victims. The swindler spent only two years in prison (22 months), and was released in April 2006. Belfort had the idea of writing his biography in prison, being advised in that project by his literary agent Joel Gotler and Irwyn Appelbaum, the director of the publishing house, who saw a good opportunity to earn more money at the expense of the goyim. The book was published in 2007.

The con man was now lecturing on sales strategies for the modest sum of $30,000 per show. He lived in a house in the residential neighborhood of Manhattan Beach, claiming to be remorseful, although he continued to recount his past exploits with glee. The release of the film, in December 2013, filled him with satisfaction, despite having only repaid $11.6 million of the $110 million owed to the victims.

Jordan Belfort claimed to *have* only *"swindled the rich"*. An article by Susan Antilla, published in the *New York Times* on December 19, 2013, showed on the contrary that his numerous victims were from the middle class. Peter Springsteel, an architect living in Mystic, Connecticut, stated that he had just launched his firm when he was contacted by a Stratton broker in the early 1990s, causing him to lose half of his savings. *"My father lost almost a quarter of a million dollars,"* said Louis Dequine, a veterinarian from Oak Creek, Colorado. Diane Nygaard, an attorney who defended some of the victims, noted that *"Jordan Belfort had ruined many middle-class citizens, retirees and small businesses."* According to her, Belfort was not sincere in his repentance or when he pretended to have changed and *"found God in his path."* In fact, none of his thousands of victims were even mentioned in his book. Scorsese had also accomplished the feat of concealing the Jewishness of the "hero" and his gang.

In an article in the American Jewish press, entitled *The Wolf and the jewish problem*, Jewish writer Ron Eshman nevertheless declared himself a bit disappointed that Scorsese erased the Jewishness of the protagonists: *"I get it: to do otherwise might give the image of an anti-Semitic film. Scorsese is much more comfortable portraying the Italianness of violent gangsters than the Jewishness of Jewish hustlers."*

He also wondered about the fact that the big swindlers were always Jewish: *"The question I ask myself and that haunts me is whether there is something wrong with the vast gray area that leads them to cross this line. Are the Belfort's and the Madoffs unnatural mutations, or are they the inevitable consequence of deeply rooted attitudes in our community[227]?"* Good question.

The dotcom bubble scam

The tactics of the Jordan Belfort scam were replicated in the great Internet bubble scam of 1999: companies that were mere ideas were floated on the stock market; and thanks to media hype, they were sold for billions to the public. Analysts at Goldman Sachs artificially inflated the stock, trumpeting that the *pedazodegoy.com* share was worth $100.

In an article published in the July 2009 issue of *Rolling Stone* magazine, journalist Matt Taibbi used this original metaphor to describe the situation: *"It was as if the banks, including Goldman Sachs, had wrapped some watermelons in pretty wrapping paper and tossed them off the fiftieth floor while making a phone call to put them on the market for sale. In this game, you could only win if you got your money back before the watermelons exploded on the sidewalk."*

Matt Taibbi provided some explanations: Since the Great Depression of 1929, there were strict rules that Wall Street respected during an IPO. The company had to have been in existence for at least five years and had to have generated a profit for at least three consecutive years. But these rules were gradually abolished. After that, a single profitable year was sufficient, even a single quarter. During the time of the Internet bubble, banks did not even ask for a profitability forecast.

In 1996, after listing Yahoo, a then little-known company, Goldman Sachs had become a specialist in this type of operation. But of the twenty-four companies that the bank floated in 1997, a third were loss-making. By 1999, at the height of the bubble, the bank had listed 47 companies, including zombie companies such as *Webcam* and *eToys*. That year, the shares of these companies rose 281% above their entry value, compared to an average of 181% for all Wall Street indexes. In

---

[227] *Jewish Journal*, December 31, 2013. The answer to this distressing question is found in our *Psychoanalysis of Judaism*, 2006.

the first four months of the following year, Goldman listed another 18 companies, 14 of which were loss-making at the time.

To manipulate stock prices, Goldman used a tactic called *laddering*: a company would ask Goldman for a listing on the stock exchange. The bank would agree with the company *pedazodegoy.com* on the number of shares to offer to the public, the commissions (say 6 or 7% of the capital raised) and the agreements with potential large investors. Goldman then offered its best clients the right to acquire large blocks of shares at the introductory price in exchange for a commitment to buy additional shares later on in the market. These agreements ensured that the price would rise, since these large investors who had bought shares at the introductory price of $15, for example, would have to buy more for $20 or $25 at a later agreed date, thus guaranteeing that the price would rise to more than $25. In this way, Goldman had been able to artificially inflate the share price and receive a 6% commission on hundreds of millions of dollars.

Goldman Sachs was prosecuted several times by shareholders for this practice, *laddering*. These fraudulent maneuvers had attracted the attention of Nicholas Maier, manager of Cramer & Co, a hedge fund run at the time by Jim Cramer, himself a former Goldman Sachs employee who later became a famous television presenter. Maier had testified to the SEC that while working for Cramer, between 1996 and 1998, he had been forced several times to participate in *laddering* operations for Goldman's IPO. In 2005, Goldman agreed to pay $40 million for his frauds—a ridiculous fine compared to the gigantic profits the bank had pocketed.

Goldman Sachs also engaged in *spinning* during the dotcom bubble. It offered the managers of the listed company preferred shares in exchange for future customers. The initial IPO price was voluntarily undervalued, with the agreement of the company's management. Instead of setting the *pedazodegoy.com share* at $20, he set it at $18 and bought one million shares on behalf of the company's CEO, not the company itself. Goldman had thus offered several million dollars to eBay's president, Meg Whitman, in exchange for eBay's future clientele. Whitman later joined Goldman's board of directors.

Such practices had contributed to making the Internet bubble a real scam. When investors lost confidence and panic set in, $5 billion vanished from the Nasdaq index alone. But the money was not lost for everyone. Between 1999 and 2002, Goldman Sachs had distributed $28.5 billion to its brokers, an average of $350,000 per year for each one. In 2002, after the collapse of the dotcom bubble, a report by the House of Representatives accused Goldman Sachs of having made these preferential offers to the managers of 21 companies it had listed on the stock exchange. Goldman vehemently denounced the report, before finally paying $110 million to settle the investigation launched by the State of New York. For a bank that paid $7 billion in salaries, a fine of $110 million to be paid over 5 years did not seem much of a deterrent. Jon Corzine, who ran Goldman from 1994 to 1999, denied any fraud on the part of the bank's management. Asked by a journalist during an interview, he had replied, "*I had never heard that term laddering until today!*"

Insider trading

This is a crime that consists of using or passing on inside information not known to the public when it would otherwise have had a positive or negative impact on the value of the securities listed on the stock exchange. The insider, for example, may buy a security shortly before a takeover bid that he knows is imminent and then resell it at a significant capital gain. Let's look at an example:

In 2001, David Zilkha was working at Microsoft but was about to leave the company to join the hedge *fund* Pequot Capital. Two weeks before the end of his contract at Microsoft, Arthur Samberg, president of Pequot Capital, had sent him an e-mail concerned about the performance of Microsoft, a company in which the fund owned shares. After asking his colleagues by internal mail, David Zilkha reassured his future boss: the figures soon to be published by the computer giant would not be disappointing. The latter then bought Microsoft shares whose price rose by one euro the next day, when the company's results were published. The capital gain generated by the information amounted to 14.8 million dollars. The Securities and Exchange Commission (SEC) did not have enough evidence to convict David Zilkha of "insider trading". But in 2009, his former wife found his compromising emails and turned them over to the SEC, pocketing 10% of the fine, or $1 million, in the process.

Ivan Boesky: the reference in this field

Ivan Boesky had created his business partnership in New York in 1975. In 1986, he had already amassed a fortune of more than 200 million dollars. Boesky had earned 65 million dollars in 1984 when Chevron bought Golfe and when Texaco bought Getty. He had also earned close to $50 million in 1985 when Philip Morris acquired General Foods. Ivan Boesky was actually buying thousands of shares of the company to be acquired in order to resell them at a very high price a few days before a company announced a takeover bid.

This was clearly insider trading. Boesky was an accomplice of Dennis Levine, the director of Drexel Burnham Bank. Dennis Levine, himself indicted, had reported Boesky, and the two were arrested in 1986 for this crime. In September, Boesky finally decided to cooperate with the SEC to save his own skin and provided federal investigators with a lot of valuable information about stock fraud. It was he who blew the whistle on Michael Milken. Thanks to wiretaps and recordings, investigators were able to prosecute fourteen people, earning Boesky the honor of being featured on the cover of the December 1, 1986, issue of the *Times* magazine. Dennis Levine, as president of Drexel Bank, was ordered by the SEC to pay a $1.1 billion fine, but the bank was bankrupted. Boesky had to pay a $100 million fine. In December 1987, at the age of 50, he was sentenced to three years in prison. He was released two years later, but was banned from the securities markets.

Ivan Boesky was a major donor to the worldwide Jewish charity CJA. His "wikipedia" file contained a good dose of humor. Listen: *"Later, Boesky began practicing Judaism and attended classes at the Jewish Theological Seminary of America, of which he had been a major donor."* We must understand that he was not Jewish when he was delinquent, but that upon discovering his Jewish roots he had redeemed himself and become an honest man and a philanthropist. It is useless to try to find out who wrote this record. In any case, part of Ivan Boesky's famous speech delivered at Berkeley in 1986, the University of California, has remained for posterity: *"I believe that greed is healthy. You can be greedy and still feel good about yourself."*

Steven Cohen: "You eat what you kill".

In January 2014, another such case was tried in the United States. A broker of an investment fund called SAC Capital was suspected of having benefited from confidential information. In 2008, he was reportedly informed by a doctor that a drug against Alzheimer's disease developed by two subsidiaries of the US laboratory Pfizer[228]—the companies Elan and Wyeth—was not going to be approved by the FDA (the US Food and Drug Administration). The following day, the investment fund SAC Capital had sold all its shares in these two companies, thus avoiding significant losses, short-selling nearly $1 billion in Elan and Wyeth shares before the official publication of the agency's report, generating a profit of $276 million[229]. It was *"the most lucrative insider trading operation in history,"* according to Manhattan U.S. Attorney Preet Bharara, who added that the magnitude of the crime was *"historically unprecedented"*.

Prosecutor Preet Bharara had an impressive list of successes, having already prosecuted 78 cases of insider trading without losing a single one. Since 2009, he had nabbed nine SAC Capital employees. A month earlier, he had obtained the indictment of Michael Steinberg on insider trading charges, facing an 80-year prison sentence. Six of them had been convicted after pleading guilty, and four had agreed to cooperate with the authorities.

The chairman of SAC Capital was a billionaire, a legendary and controversial Wall Street figure at the same time: Steven Cohen. For a decade, the U.S. justice system had been trying to corner him. According to investigators, the illegal use of sensitive and non-public information obtained thanks to a large network of friends—mainly doctors—was his main business.

In March 2013, two subsidiaries of SAC Capital had agreed to pay 600 million dollars to end the legal actions against this crime. This was the largest sum ever paid in this type of case in the United States. At first glance, Steven Cohen seemed to be off the hook, but the fine did not put an end to the investigations initiated by the federal authorities. Steven Cohen, 56 years old, the 35th richest man in the United States,

---

[228] Between 1995 and 2009, 40 cases were brought to court for malpractice and fraud. Pfizer paid a total of 6171 million dollars in fines.

[229] Article from *France24.com*, dated January 7, 2014. You can bet on the upside of a stock, a bond or a commodity by buying it. But you can also bet on the downside by selling what you don't own (the asset in question can be acquired for sale through a securities loan), with a promise to buy it later. This is called short selling, or short position. The person who carries out the operation expects to obtain an economic benefit to the extent that the value of the security has fallen because he sells it at a higher price (initial moment) than when he buys it (later moment). If, on the other hand, the securities were to rise, he would suffer a loss.

whose funds managed some 14 billion dollars, had not yet been indicted personally.

In November 2013, however, after months of investigation, Steven Cohen was finally charged with insider trading and agreed to pay $1.2 billion to settle the criminal proceedings, in addition to the $616 million paid in March as part of the civil proceedings. With annual returns of over 25% for 20 years, SAC Capital was forced to give up its *hedge fund status* to become a simple *"family office"*: Steven Cohen would have to limit himself to managing the $9 billion that belonged to him and his close associates.

He could continue to occupy his 3251 m² villa in Connecticut where he had built up an impressive collection of contemporary works of art. An article in the weekly *Le Point* of February 9, 2006 entitled "Steven Cohen, the Wall Street Boss" described him as follows: *"The real boss of Wall Street does not live in Manhattan, but secluded in a house in Greenwich (Connecticut) enclosed by a four-meter high wall. Steven Cohen, 49 years old, hardly ever shows himself... In 2005, he pocketed 500 million dollars. What is his secret? Knowing everything before anyone else. With his eyes glued to the control screens, he analyzes thousands of data and gets furious when Wall Street analysts don't give him the scoop on a piece of information. The investors who entrust him with their money ($4 billion) pay him dearly for his services: Cohen receives 3% of the sums as management fees (against 1.44% on average) and 35% of the profits (against 19.2% on average)."* Cohen *"professes total capitalism:" You eat what you kill,"* he tells his brokers, *remunerated on the basis of their skills and performance*[230]*."*

---

[230] In *Psychoanalysis of Judaism (2006)* and *Jewish Fanaticism (2007)*.

3. The Federal Reserve heist

At the beginning of October 2008, the U.S. government had received authorization from senators and representatives to bail out the ailing banks. No less than 700 billion dollars were taken from the pockets of the US taxpayer.

It had all started with a real estate crisis: the famous *subprime* crisis[231]. The "predatory lending" that underpinned the bottom of the pyramid had been granted by lending institutions to millions of households who had been promised a bright future. For years, the bankers had profited immensely, but when the bill for the party had to be paid, the U.S. government had found only the taxpayer to search and empty its pockets.

At the time, economists had privileged the explanations of economic cycles, and it took a few years before more conscientious analysts demonstrated that this crisis was of criminal origin. In his book *The Great Fraud (La grande Fraude,* 2011), Jean-François Gayraud denounced the thesis according to which the crisis would have been a fatality of economic cycles. The dominant explanation of economic cycles was indeed *"very comfortable for financial actors,"* since thus *"everyone and no one is really responsible*[232]*."* The system being fallible, men were victims of phenomena beyond their control. The approach of the fatality of cycles is very comfortable because it makes it possible to evade nagging questions about the real causes of financial crises. *"In reality,* wrote Jean-François Gayraud, *financial crises are human tragedies, and not natural catastrophes*[233]*."*

---

[231] About this crisis you can watch the interesting film, *The Big Bet* (*The Big Short,* 2015). It is based on the book of the same name by Michael Lewis, about the financial crisis of 2007 to 2010 due to the accumulation of housing and the economic bubble. The book highlights the eccentric nature of the type of person who bets against the market or goes against the grain. This is reflected in the film adaptation, although, thank God (YHWH), the voice of universal moral conscience is raised in the wilderness through the character played by a Jewish hedge fund manager to condemn the folly of men and the market. (NdT)

[232] Jean-François Gayraud, *La grande Fraude,* Odile Jacob, 2011, p. 15.

[233] Jean-François Gayraud, *La grande Fraude,* Odile Jacob, 2011, p. 16.

Jean-François Gayraud insisted on the criminal dimension of the crisis, just as the journalist William Black had done for the Savings Banks crisis in the 1980s. William Black—a specialist in financial delinquency who denounced the *"managerial swindlers"*—was an apologist for the authors George Akerlof and Paul Romer who had jointly written an article that went to the heart of the matter: *"Only a small percentage of university studies and economic books on the current crisis mention this fundamental text, or consider fraud as a driving force of the crisis"*, wrote William Black.

George Akerlof had received the Nobel Prize in 2001, largely for his work on another form of corporate fraud, and Paul Romer was also a highly respected economist. *"The economists' guild still refuses to analyze corporate fraud or to take an interest in criminological studies of the scams that are at the root of our recurrent, and increasingly severe, financial crises: this does not honor the discipline. Moreover, ignoring a Nobel laureate in one of his main areas of expertise evidences a reckless disregard for the truth[234]."*

The criminal dimension of the *subprime* crisis is now absolutely evident. Nobel Prize winners Paul Krugman and Joseph Stiglitz denounced the abuses generated by deregulation. In 2010, in his book *The Big Bet*, Michael Lewis pointed the finger directly at the *"swindling managers"*. But even more the journalist Charles Ferguson, who brought the whole phenomenon to light. Charles Ferguson won the Oscar for best documentary in 2011 for his *Inside Job*, which exposed the 2008 financial crisis. In 2012, in his eponymous book *Inside Job*, Ferguson expanded on his research. At the beginning of the book, he was surprised that no protagonists were still behind bars. *"At the beginning of 2012, no criminal charges have yet been brought against any senior financial executives in connection with the financial crisis."* He denounced *"widespread and unpunished criminal behavior in the financial sector"* dating back to the times of the criminogenic

---

[234] *"One of the most pertinent checks a reader can make before buying (or not) an economics book on the crisis is to verify whether the author cites the 1993 article by George A. Akerlof and Paul M. Romer: "Looting: the Economic Underworld of Bankruptcy for Profit"* (William Black, *Une Fraude presque parfaite, Le pillage des caisses d'épargne américaines par leurs dirigeants*, Éditions Charles Léopold Mayer, 2012, p. 440)." (William Black, *Une Fraude presque parfaite, Le pillage des caisses d'épargne américaines par leurs dirigeants*, Éditions Charles Léopold Mayer, 2012, p. 440).

deregulation of the 1980s: *"We have irrefutable evidence that over the last thirty years the US financial sector has become a rogue industry[235]."*

Charles Fergusson confessed—a bit naively to be honest—his disappointment at the inaction of the Obama administration. What did he think? One only had to look at the entourage of the first black president Barack Obama and see that it was composed of the same people from the same sect as those who had preceded them. In fact, neither Charles Ferguson, nor Michael Lewis, nor William Black, nor the Nobel laureates pointed out the particularly nefarious role played by the members of this omnipresent sect in the business world. Jean-François Gayraud went even further, grotesquely denouncing the control of the Sicilian Mafia whenever an Italian surname appeared. None of these researchers therefore saw what was to be seen: namely that the *subprime* crisis had its origin in a very particular mentality that has spread by contagion throughout the West and the world. From this point onwards, all the regulatory measures that may be proposed will only be more or less solid and ephemeral dams, which will always be circumvented by the malice of the money men.

Predatory lending and the subprime crisis

The global financial crisis of 2008 had begun the previous year with the contraction of the U.S. housing market. The market had experienced an extraordinary boom up to that point, with two million homes built each year for a decade. This growth had been fueled by historically low interest rates. After the bursting of the Internet bubble in 2000 and the attacks of September 11, 2001, the US Federal Reserve (the Fed: the central bank) had opted for this policy to strengthen investments and avoid a recession. Thus, Fed Chairman Alan Greenspan had lowered the interest rate eleven times in a row, bringing it from 6.5% at the end of

---

[235]Charles Ferguson, *Inside Job, the financial crisis...* Ediciones Deusto, Barcelona, 2012, p. 15–16. [*With each new step in the process of deregulation and concentration, the U.S. financial sector became an almost criminal industry, whose behavior ended up producing a gigantic Ponzi scheme on a global scale: the financial bubble that provoked the 2008 crisis was literally the crime of the century, one of whose collateral effects will continue to weigh on the world for many years to come in the form of economic stagnation in the United States and the debt crisis in Europe". Inside Job,* p. 33.

2000 to 1% in July 2003, its lowest level since 1954[236]. Taking inflation into account, real interest rates were thus negative.

Real estate lending had been facilitated by successive governments aimed at enabling the neediest Americans to become homeowners. A 1977 law (the Community Reinvestment Act)—strengthened in 1995 under President Bill Clinton and in 2002 by Republicans—encouraged banks to lend to families in disadvantaged neighborhoods. President Bill Clinton had strongly insisted on access to property for the poor and Hispanic and black minorities, even under the cover of judicial threats. Roberta Achtenberg, a senior city planning official and homosexual activist, had played an important role: *"Roberta Achtenberg provided teams of investigators and prosecutors with significant resources to root out discriminatory practices in mortgage companies. She promised to prosecute them at the first sign of bad behavior. These companies, naturally inclined to be lenient on lending criteria, were encouraged by Washington to turn a blind eye to the creditworthiness of applicants. Like deposit banks, they were even rated on the volume of loans granted to low-income individuals. A good rating then allowed them to open new branches or undertake mergers[237]."* Republican George Bush, who had succeeded Bill Clinton, had practiced the same policy in hopes of capturing the votes of black and Hispanic voters. The Community Reinvestment Act is, despite what has been described, generally considered by "Republicans" (the "right-wing" liberals) as one of the main explanations for the financial crisis.

But mortgage lending was mainly encouraged by banks and lending institutions thanks to set-ups and mechanisms that protected them from the risk of non-repayment: with the real estate mortgaged and the rapid and continuous rise in real estate market prices, a foreclosure (eviction)

---

[236] *"Federal Reserve Chairman Alan Greenspan, the man who was supposed to be protecting the country from excessive risk-taking, in fact encouraged it... Typically, markets project that interest rates will remain roughly where they have been—except in exceptional periods. But in 2003, Greenspan had done something unprecedented: he lowered interest rates to 1 percent... That meant that anyone with a variable-rate mortgage was almost certain to see their interest payments rise in the future, and perhaps by a large amount. And boy, did they go up, as the short-term interest rate rose from 1 percent in 2003 to 5.25 in 2006."* Joseph Stiglitz, *Free Fall, the Free Market and the Collapse of the World Economy*, Taurus, Madrid, 2010, p. 124.

[237] Jean-François Gayraud, *La grande Fraude*, Odile Jacob, 2011, p. 26.

allowed them to recover the money lent in case of non-payment. In fact, from 1999 to 2005, house prices had increased by 42%[238].

Borrowers were rated on the basis of their socio-professional characteristics (employment, unemployment, marriage, incident of default, bank overdraft, etc.) using *"FICO scores"*, invented in the 1950s. Creditworthiness levels were evaluated on the basis of a score ranging from 300 to 850 points. Borrowers with the highest score were referred to as *"prime"* (above 700), while the *"subprime"* category corresponded to borrowers whose *score was* below 620. However, the evaluation of borrowers was not always very reliable. An immigrant who had never failed to repay a loan, for the simple reason that he had never been granted a loan, often had a surprisingly high *score*.

Most of the time, poor families could get a mortgage with a fixed and very low interest rate for the first two years; then this rate became variable according to the value of the real estate; the more valuable the house, the lower the rate; and conversely, when the house lost value, the interest rate increased. Lending institutions agreed to lend up to 110% of the value of the mortgaged property. In the worst case scenario, they would benefit from the first two years of repayments on a property that they would end up recovering and selling more expensively thanks to the continuous boom in real estate market prices, which had never fallen since the 1930s. The borrower, for his part, knew that if he found himself in trouble he could resell the house and even earn a capital gain. The great Temple treasurer Alan Greenspan directly encouraged all households to take out variable rate mortgages[239]: proof that there was no risk.

Mortgage lenders, attracted by the high profitability of these loans, thus granted millions of loans to poor families, little informed of the risks of over-indebtedness, and who were promised that they would earn a lot of money by reselling their house two or three years later at a substantial profit. These lenders were negligent about the creditworthiness of the borrowers, as most of them resold their loans to the big Wall Street

---

[238] Joseph Stiglitz, *Caída libre, el libre mercado y el hundimiento de la economía mundial*, Taurus, Madrid, 2010, p. 123. *"Between 1999 and 2005, housing prices rose by 42 percent"*, but according to Paul Krugman, in 2006, the market was overvalued by 50%. (Jean-François Gayraud, *La grande Fraude*, Odile Jacob, 2011, p. 27).
[239] Joseph Stiglitz, *Free Fall, the Free Market and the Collapse of the World Economy*, Taurus, Madrid, 2010, p. 124, 153.

investment banks that took care of the repossession. The risk was no longer theirs.

The business was so booming that tens of thousands of independent loan brokers, working with various lender banks, scoured the cities and countryside looking for someone to scam[240]. The broker could set up shop in a prefabricated storefront near the showings of homes in a development for sale or canvass the Internet. In the United States, anyone could be a loan broker. Unlike banks, real estate brokers and lending institutions were not controlled by federal banking regulations, so the profession attracted many scammers and abuses multiplied[241]. To attract clients, all means were good: loans granted with no cash down payment, no documentation, discounted or "balance" rates (at the beginning of the borrowing period). There were no limits to the brokers' imagination, since they did not assume the risk and knew that the local bank would validate the application. The interest of the brokers was even to conceal from the lenders the information that could prevent the signing of the contract, in order to collect the commissions. Many applications were thus filled out with false declarations, or even without any declaration at all. While in 2001, 80% of *subprime* loans were processed with "complete documentation", by 2006 this share had fallen to 50%[242]. For example, when a borrower did not have sufficient income to repay the loan he was applying for, it was sufficient to attribute extraordinary income "declared on the honor".

The largest lender specializing in real estate loans, Countrywide Financial, which had blanketed the country with branches and financed one real estate loan out of six across the country, had by 2008 earned a very bad reputation[243]. The more dubious lenders, such as Long Beach Savings in California, were making loans with no income disclosures, and no input from the borrower. California real estate blogs are still replete with stories of floating interest rate scams. Former employees

---

[240] Credit brokerage companies grew from 37,000 in 2001 to 53,000 in 2006, and accounted for 68% of credit operations (Jean-François Gayraud, *La grande Fraude*, Odile Jacob, 2011, p. 64).

[241] In Florida, from 2000 to 2007, more than 10,000 brokers had criminal records (Jean-François Gayraud, *La grande Fraude*, p. 76).

[242] Jean-François Gayraud, *La grande Fraude*, Odile Jacob, 2011, p. 66.

[243] *Countrywide Financial was* created in 1970 by Angelo Mozilo and David Loeb (Olivier Pastré, Jean-Marc Sylvestre, *Le Roman vrai de la crise financière*, Perrin 2008, coll. Tempus, p. 107). From 2004 to 2007, *Countrywide Financial* had processed 150 billion bad loans (Jean-François Gayraud, *La grande Fraude*, p. 71).

of a major lender, Washington Mutual, had testified in court *"that each originator had to sign for five loans a day, and at that number the premiums started accruing; that the lending criteria changed almost daily[244]"*. The president of Washington Mutual was not Jewish, but a Goy: Kerry Killinger. New Century, the second operator in the market, used similar methods. Their remuneration depended on the volume of loans they granted and not on their quality. They therefore had an interest in granting very expensive loans at the highest possible interest rate.

The most fraudulent transactions involved false payrolls and false identity documents. Real estate prices were fraudulently overvalued by experts and appraisers, with the consent of borrowers and brokers. *"In 2007, 90% of the more than 1,200 appraisers questioned admitted to having been pressured to change their evaluation of real estate, pressure that came from brokers, lenders and real estate agents,"* wrote Jean-François Gayraud. In his book *Confessions of a Subprime Lender*, Richard Bitner, who headed a lending company, also provided a blunt assessment of these brokerage and appraisal professionals: *"The number of questionable appraisals was as high as 80%*. More than 70% of the mortgage loans he had processed were "*misleading*"; according to him no more than a third of the brokers were honest[245].

It was enough to drive past a bank for a salesman to grant you a loan of hundreds of thousands of dollars. In the small town of Bakersfield, California, a Mexican strawberry picker, who earned $14,000 a year and did not speak a word of English, took out a loan of $724,000 to buy a house. A nanny of Jamaican origin had become the owner of six houses in Queens, a borough of New York. She had bought one; and then, as its value had increased, she was offered another loan of $250,000 to buy a second, and so on[246]. A penniless web designer had

---

[244] Charles Ferguson, *Inside Job, the financial crisis*… Ediciones Deusto, Barcelona, 2012, p. 92.

[245] Jean-François Gayraud, *La grande Fraude*, Odile Jacob, 2011, p. 68, 69. ["A high-level appraiser testified that loans rejected by her reappeared many times approved by higher management. Dozens of former employees have come forward with similar testimony. The New York state attorney general has also brought charges against Washington Mutual for exerting financial pressures to get appraisers to inflate property values." Charles Ferguson, *Inside Job, The Financial Crisis*… p. 92. Also read note 21, page 368, in Joseph Stiglitz, *Free Fall, The Free Market and the Collapse of the World Economy*, Taurus, Madrid, 2010 (NdT)].

[246] Michael Lewis. *La gran apuesta*, Debate Penguin Random House, Barcelona, 2013, p. 123, 124.

been able to buy seven houses by borrowing two million dollars without a fixed salary. A Chilean cleaner who spoke no English and was in an illegal situation had received a loan of $400,000 in 2003 to buy an apartment in New York. Unable to repay it, she was refinanced twice in a row. In general, the aim was to ensure that, at the end of the fixed-rate period, borrowers could refinance their loans.

Some brokers had scoured the most dangerous neighborhoods in Los Angeles, where they would give $400 to people totally broke to put a signature under a mortgage contract. Joseph Stiglitz, Nobel laureate in economics, transcribed this testimony: "*They would just call and say, "Hey, do you need money in the bank? And I would say, "Yes, I need money in the bank*[247]"" Only after two years of low interest rates, they could go up to 15%. These abusive loans were nothing less than usurious, the same usury practiced by the Jews since high Antiquity and complained about by the peasants driven to ruin[248].

The *subprime* market developed at a dizzying pace, growing from $200 billion in 2002 to $640 billion in 2006, which then represented 23% of the country's total real estate loans. Between 2004 and 2008, there was $1.8 trillion of *subprime*, but the "Alt A" loans, above 680 FICO, were also dubious as they were poorly documented as well, with borrowers not presenting solid proof of income.

When, at the beginning of 2005, the great Treasurer Alan Greenspan readjusted the interest rate to deflate the housing bubble and contain inflation, the edifice faltered before collapsing. The Fed's interest rate rose seventeen times, first under Alan Greenspan, then under his successor and congener Ben Bernanke, to 5.25% in mid-2006. Lending had become less attractive and prices in the sector began to fall in several regions of the United States. The market eventually lost about 20% during the 18 months before the crisis—fluctuations differed from state to state, city to city and neighborhood to neighborhood.

Thus, in the summer of 2006, tens of thousands of U.S. households began to default on their mortgages and evictions multiplied. At first, only *subprime* loans were affected; then foreclosures affected

---

[247] Joseph Stiglitz, *Free Fall, the Free Market and the Collapse of the World Economy*, Taurus, Madrid, 2010, p. 114.
[248] In this regard, read the testimony of Guy de Maupassant in *The Jewish Fanaticism* (2007), and *History of Antisemitism* (2010).

homeowners who had a conventional mortgage but had lost their jobs (at a time when companies were relocating to emerging countries with cheap labor). In June 2007, more than one million people who had signed a mortgage were insolvent (15% of *subprime* loans), and three million households were at risk of becoming insolvent. In July 2009, *"more than 15.2 million U.S. mortgages, nearly one-third of all mortgaged real estate were "underwater"[249]."*

Lenders should have been able to recover the principal by selling foreclosed homes, but the number of homes put up for sale had aggravated the market imbalance and real estate prices collapsed. Houses had lost more than a third of their value, so that for eleven million households their mortgage loan exceeded the value of their home. Those who were still able to pay their installments had no reason to continue paying. But with the other debtors, the banks were inflexible, after having been falsely generous: *"Doris Canales' home was threatened with foreclosure after she refinanced her home thirteen times in six years with "no-doc" [no documentation] mortgages, which required little or no documentation of income or assets."*

In reality, these loans were more like "neutron loans," as they were called at the time: they destroyed families, leaving homes empty and untouched. *Subprime* loans were also nicknamed *"liar loans"*, whose victims were usually the most vulnerable people: the poor, the elderly and ethnic minorities, especially Hispanics, newly arrived immigrants with no command of English and unable to understand the contracts.

Moody's Economy website *"predicted that a total of 3.4 million homeowners would default on their mortgages in 2009, and 2.1 million would lose their homes. Many millions more are expected to have their mortgages foreclosed on between now and 2012[250]."* On average, one loan in eight had defaulted. More than half of the foreclosures (evictions) had occurred in four states: California, Florida, Arizona and Illinois. The states of Michigan, Ohio, Texas and Georgia had also been widely affected.

Other statistics were even more alarming. In January 2010, the Californian company RealtyTrac, which specializes in housing market

---

[249] Joseph Stiglitz, *Free fall, the free market and the collapse of the world economy*, Taurus, Madrid, 2010, footnote 33 page 370.
[250] Joseph Stiglitz, *Free Fall, the Free Market and the Collapse of the World Economy*, Taurus, Madrid, 2010, p. 114, 115.

statistics, counted a record 3.9 million homes that had been foreclosed on in 2009. On March 26, 2010, President Barack Obama unveiled a new plan to curb home foreclosures: an additional $14 billion to enable distressed borrowers to refinance their mortgages and avoid default. But the decline in foreclosures did not begin to be significant until December 2013, reducing the divorce and suicide rate in the process. In the meantime, hundreds of thousands of people had returned to live at home with their parents or directly in makeshift shelters or in their vehicles. In total, an estimated fifteen million homes were evicted between the beginning of the crisis in 2006 and the expected return to normality in 2015.

Alan Greenspan's responsibility was all the greater because as early as 2002 he had been warned by the Fed's board of the dangers of the *subprime* market. The Fed could, for example, *"have reduced loan-to-value ratios as much as possible instead of allowing them to rise. It could have restricted adjustable-rate mortgages. Instead, Greenspan encouraged them. He could have restricted loans with negative amortization and insufficient documentation (liar's credit). He had many tools at his disposal*[251]*."*

The causes of the crisis were structural: if credit institutions were able to lend so easily to people who clearly did not have the capacity to repay, it was because they had resold the loans to investment banks.

The CDO scam

Whether the mortgage was toxic, i.e. risky or fraudulent, was no longer a problem for the lender, since it was immediately resold on Wall Street. And the big Wall Street banks had a great interest in buying and managing these loans to the extent that they could be "securitized", i.e. transformed into securities tradable on the stock exchange to be bought and sold by investors: banks (in the United States or abroad), insurance companies, pension funds, municipalities or hedge *funds*. A long-term,

---

[251] Joseph Stiglitz, *Free Fall, Free Markets and the Collapse of the World Economy*, Taurus, Madrid, 2010, p. 315. "In *fact, Alan Greenspan blocked a proposal to increase oversight over subprime lenders under the Federal Reserve's broad authority. Greg Ip, "Did Greenspan Add to Subprime Woes?", Wall Street Journal, June 9, 2007, p. B1.",* footnote 10 page 367.

illiquid commercial contract (mortgage, real estate loan) was transformed into a market product, liquid and sellable at any time.

The securitization of debts consisted in grouping them all together in packages (up to several thousand), in order to diversify the risk. A certain number of borrowers could default; but if a large number of borrowers were put together, diversifying their origin, it was possible to reduce the overall risk. The loans were thus transformed into mortgage bonds called "MBS" (*mortage-backed securities*, or "mortgage-backed securities" [252]). Securitization created an uninterrupted flow of fees that generated unprecedented profits, all the more so as financial engineers managed to create ever more sophisticated new products. In 2005, there were "*$625 billion in junk mortgage loans, of which $507 billion ended up as mortgage bonds. Half a trillion dollars in subprime mortgage-backed bonds in a single year*[253]." By 2006, 75% of the $665 billion in *subprime* loans had been securitized[254].

In 2000, five investment banks dominated the market: Goldman Sachs, Merrill Lynch, Morgan Stanley, Lehman Brothers and Bear Stearns. There were also the subsidiaries of the three financial conglomerates Citigroup, JP Morgan Chase and Bank of America. Some European banks shared the rest: Deutsche Bank, UBS and Credit Suisse.

The most popular securities for large investors were CDOs ("*collateralized debt obligation*" or collateralized debt obligations[255]), which pooled MBS and traded for hundreds of millions of dollars. In 1983, Larry Fink and his team at First Boston had invented

---

[252] Other types of receivables can be used as collateral: auto loans, student loans, consumer loans, outstanding credit card payments. These are called *asset-backed securities* (ABS).

[253] Michael Lewis, *La gran apuesta*, Debate Penguin Random House, Barcelona, 2013, p. 44.

[254] Jean-François Gayraud, *La grande Fraude*, Odile Jacob, 2011, p. 30. Securitization was invented in 1977 by Salomon Brothers. In the 1980s, the Savings Banks had thus been able to sell their loss-making mortgage loans by transforming them into MBS (*mortgage-backed security*). The perverse mechanism that disconnected risk and profit was already in place.

[255] A *Collateralized Debt Obligation* (CDO) is a type of structured financial product backed by asset-backed security (ABS). Originally developed for the corporate debt markets, CDOs were expanded over time to include mortgages and mortgage-backed securities (MBS) as well.

collateralized debt obligations[256]. Fink had innovated by cutting the obligations into several tranches. All payments made by borrowers went first to the most secure tranche, but with the lowest interest rate for the investor. When the first tranche received the full amount due, payments went to the second tranche, then the third, and so on. The last tranche was the riskiest, but the interest for investors was also much higher.

Each CDO contained several tranches of about one hundred different mortgage obligations (bonds), themselves composed of thousands of different loans. Investors who bought them were remunerated with the cash flows generated by the assets contained in the CDO. The decline in some securities was offset by the rise in others.

But there were also several modalities. Investors could have preferences, such as, for example, to buy the part of the credits whose duration did not exceed 5 years, or to buy only credits whose borrowers were civil servants; or credits that served only to finance houses located in a specific geographic area. The bank collected the credits by maturity, duration, or taking into account all kinds of criteria, and issued the securities.

Banks created more and more CDOs. At Goldman Sachs, as at Morgan Stanley, hundreds of employees bought *subprime* loans, assembled them into bonds and resold them. Another group transformed the most repulsive and unsaleable tranches of these bonds into CDOs. The

---

[256]Laurence Douglas Fink, known as Larry Fink, is a Jewish-American entrepreneur Chairman and CEO of BlackRock, the world's largest asset and investment management firm, with nearly $9.5 trillion under management as of mid-June 2021 (of which approximately two-thirds worldwide was related to retirement savings at the end of 2018). In the late 1980s, BlackRock launched its revolutionary Aladdin program. Aladdin (*Asset, Liability, Debt and Derivative Investment Network*) is an electronic system from BlackRock Solutions. In 2013, it managed approximately $14 trillion in assets (including BlackRock's more than $6 trillion), or about 7% of global financial assets, and monitored about 30,000 investment portfolios. By 2019, Artificial Intelligence (AI) was managing $18 trillion in assets. Adam Curtis' 2016 documentary *HyperNormalisation* cites the Aladdin system as an example of how modern technocrats attempt to manage real-world complications. The 2019 *Art* documentary *These Financiers Who Run the* World—*BlackRock* claims that this artificial intelligence is driving a standardization of global investing that could amplify the ripple effect of the next financial crisis. In an article critical of BlackRock's role in the expansion of the funded pension model, *Le Monde diplomatique* highlights Aladdin's prominent role in the concentration of capital and the financialization of the economy. In 2022, the YouTube channel *Science4All* ranked Aladdin as the most "terrifying" artificial intelligence. [wikipedia (NdT).

originating bank could also create securities. In this case, the bank had to verify the loan applications twice: as a lender and as a securitizer in order to be rated, since this second verification consisted of checking the lender's financial statements and hiring criteria.

In reality, the CDOs' objective was to hide the rotten apples in a basket with some healthy fruit. In any case, the complexity of the products was so great that investors didn't understand anything either.

"Looking for bad bonds inside a CDO was like fishing for shit in a latrine: the question wasn't whether you'd catch any or not, but how soon you'd let it run disgusted. The CDO names themselves were fake and told you nothing about their contents, their creators or their managers: Carina, Piedra Preciosa, Octanos III, Glaciar Financiación...[257] "

Given the complexity of these financial products, it was almost impossible to find out what tranches and loans they were composed of, and not even the rating agencies, supposedly the best source of information in the market, had the remotest idea[258]. *"Everything was done so that the buyer of the CDO would not know, or too late, that these products contained "toxic assets"*[259]*."*

These new products had triggered a securitization rush. From late 2005 to mid-2007, Wall Street banks had created hundreds of billions of dollars in CDOs collateralized with *subprime*. No one knew the exact amount. Between 2004 and 2006, Bear Stearns (14,000 employees) securitized nearly one million mortgage loans worth $192 billion. Of the four people responsible for the securitization of Bear Stearns' mortgage loans, two co-headed the finance arm (Mary Haggerty and Baron Silverstein), whose responsibility was to ensure that the loans met the bank's requirements; and two co-headed the trading arm (Jefrrey Verschleiser and Michael Nierenberg), who negotiated the securitized loans with investors[260].

---

[257] Michael Lewis, *La gran apuesta*, Debate Penguin Random House, Barcelona, 2013, p. 161.

[258] Michael Lewis, *La gran apuesta*, Debate Penguin Random House, Barcelona, 2013, p. 160.

[259] Philippe Quême, *Monnaie bien public ou "banque-casino"?*, Édition L'Harmattan, 2011.

[260] We see that there were not only Jews in the system, although they may have played a driving role, as always in this type of business. The chairman of Bear Stearns, James Cayne, was (perhaps) not Jewish, but his wife was; moreover, the bank was co-managed

CDOs increasingly integrated more and more *subprime* mortgage bonds, often up to 80%. But the 20% of healthy assets were always enough for rating agencies such as Moody's, Standard and Poor's and Ficht to award the famous "Triple A", the best rating, which represented the best guarantee for all investors. *"It's a safe security!"* The CDO was therefore a mechanism that succeeded in transforming lead into gold.

CDOs were resold to large investors around the world. It was in this way that the risk of US *subprime* loans was transmitted to all developed economies. The Germans were especially fond of this New York-prepared junk. In fact, at the beginning, *"a large number of the subprime investors seemed to live in Germany, specifically in Düsseldorf*^{261}*"* "

The rating agencies gave the go-ahead at every step of the process, blessing a lot of junk loans in the end. The fact is that they received hefty fees for each rated security, which seemed to be enough for them^{262}. On the eve of its collapse, a month before its failure, Bear Stearns was still highly rated (A2), as was Lehman Brothers on the eve of its failure.

In a well-conceived and orderly system, the most competent and experienced broker should end his career in a rating agency with flying colors. As a financial analyst, there should be no more rewarding profession. But the opposite was true: a Moody's analyst, i.e. the aristocracy of the business, was actually very poorly paid. The rating agencies were at the bottom of the ladder; and their employees worked like brokers, paid according to their productivity: *"During the first week of July 2007, Standard and Poor's rated 1,500 new mortgage-backed securities, a rate of 300 per working day. It was a production line*^{263}*."*

CDS: weapons of mass destruction

According to Michael Lewis, in his book *The Big Bet* (2010), very few actors had realized that the tower was going to collapse; at most a dozen

---

by Warren Spector; and James Cayne was replaced by Alan Schwartz in 2008. Prior to James Cayne, the bank had been run by Alan Greenberg.

[261] Michael Lewis, *La gran apuesta*, Debate Penguin Random House, Barcelona, 2013, p. 91.

[262] In 2006, Moody's made 44% of its turnover from *subprime* ratings (Jean-François Gayraud, *La grande Fraude*, Odile Jacob, 2011, p. 49).

[263] Charles Ferguson, *Inside Job, the financial crisis...* Ediciones Deusto, Barcelona, 2012, p. 144.

people. Among them was a small goy investor from the West Coast, one Michael Burry. Alone in his San Jose, California office, Michael Burry had taken the trouble to read the 130-page brochures that accompanied each mortgage obligation. *"As early as 2004, if you looked at the numbers, you could clearly see the deterioration in credit standards. In Burry's view, those standards had not only fallen, they had hit rock bottom*[264]*."* He was convinced that the *subprime* loans made in early 2005 would spiral out of control. Michael Burry then looked for a way to bet on a collapse by buying a kind of insurance to hedge against the risk of an asset you don't own. This financial product existed and was called a *"credit default swap"* (CDS, or "credit default swap")[265].

A wife can buy insurance in case of her husband's death; a company can buy life insurance on the life of an important member of its staff. But if John takes out an insurance policy on Paul, with whom he has no relationship, this policy creates a perverse incentive: John then has an interest in precipitating Paul's death. Similarly, if a financial institution were to take out an insurance policy against the death of Lehman Brothers Bank, it would automatically have an interest in seeing Lehman fail.

---

[264] Michael Lewis, *The Big Bet,* Debate Penguin Random House, Barcelona, 2013, p. 48. See also the film *The Big Bet* (*The Big Short*, 2015), Christian Bale plays Michael Burry.
[265] A *swap* is a contract by which two parties agree to exchange a series of amounts of money on future dates. Normally future money exchanges are referenced to interest rates, being called IRS (*Interest Rate Swap* or Interest Rate Swap) although more generically a swap can be considered to be any future exchange of goods or services (including money) referenced to any observable variable. A credit default swap (also known as a CDS) is any future exchange of goods or services (including money) referenced to any observable variable: *Credit Default Swap* CDS) is a financial product consisting of a financial risk hedging transaction, included within the category of credit derivative products, which is materialized through a *swap* contract (swap) on a certain credit instrument (usually a bond or a loan) in which the buyer of the swap makes a series of periodic payments (called *spread*) to the seller and, in exchange, receives from the seller an amount of money in the event that the security serving as underlying asset to the contract is unpaid at maturity or the issuing entity incurs in suspension of payments. Although a CDS is similar to an insurance policy, it differs significantly from it in that the buyer of the swap is not required to be the owner of the security (and therefore to have incurred the actual risk of purchasing the debt). In other words, insurance is placed on something that is owned by the insured, but a CDS is placed on an asset that is not owned by the swap counterparty. This type of CDS is called *"naked"*, and is actually equivalent to a bet. The European Parliament banned "naked" CDS on government debt as of December 1, 2011. (wikipedia, NdT).

The first major CDS was developed by a banker named Blythe Master of JP Morgan after the 1989 sinking of the Exxon Valdez oil tanker off the coast of Alaska and the resulting oil slick. In 1993, the Exxon company, which was at risk of having to pay a $5 billion fine, had contracted a $4.8 billion credit facility with JP Morgan. The problem was that the bank had to keep capital on its balance sheet proportional to the size of the loan, in case of a severe setback, and that this tied-up capital was unusable. A way had to be found to eliminate the risk from the Exxon transaction, but without selling the high-interest loan. In the fall of 1994, Blythe Master proposed to the EBRD (the European Bank for Reconstruction and Development) an annual fee in exchange for insuring JP Morgan against the risk of default on the Exxon loan. If Exxon defaulted on its commitment, the EBRD would be obliged to indemnify JP Morgan for the loss. Otherwise, the EBRD would make a handsome profit on the quarterly commissions paid by JP Morgan. In this way, the JP Morgan bank had protected itself from the risk of not being paid by transferring it ("*swap*") to another bank. This is a "CDS".

In 1998, JP Morgan decided to increase its "credit derivatives" operations. JP divided its portfolio of loans granted to its 306 clients into different tranches, with different levels of risk, so that investors could choose the risk they were willing to take, knowing that the higher the risk, the higher the fees. The bank thus began to market "credit derivatives" on all types of portfolios, its own or others'.

However, *credit default swaps* were not exactly insurance policies, which would have obliged banks to comply with strict regulations and provide funds commensurate with the risks assumed. It was a kind of under-the-table insurance contract, unregulated[266]. Credit derivatives were a very important financial innovation, as they allowed a bank to avoid the obligation to have consistent own funds. The amount of capital that banks had to hold was considerably reduced and banks were able to grant more and more loans while eliminating risk. CDS

---

[266] Credit default swaps were traded over-the-counter (OTC), i.e. they were not traded on an organized official market. They were tailor-made contracts between the two contracting parties. The international association of derivatives market operators ISDA (International Swaps and Derivatives Association) provides models of this type of contract. While the equity market was under scrutiny, the bond market, mainly composed of large institutional investors, had not come under political pressure of any kind and increasingly overshadowed the equity market. (NdT).

encouraged banks to lend beyond all limits, ignoring all prudential rules. It was the dawn of a new banking era[267].

For Michael Burry, CDS was a purely speculative product and by no means insurance, since he did not own the CDOs he was "insuring". *"Whoever sold him a credit default swap (CDS) on a junk mortgage bond would one day owe him a lot of money. He suspected that traders might try to get out of paying him. A contract would make it harder for them to do that and easier for him to sell to one trader what he had bought from another, and thus get better prices... There was an event, called a default, that either happened or it didn't. If the company defaulted on a payment, the company would either default or not. If the company defaulted on an interest payment, you had to pay. The buyer of the insurance might not get 100 cents on the dollar just as the bondholder might not lose 100 cents on the dollar, given that the company's assets had some value—but an independent judge could decide, in a way that was generally fair and satisfactory, how much would be recovered. If the bondholders received 30 cents on the dollar—thus experiencing a loss of 70 cents—the guy who had bought the credit default swap earned 70 cents[268]."* When Burry wanted to "bet" on the downside, CDS on *subprime* mortgage obligations did not yet exist. But he managed to convince some banks to sell him this product, and three years later CDS were a multi-billion dollar market.

After having read hundreds of brochures, Michael Burry had been hard at work to find exactly the bonds he wanted to bet on. What he was looking for were not the best loans, but on the contrary the worst ones, those that he believed could never be repaid. In May 2005, he bought (with the money of his trusting investors) a modest 60 million CDS

---

[267] Securitization also made it possible to lighten banks' balance sheets, since the securitized products were placed in SIVs (Structured Investment Vehicles). The SIV was a type of financial operating company created to earn a spread between its assets and liabilities like a traditional bank. The strategy of SIVs was to borrow money by issuing short-term securities, such as commercial paper, medium-term securities and government bonds at low interest rates and then lend that money by purchasing longer-term assets at higher interest rates, with the difference in rates being attributed to the investor as profit. Longer-term assets could include mortgage securitizations, auto loans, student loans, credit card securitizations, and bank and corporate bonds. As a consequence of this structure, SIVs were considered part of the shadow banking system. In October 2008, following the *subprime* mortgage crisis, all SIVs disappeared (NdT).
[268] Michael Lewis, *La gran apuesta*, Debate Penguin Random House, Barcelona, 2013, p.71, 72.

from Deutsche Bank on six different bonds. Burry was surprised to find that the bank was totally indifferent to his choice of bets.

> "The price of insurance was not given by an independent analysis, but by the ratings given to the bonds by the rating agencies, Moody's and Standard & Poor's. If you wanted to buy insurance on the triple-A rated tranche, supposedly risk-free, you could pay 20 basis points (0.20 percent); on the riskier AA rated tranches, you could pay 50 basis points (0.50 percent); and on the even less safe triple-B rated tranches, 200 basis points, or 2 percent (a basis point is one hundredth of a percentage point). The triple-B tranches—those whose value would be zero if the underlying mortgage pool experienced a loss of only 7 percent—were the ones he was looking for... Anyone who even glanced at the prospectuses could see that there were many critical differences between one triple-B bond and the next... He was intent on carefully selecting the absolute worst ones, and he was a little concerned that investment banks would find out how much he knew about particular mortgage bonds, and adjust their prices accordingly... Goldman Sachs e-mailed him a very long list of bad mortgage bonds to choose from: "It was really shocking to me. They were all priced according to the lowest rating from one of the big three rating agencies." He could pick from the list without alerting them to the depth of his knowledge. It was as if you could buy flood insurance for a house in the valley for the same price as flood insurance for a house high on the mountain. The market didn't make sense, but that didn't stop other Wall Street firms from joining it[269]."

Michael Burry harassed Bank of America until it agreed to sell him 5 million CDS. He went on to do so with half a dozen other banks, for packages of $5 million. At the end of June 2005, Goldman Sachs offered him $100 million worth of deals, so that by the end of June he owned CDS on $750 million of *subprime* mortgage bonds, with the near certainty that the house of cards would collapse two years from now when the fixed rates on the mortgages moved to the devastating variable rates. And he kept asking himself what kind of crazy people could sell him insurance on so many junk bonds. However, Burry was up against his skeptical investors, who were relentlessly hounding him to get their money back! If the borrowers succeeded in paying off their mortgages, Michael Burry would have to pay premiums equivalent to 2% per

---

[269] Michael Lewis, *La gran apuesta*, Debate Penguin Random House, Barcelona, 2013, pp. 73–75.

annum. With CDS on $100 million of *subprime* mortgage bonds, this amounted to Burry paying a premium of $12 million over six years. But if all went according to plan, he would earn close to $100 million.

At the end of 2005, mortgage lending began to deteriorate, so that in November, banks called Michael Burry to buy back the CDS they had sold him. On November 5, 2005, a *Wall Street Journal* article explained that a portion of variable rate borrowers were unable to pay their payments. The word was out, Michael Burry thought. From now on, no broker in his right mind would sell CDS on *subprime* bonds at the price he had bought them.

In 2006, a hundred or so investors had timidly entered the CDS market on *subprime* mortgage bonds; most of them were buying this insurance not to bet directly on the downside, but to protect their own bond portfolios (*subprime* bonds). Only a small group operated in the market to make bets. They were betting, for example, that bonds made up of a large number of loans made in California would perform worse than those in the rest of the country, or "*that bonds issued by Lehman Brothers or Goldman Sachs (both notorious for packaging the worst home loans in the United States) would perform worse than those packaged by JP Morgan or Wells Fargo (who actually seemed to care a bit about which loans they packaged into bonds).*"

"*A smaller number of investors—more than ten and less than twenty—made a direct bet against the integrity of the multibillion-dollar subprime market and, by extension, the global financial system. In itself, this was a remarkable fact: the catastrophe was foreseeable, but only a few investors warned of it. Among them were a Minneapolis hedge fund called Whitebox, a Boston hedge fund called The Baupost Group, a San Francisco hedge fund called Passport Capital, a Westchester (New York) hedge fund called Elm Ridge, and a few New York City hedge funds... What most of these investors had in common was that they had heard, directly or indirectly, Greg Lippman's* [a Jewish fund manager at New York's Deutsche Bank, NDT] *argument... A wealthy U.S. real estate investor named Jeff Greene bought multibillion-dollar credit default swaps on junk mortgage bonds after hearing about it from a New York hedge fund manager, John Paulson. Paulson had also heard Greg Lippman's speech.*" John Paulson sold short[270] *subprime* mortgage

---

[270] You can bet on the upside of a share, a bond or a commodity by buying it. But you can also bet on the downside by selling what you do not own (the asset in question can

bonds (he bet on the downside) by placing $25 billion in CDS. In the stock market, the price would have plummeted; but the mortgage bond market was very opaque. John Paulson had by far the most money to play with, so he was the most obvious example of this, but *"if you were to chart the spread of the idea as you would a virus, most of the lines would point to Lippmann: he was 'patient zero'. Only one of the carriers of the disease could plausibly claim to have infected him first. But Mike Burry kept himself hidden in his office in San Jose, California, and spoke to no one[271]."*

In three years—from the beginning of 2003 to the beginning of 2006—real estate prices grew faster than during the last thirty years. In February 2006, they had not yet collapsed, but had stopped rising; and the proportion of bad loans in their first year amounted to 4%[272].

Goldman Sachs then bet against the CDOs it sold to its clients by insuring them with the leading US insurer, AIG (American International Group). As of February 2007, Goldman Sachs had underwritten $20 billion in *subprime* CDS with AIG. The CDS that Goldman Sachs requested from AIG were no longer 2% *subprime*, but 95%! However, Martin Sulivan, the chairman of AIG, and its CEO Joe Cassano, insured everything that came through their door. Within a few months, they insured $50 billion against default on triple-B *subprime* mortgage obligations.

Michael Lewis recounted in his book: *"The more we saw what a CDO really was, the more we said to ourselves, 'Holy shit! It's a fucking nut job. It's a fraud. It may not be provable in a court of law. But it is a fraud. However, it was also a sensational opportunity, as the market seemed to believe its own lie. It charged far less to insure a supposedly safe portion of a CDO rated triple A than it did to insure clearly risky bonds rated triple B. Why pay 2 percent a year to bet directly against triple B bonds when it could pay 0.5 percent a year to actually make the same bet against the double-A portion of the CDO? If they paid four*

---

be acquired for sale through a securities loan), with a promise to buy it later. This is called short selling, or short position. The person who carries out the operation expects to obtain an economic benefit to the extent that the value of the security has fallen because he sells it at a higher price (initial moment) than when he buys it (later moment). If, on the other hand, the securities were to rise, he would suffer a loss. You can also bet on the downside with CDSs.

[271] Michael Lewis, *La gran apuesta*, Debate Penguin Random House, Barcelona, 2013, p. 132, 133.

[272] A default of only 7% would collapse any CDO composed of triple-B bonds.

times less for making what was in practice the same bet against triple B junk mortgage bonds, they could afford to multiply that bet by four[273]." Even more so when in June 2006, for the first time, real estate market prices began to decline.

Of course, AIG was also selling CDS on triple-A subprime bonds for a derisory 0.12% per annum, and Goldman Sachs underwrote some $20 billion. In other words, in exchange for annual premiums of several million per year, AIG stood to lose $20 billion! AIG was also buying a lot of CDOs, as these triple-A rated products were safe! At the end of 2007, AIG was insuring no less than 62 billion CDOs to Goldman Sachs, and some of Goldman's CDOs turned out to be the worst in AIG's CDS portfolio. In addition to the CDS that AIG was carrying on its back, AIG had some $50 billion in CDOs, as *"Goldman had also created and sold part of the $75 billion in mortgage CDOs that had been naively purchased by another arm of AIG—its credit and investment securities division [AIGFP]—CDOs that had begun to lose value very quickly[274]."* In short, AIG was playing the useful fool[275]. When it stopped buying them, the major Wall Street banks (Goldman Sachs, JP Morgan, Bear Stearns, Merrill Lynch, Lehman Brothers, Bank of America, Morgan Stanley, Citigroup, UBS[276]) found new CDO buyers and the machine kept running.

In 2007, the loans contracted in 2005, amounting to 750 billion, were now reaching the two-year maturity of the low fixed rate at the start and were switching to a higher variable interest rate. The consequences were not long in coming, since the Federal Reserve had also raised the interest rate: at the beginning of February 2007, Mortage Lenders Network, one of the top twenty *subprime* lenders, declared bankruptcy,

---

[273] Michael Lewis, *La gran apuesta*, Debate Penguin Random House, Barcelona, 2013, p. 159.
[274] Charles Ferguson, *Inside Job, the financial crisis...* Ediciones Deusto, Barcelona, 2012, p. 183.
[275] Its managers and employees were lining their pockets while waiting for the apocalypse. "The business *was run by a very autonomous 375-person unit based in London, AIG Financial Product (AIGFP), the personal fiefdom of a man named Joseph Cassano. AIGFP kept 30 percent of the annual profits in the form of cash bonuses, and gave the rest to the parent company. During the bubble, AIGFP paid itself more than $3.5 billion in bonuses.*" Charles Ferguson, *Inside Job, The Financial Crisis ...* p. 148.
[276] Although JP Morgan had exited the market in the late fall of 2006. Deutsche Bank had never really been fully involved.

and at the beginning of April the second largest in the country, New Century, declared bankruptcy, collapsed by defaults.

Bankruptcies followed one after the other. Banks had stopped selling CDS on *subprime* bonds and CDOs. By the end of February 2007, "overnight, *Morgan Stanley had gone from being tremendously eager to sell insurance on the subprime market to wanting nothing to do with it at all*[277]."

On July 17, two hedge funds owned by Bear Stearns bank failed miserably with a brand new triple-A rating from Moody's. Savers were left with only their eyes to mourn for their savings that had gone up in smoke. Savers had only their eyes left to mourn for their savings that had vanished. But the loans issued in 2006 would be even worse than those of 2005; the crisis had just begun.

In October, banks announced massive losses never before seen on Wall Street. Merrill Lynch announced 8 billion in losses, Citigroup lost 11 billion, Bank of America 3 billion, and so on. Michael Burry made good on his CDS in August 2007 and his investors breathed a sigh of relief. But no one thanked him.

The whole system relied on the work of the banks that had set up the lending operations, whether or not they were the managers of those operations. If the banks had not selected good borrowers, the quality of the loan portfolio was in question. But often, the analysis of the loan applications had not been carried out by the lending banks, but by simple (commercial) brokers who had an interest in closing as many contracts as possible, and the larger the better, since they were paid on commission. It can be said—caricaturing a bit—that all sorts of individuals, from indigent alcoholic Americans, drug-addicted blacks and newly arrived Mexican strawberry pickers, were able to benefit from the banks' generosity. Too many borrowers labeled *"prime"* or *"subprime"* were actually *"junk."* These new-fangled borrowers nicknamed "Ninjna" (an acronym for *"No income, no job, no asset"*— no income, no job, no wealth) carried the world's economy on their shoulders!

---

[277] Michael Lewis, *The Big Bet*, Debate Penguin Random House, Barcelona, 2013, p. 193.

Foreclosure scandal

How do you explain to the man in the street all the importance of a CDS on the double-A tranche of a CDO collateralized by *subprime* mortgage bonds? Now you get the picture. What followed was more prosaic.

Since the summer of 2006, real estate bond exchanges had begun to slow down, before coming to a complete halt a few months later. It was a case of every man for himself. The banks hurriedly foreclosed on homes in such a disorderly fashion that thousands of interims—the *"robo-signers"*—were hired to sign eviction documents in chains. At the end of 2010, the *Wall Street Journal* revealed that JP Morgan employees had admitted to having each signed 10,000 foreclosure documents per month, with no real control, and above all no respect for the rules set for foreclosures. According to the *New York Times,* Citigroup had even relocated the processing of the files to the Philippines and Guam. This did not prevent Citigroup from claiming that its foreclosure proceedings were entirely legal and that there was no need to suspend anything. There were also many cases of families evicted from their homes who were not in arrears at all.

Two weeks later, in October—when the full implications of these dishonest practices became public knowledge—the *"robo-signer"* scandal was renamed the "foreclosure gate" scandal. In the meantime, it had come to light that some bankers had falsified documents to speed up foreclosure proceedings: forged signatures, false letterheads, backdated acts, unfounded evictions... In fact, as mortgage registration was costly in terms of procedures, the big banks and the two federally subsidized credit institutions, "Fannie Mae" (nickname of the Federal National Mortgage Association) and "Freddie Mac" (Federal Home Loan Mortgage Corporation), had created in 1997 an agency to speed up the long and costly registration procedures [278]. The "MERS" (Mortage Electronic Registration Systems) system allowed the computerized registration of mortgage purchases and sales, so that paper documents had been destroyed. This system also avoided owing fees to states and municipalities for each loan registration or modification. Thus, MERS

---

[278] Fannie and Freddie had acquired numerous portfolios of mortgage-backed securities for investment purposes. From 2004 to 2006, they had purchased $434 billion. At the end of 2010, their losses amounted to $147 billion. It is true that the Obama administration had forced them to grant payment facilities to unemployed borrowers.

owed between $60 million and $120 million to the State of California alone to regularize uncollected recording fees. In the midst of the evictions, the procedures recorded by the MERS system were declared illegal, or at least not admissible in court, and incomplete. Many banks were prohibited from foreclosing on homes because they did not have the original loan agreements and mortgages in order. To remedy this problem, many banks, assisted by lawyers of dubious morality, had produced false mortgage documents or backdated documents that amounted to forgery of public deeds. This was the reason for the hiring of *"robo-signers"*. The MERS company had even allowed itself to launch foreclosures without prior notice to the courts.

The banks had created MERS, with its easy mortgage loan registration system, to disguise the fact that there were too many loans granted to insolvent families, and that the loans were often not even *subprime*, but straightforwardly *junk*. Now, if the banks were found guilty and ordered to reimburse the homeowners who had been harmed and the states that had not collected the registration fees, then the banks that had bought the rotten CDOs and the insurers that had insured the CDOs would surely all go bankrupt.

With the computerization of the sale and purchase documents, many documents had been lost and the banks were unable to prove that they actually owned a mortgage. And since MBS and other CDOs had been sold and resold, the mess was enormous.

And that's not all: we then learned that many bankers had resold the same "MBS" mortgage bonds to different investors[279]. Bear Stearns had set up a Madoff pyramid using the proceeds from each sale to pay interest to each new group of investors. The case had exploded when two entities (JP Morgan and Washington Mutual) had at the same time claimed foreclosure on the same real estate, each claiming ownership of the mortgage. Some homeowners had found themselves in the position of going up against several different banks with the intention of foreclosing on the same property. Subsequent investigation eventually revealed that the true owner was the lender Fannie Mae, but that the bankruptcy firm (Shapiro & Fishman) had created false backdated documentation.

---

[279] This history of selling the same mortgages to numerous different buyers is confirmed by economics professors William Black and L. Randall Wray, who cite the case of Bear Stearns Bank, one of the big players in this debacle.

A well-known American journalist, Gretchen Morgenson, reported in a *New York Times* article on this common practice of destroying the original physical mortgage document when an electronic notice was created to "avoid confusion". This could then be resold several times, although the mortgage payments could only be applied to one of the copies; for the other buyers, the obligation appeared unpaid, which further contributed to the collapse of MBS and CDOs[280].

The FBI was aware of these practices, as in 2004 one of its press releases warned of "an epidemic of fraudulent mortgage lending". The problem was also mentioned in the 2005 *Financial Crimes Report*. In 2006, the FBI services had published a report entitled "Mortage Fraud report", explaining that between 30 and 70% of the defaults on 3 million loans analyzed were due to malfunctions in the granting of such loans. But of the 14,000 FBI agents, only a small group (120) worked on this type of fraud, i.e. two agents per state. The U.S. was then focusing on counterterrorism[281]. However, given the hundreds of thousands of abandoned and half-destroyed houses that disfigured many cities and neighborhoods in the country, one could think that the enemy was clearly within the borders.

Making the taxpayer pay

Since the beginning of the crisis, the securitization market had been virtually closed, so that investors were left holding securities whose value had fallen sharply. The exact composition of these securitization vehicles was so opaque that no one knew exactly which ones contained *subprime* and in what proportion. And no one knew which entities were most exposed to *subprime* and at what level. Banks had therefore stopped trusting each other and were not lending to each other. This crisis of confidence paralyzed the markets.

---

[280] According to one "conspiracy theorist" analysis, the government allegedly encouraged an upward movement in real estate prices with attractive interest rates. MBS and CDOs were then resold up to twenty times to investors. Finally, unable to pay for the 2000% oversold MBS and CDOs, it was necessary to intentionally collapse the housing market, thanks to the complicity of Alan Greenspan who raised interest rates out of all proportion. November 7, 2010 article by François Margineau on www.mondialisation.ca.

[281] Jean-François Gayraud, *La grande Fraude*, Odile Jacob, 2011, p. 103.

On Thursday, August 9, 2007, BNP Paribas announced the freezing of three *subprime* funds. On August 23, Countrywide Financial, in great difficulty, was rescued from bankruptcy by Bank of America with an investment of 2 billion. On September 14, customers of the British bank Northern Rock were waiting in long lines in front of ATMs to withdraw their deposits, which were not guaranteed beyond 2,000 pounds sterling. The banking panic was stopped thanks to the Bank of England's guarantee on all deposits, but the hemorrhage continued nonetheless, and the bank was nationalized months later.

Central banks became aware of the monetary risk. On August 9, the ECB (European Central Bank) was the first to inject liquidity (loans to banks). It was followed by the Fed and the British central bank. In total, 330 billion was injected into the banking system in August. At the end of January 2008, the Fed readjusted its rate to 3% (instead of 5.25% in August 2007).

In March 2008, it became clear that all the *subprime* mortgage bonds had not been sold by the banks to South Korean pension funds or German banks: the fifth Wall Street bank, Bear Stearns (14,000 employees), which had invested massively in *subprimes*, was on the verge of bankruptcy. Unlike Northern Rock, Bear Stearns was an investment bank, which meant that it did not collect money in the form of customer deposits, but by issuing securities. By mid-2007, the bank had tried to get rid of its loans still in stock as quickly as possible by securitizing them and placing them in the market. Because it was heavily "leveraged" ([282]) (relying heavily on short-term borrowing), Bear Stearns became insolvent when the situation worsened, as other banks stopped lending funds. The *bank run* this time came in the form of electronic transactions, and money came rushing out. In an instant, the share price was divided by 80. The 17 billion of liquidity was lost in 48 hours, i.e. the bank had lost 100,000 dollars per second. The other banks were also both accomplices and victims of the system.

---

[282]Leverage is the ratio between equity capital and total investment (equity + credit) in a financial operation. The higher the credit, the higher the leverage and the lower the equity investment. In other words, leverage is simply using debt to finance a transaction. By reducing the initial capital that needs to be contributed, there is an increase in the profitability obtained. Increased leverage also increases the risks of the operation, since it results in less flexibility or greater exposure to insolvency or inability to meet payments. (NdT).

Tim Geithner, who headed the New York "Federal Reserve", Ben Bernanke (Alan Greenspan's successor at the Fed) and Henry Paulson[283], the Secretary of the Treasury, decided to save the bank and managed to convince JP Morgan to buy it with a $30 billion loan from the State. Although Paulson warned Wall Street that this operation would not be repeated.

The crisis spread to the rest of the world, as nearly 25% of U.S. mortgage loans had been purchased abroad. And the insurance mechanisms proved useless, given the amount of the sums at stake. Lacking sufficient capital of their own to meet their commitments, the insurers went bankrupt, dragging the banks down with them.

The situation worsened rapidly at the beginning of September 2008. Fannie Mae and Freddie Mac, the two managers of real estate loans to households that guaranteed nearly 5.3 trillion dollars of loans (40% of US real estate credit), were under State supervision. The US Treasury invested $200 billion to save them and on September 8 the two entities were practically nationalized.

On September 10, Lehman Brothers, a 25,000-employee bank and the world's fourth largest investment bank, reported a loss of almost four billion dollars for the third quarter. The British bank Barclays could have bought Lehman, but Barclays could not carry out the operation without the endorsement of the British regulatory authorities, which had opposed it.

The bombshell exploded on Monday, September 15: Lehman Brothers declared bankruptcy. This staggering news triggered a full-blown panic and stock indices plummeted. Lehman Brothers shares fell 94% to 21 cents, reducing the company's capitalization to $145 million against $46 billion six months earlier. The contagion spread to all world markets.

Richard "Dick" Fuld, the chairman of Lehman Brothers Bank, had believed that his bank was too big for the government to let it go under. *"Too big to fail,"* Americans used to say. But the bank had finally been left to its fate. On the night of September 14–15, 2008, after four days of negotiations, the U.S. government had decided to let Lehman

---

[283]Paulson and Bernanke had a very questionable role and responsibility in the most pressing moments of the 2008 crisis, read in Charles Ferguson, *Inside Job, la crisis financiera...* Ediciones Deusto, Barcelona, 2012, p. 194-195. (NdT).

Brothers fail without intervening after ensuring that there were enough creditors to absorb the impact. In his report to the Bankruptcy Court for the Southern District of New York, Ian Lowitt, Lehman Brothers' chief financial officer, declared a balance sheet with 639 billion in assets and 613 billion in liabilities, but this was without counting the billions in debt disguised by accounting shenanigans. It was the largest bankruptcy in the history of the United States.

The following day, on September 16, 2008, George Bush's administration gave the green light for the multi-billion dollar bailout of AIG, the country's leading insurer, which guaranteed the default risks of hundreds of entities around the world. The federal government acquired 79% of its capital. During 2008, after each drop in the stock price, Goldman Sachs had demanded immediate cash compensation from AIG, *"leading to fierce disputes between it and AIG over the value of the securities and the amount of payments required."* *"By mid-2008, perhaps even earlier, Goldman knew that its CDS claims alone could easily cause AIG's bankruptcy... Given all of the above, it can be said that Goldman knew beyond a shadow of a doubt that AIG was in dire straits... Goldman Sachs became even more aggressive in its demands for payment for its CDS, so as to get its money before everyone else and to forestall AIG's downfall."* *"On September 12, shortly before AIG's bankruptcy, its accumulated payments on account of its mortgage CDS amounted to $18.9 billion, of which $7.6 billion, more than 40 percent, had gone directly into the coffers of Goldman, which was demanding even more[284]."* It should be noted that Goldman Sachs management had protected itself from bankruptcy by spending $150 million on AIG CDS, so as to pocket $2.5 billion in the event of a widespread default.

After the collapse of Lehman Brothers, one could wonder what the next big bank on the list would be. A bank with a market capitalization of $1 billion could have $1 billion of CDS outstanding. No one knew how many it had or where they were. Phil Angelides, who would later serve on the Financial Crisis Inquiry Commission, explained in his reports that neither the regulators at the Federal Reserve nor the financial markets authority had seen the warning signs of the crisis. Regulations had not been in place for years, and no official had any idea what was happening in the markets. AIG thus held 440 billion credit default

---

[284] Charles Ferguson, *Inside Job, the financial crisis...* Ediciones Deusto, Barcelona, 2012, p. 184-185.

swaps, and it was clear that the firm would not be able to repay these CDS, although no one knew it, including the other banks.

Merrill Lynch, which had lost 27 billion in CDOs in 2008 alone, was bought by Bank of America. Morgan Stanley suffered a loss of 9 billion for having invested massively in CDOs. Citigroup, UBS and many more also took terrible losses. *"Citigroup had a much larger position in the market—more than 50 billion subprime mortgages on its balance sheets—and its leaders didn't realize they had a problem until the market began to crack*[285]*."*

It turned out then that the Federal Reserve's covert bailouts were no longer enough to reassure the markets. On September 18, Henry Paulson and Ben Bernanke appeared before Congress. The situation was catastrophic. Confidence had to be restored at all costs to get the banks back to lending to each other. The government had to buy the banks' toxic assets and ask Congress for a blank check of 700 billion, free from any parliamentary supervision and any possibility of judicial opposition. On September 29, the bill was rejected by the House of Representatives.

On the same day, in Europe, Fortis bank was nationalized in Belgium and the Netherlands, whose governments injected 11 billion euros and took control of 49.9% of the capital in order to prevent savers from panicking. A few days later, the United Kingdom recapitalized the Royal Bank of Scotland and Lloyd's Banking Group to the tune of 46 billion euros. Following this, the Franco-Belgian bank Dexia was in turn recapitalized to the tune of 6 billion euros by Paris and Brussels.

In October, the Icelandic banking system collapsed dramatically. As the Icelandic government refused to compensate British and Dutch customers, Great Britain invoked the anti-terrorism law to blacklist Iceland.

On October 3, an amended version of Henry Paulson and Ben Bernanke's bailout plan was finally accepted by Congress, in exchange for fiscal aid that had convinced dozens of parliamentarians, both Democrats and Republicans. Henry Paulson, the US Secretary of the Treasury, had this plan (TARP: *Troubled Asset Relief Program*), which provided for the purchase by the federal government of $700 billion of

---

[285] Charles Ferguson, *Inside Job, the financial crisis...* Ediciones Deusto, Barcelona, 2012, p. 172.

toxic, high-risk assets, adopted in two phases. But just ten days after the adoption of the rescue plan, Henry Paulson decided to radically modify the project in imitation of the Swedish government: the US Treasury would take a stake in the capital of the most fragile financial institutions, thus increasing their liquidity. The U.S. government now planned to take a stake in the capital of some financial institutions.[286]

On October 13, 2008, Henry Paulson summoned the presidents of nine of the largest U.S. banks to a secret meeting in Washington. Nine of the country's leading banking institutions were forced to accept the purchase of preferred shares from the State. Thus, half of the first tranche, i.e. $125 billion, had gone to Citigroup, JP Morgan Chase, Bank of America, Wells Fargo, Goldman Sachs, Morgan Stanley, Merrill Lynch, Bank of New York Mellon and State Street. The second half of the tranche would be earmarked for the recapitalization of smaller banks[287].

Of the first $350 billion of the bailout paid out, some $335 billion had already been distributed by mid-December 2008. *"Before Bank of America took over, despite Merrill's $50 billion in losses, bonuses totaled nearly $4 billion in cash, and were heavily concentrated at the top of the ladder. More than 700 people received bonuses of more than $1 million, and several were in the tens of millions."* During the meeting with Paulson, Merrill Lynch's new president, John Thain, *"had a single concern, and he shared it with Paulson: would that affect the freedom to pay bonuses? The answer was no[288]."*

This direct intervention of the State in the markets was totally unprecedented in the history of the United States. The insurer AIG had benefited from three bailouts of 60, 70 and 52.5 billion dollars. Part of them had been paid under the administration of President Barack Obama, elected president on November 4, 2008. No sooner had the money been released than Goldman Sachs had obtained the

---

[286] In Europe, the various national plans announced around the weekend of October 11, 2008 amounted to several hundred billion euros in bank recapitalization-nationalization measures. In the following months, the British government dedicated 118 billion euros to the rescue of its banks.

[287] The TARP plan helped 650 banks. But 140 had failed anyway in 2009, and another 139 in 2010.

[288] Charles Ferguson, *Inside Job, the financial crisis...* Ediciones Deusto, Barcelona, 2012, p. 201.

$12.9 billion owed to it by AIG. In France, Société Générale had received $12 billion from AIG, and BNP about $5 billion.

The banks had enjoyed full compensation instead of assuming part of the losses as they should in these bailout cases. *"When the government decided to cancel AIG's [CDS] policies with Goldman Sachs, it paid out as if the house had burned down completely. There was no justification for such largesse: other credit default swaps had been settled for thirteen cents on the dollar[289],"* wrote economist Joseph Stiglitz. *"To put it bluntly, the US taxpayer saved the ghost ship that AIG had become, only for Goldman Sachs—with others—to come in and help itself. Washington has never really explained this exceptionally generous decision: to reimburse the establishment for all its losses[290],"* wrote Marc Roche. The government had used public money to save a small clique of bankers who shared out million-dollar bonuses.

The cynicism of the Paulson plan will forever remain in the annals of history. The banks' profits were privatized but their losses were borne by the taxpayer. And despite the fact that the US taxpayer had become the principal "owner" of several banks, George Bush's Treasury Department, and then Barack Obama's, had refused to exercise any control. Having contributed hundreds of billions of dollars, the taxpayer did not even have the right to know how that money had been spent. The AIG bailout, for example, had been made public much later, and only thanks to pressure from Congress.

Bernard Madoff had been arrested on December 11, 2008, but a number of major bank executives would have deserved to spend a vacation in prison as well.

In Great Britain, at least, the former managers had been fired and there were restrictions on the distribution of dividends to shareholders. US banks, on the other hand, had continued to pay out extraordinary dividends and bonuses to their shareholders and managers, and did not even pretend to revive credit in the economy. During the three years that

---

[289] Joseph Stiglitz, *Caída libre, el libre mercado y el hundimiento de la economía mundial*, Taurus, Madrid, 2010, p. 83.
[290] Marc Roche, *El Banco, cómo Goldman Sachs dirige el mundo*, Ediciones Deusto, Barcelona, 2011, p. 150. "*The bailout of AIG, of almost 200 billion dollars was based on credit default swap derivatives, that is, some banks betting against others.*" Joseph Stiglitz, *Free Fall* ... p. 41

followed, the banks paid their shareholders no less than 80 billion in dividends, with the blessing of the State. Executives had received record bonuses, and brokers had not played their cards badly either, for *"a study in early November 2009 suggested that traders, on average, would reap profits of $930,000[291]."* Joseph Cassano, the president of AIG who had insured almost everything put in front of him, had received an interesting severance package, a $314 million golden parachute. *"Nine lenders that together had losses of $100 billion received $175 billion in bailout money through TARP, and paid nearly $33 billion in premiums, including more than $1 million apiece to nearly five thousand employees[292]."*

In contrast to these payments, the compensation paid to evicted families has been very limited. In 2012, Charles Ferguson had made the calculation: *"Fewer than a million of those who have lost their homes will receive checks averaging $2,000 per head. Another 20 million*

---

[291] Joseph Stiglitz, *Free Fall, the Free Market and the Collapse of the World Economy*, Taurus, Madrid, 2010, p. 91.

[292] Joseph Stiglitz, *Caída libre, el libre mercado y el hundimiento de la economía mundial*, Taurus, Madrid, 2010, p. 116. ["*Such high payouts unrelated to performance were evidenced by the bonuses that banks paid in 2008, a record year for losses and a near-record year for bonuses (about $33 billion). Six of the nine big banks paid out more in bonuses than they received in profits.*" Stiglitz, note 8, p. 386. "*Executives who were paid with stock options had an incentive to do whatever they could to drive their company's stock price up, including creative accounting. The higher the stock price, the better their work was considered. They knew that the higher the reported profits were, the higher the stock price would also be, and they knew that fooling the markets was easy. And one of the easiest ways to increase reported profits was to manipulate the income statement, taking away potential losses with one hand and adding profit income with the other.*" Stiglitz, p. 196 "*U.S. banks were actively engaged in deception: they removed risk from income statements so that no one could value it. The magnitude of the deception that was achieved is mind-boggling: Lehman Brothers was able to declare that it had a net worth $26 billion shortly before it disappeared, when it had a hole in its income statement of almost two hundred billion.*" Stiglitz, p. 200. "*Executives who defended their deceptive accounting practices claimed that shareholders benefited from banks reporting high profits in their accounts. But while some shareholders won, others lost, especially those who had relied on the rigged figures and held on to their shares with expectations that were not fulfilled. When the truth was finally discovered, prices fell, sometimes (as in the case of Citibank) dramatically.*" Stiglitz, note 9 p. 386. "*The conflict over whether or not to account for stock options is an example of the disparity of interests. Shareholders would like to know the extent to which their shares lose value through the issuance of stock options. But companies (meaning their managers) have resisted improving the transparency of such issuances because they have realized that if shareholders understand the extent to which their shares lose value, they will oppose such colossal payouts.*" Stiglitz, footnote 16, p. 387. n.d.]

people whose mortgages are underwater, or who have lost their homes to evictions, will receive nothing[293]."

The Bush administration and the Federal Reserve had not prepared any contingency plan prior to Paulson's plan. In some bailouts (Bear Stearns), shareholders had received some money and bondholders had been fully protected. In other cases (Fannie Mae), shareholders lost everything while bondholders were preserved. For Washington Mutual, both shareholders and bondholders had lost everything. In total, it was estimated that $17 billion had been lost by investors, but also from the pockets of shareholders and pensioners. But the only sanction that the managers of the big banks received were their ridiculous appearances at parliamentary hearings.

It is almost certain that if the big banks had not been bailed out a general collapse of the financial system would have occurred. The fact is that some banks had become too important to be allowed to fail. The managers of these large investment banks knew that the state could not leave them to their fate without facing disastrous consequences, so they cynically took excessive risks. Wall Street had used the fear of a general economic collapse to extract gigantic sums of money from the American taxpayer.

A first measure seemed absolutely necessary: the reinstatement of the historic Glass-Steagall Act, a 1933 law voted in reaction to the Great Depression, which had imposed the separation of commercial deposit banks (which lend money) and investment banks (which organize the sale of stocks and bonds) to avoid the conflicts of interest that inevitably arise when the same bank issues stocks and lends money[294], but which had been repealed in 1999 by the Clinton administration (U.S. liberal left).

Prior to deregulation, other regulations prohibited, for example, banks from expanding from one state to another in the country, so that, apart from the large banks in New York and Chicago, the sector comprised thousands of local or regional entities. The criminogenic effects of deregulation were evident.

---

[293] Charles Ferguson, *Inside Job, the financial crisis...* Ediciones Deusto, Barcelona, 2012, p. 373.
[294] Joseph Stiglitz, *Free Fall, the Free Market and the Collapse of the World Economy*, Taurus, Madrid, 2010, p. 206.

The State had distributed most of the money to the big banks, when in practice they had not been interested in financing business and industry for years. Other solutions were possible, according to economist Joseph Stiglitz: *"Instead of trying to save the existing banks, which had repeatedly demonstrated their incompetence, the government could have given the $700 billion to the few healthy and well-run banks, or even used it to found a set of new banks. At a modest borrowing rate of 12 to 1, that would have generated $8.4 trillion of new credit—more than enough for the needs of the economy[295]."*

Irony of history: Alan Greenspan and George Bush's efforts to minimize the role of the state in the economy had resulted in the state having unprecedented power over a large number of sectors. The federal state had thus become the owner of the largest automobile company (emergency loan General Motors[296]), the largest insurance company, and in theory also some of the largest banks in the country, given the immense amounts of capital it had invested.

Synthetic CDOs, fruits of love

In 2011, the investment bank Goldman Sachs employed 34,000 people in some thirty countries, when in 1980 it had only 2,000 employees. Since the beginning of this millennium, Goldman Sachs has been the bank that symbolizes the abuses of the Western financial system.

In 2007, Goldman Sachs, which managed gigantic amounts of capital, was the only bank to have generated profits during the collapse of the *subprime* market. Unlike many big bank CEOs, whose priority was golf courses, Goldman Sachs' leaders kept a close eye on the markets.

The bank had changed its strategy in December 2006. David Viniar, the CFO, had recommended to the board to "reduce risk exposure", i.e. to

---

[295] Joseph Stiglitz, *Free Fall, the Free Market and the Collapse of the World Economy*, Taurus, Madrid, 2010, p. 174.
[296] More than 13 billion dollars had been granted in December 2008 to the *"Big Three"* (General Motors, Ford and Chrysler). Due to the great difficulties facing the automobile industry, GM and Chrysler had received respectively 9.4 and 4 billion dollars from Paulson's fund, i.e. 13.4 billion dollars in total, in exchange for extremely strict conditions to ensure their return to profitability. At the end of 2013, the State owned more than 10% of GM.

get rid of all toxic assets as quickly as possible[297]. Anxious not to reveal its policy change, Goldman Sachs had continued to be present in the buyers' market, but without bidding for the securities. In the spring of 2007, the bank began betting massively on the collapse of CDOs made up of toxic *subprime* that it was selling to its own clients, buying huge amounts of CDS derivatives. *"Goldman had bought all the CDS it could while they were cheap and then, once it found itself fully hedged, devalued its securities and sought payment from the underwriters."* In this way, he was speculating against his own clients to whom he was selling his junk. Shortly thereafter, the market collapsed. *"Although Goldman made huge profits on its short bets on mortgages, it could have made much more. But the top managers, Viniar, Cohn and Lloyd Blankfein, the CEO, did not approve of a strategy of massive short bets*[298]*."* Goldman Sachs entered Wall Street legend by generating $11.4 billion in profits in 2007, when all other banks had wrecked[299].

The bank sold its customers bonds that it knew were defective. It easily sold its entire 2006 vintage of CDOs, without disclosing to buyers that the borrowers were close to total default. Take for example a 2006 issue: GSAMP Trust 2006-S3. Goldman Sachs had issued some $494 million of this CDO. Many of the mortgage loans that comprised it were refinanced with borrowers whose average principal was worth only 0.71% of the loan! In addition, 58% of the loans were poorly or undocumented—no borrower's first and last name, no address, only a zip code. Despite this, the two major rating agencies, Moody's and Standard & Poor's, had given 93% of the issuance an "investor grade" rating, the famous "triple A". Moody's predicted that less than 10% of the mortgages would default, when in fact 18% defaulted after 18 months[300]. Buyers tended to be pension fund managers, looking for safe

---

[297] Another highly recommended film, with an outstanding cast of actors, is J.C. Chandor's *Margin Call* (2011). The film takes place almost behind closed doors in the offices of a large U.S. bank, during a night of heartbreak experienced by the board of directors. The first part tells how the terrible discovery of a young analyst rises through the hierarchy to the top, the brand new president played by Jeremy Irons. It is only to be regretted that the Jewish spirit that animates the brokers is once again blamed on the Goyim. In this case, Nordic actor Paul Bettany takes on the role of the bastard. Although it is true that Protestants, especially Anglo-Saxon Protestants, are very much steeped in "old-testamentary" and cosmopolitan values.
[298] Charles Ferguson, *Inside Job, the financial crisis...* Ediciones Deusto, Barcelona, 2012, p. 170, 171.
[299] *Bilan.ch*, July 4, 2011, in *Comment Goldman Sachs a parié contre ses propres clients.*
[300] Article by Matt Taibbi published in the July 2009 issue of *Rolling Stone* magazine.

investments, but also other banks, insurers, municipalities, etc. Goldman Sachs thus reaped billions of dollars.

The New York firm was the largest packager of *subprime subprime* distressed loans. In 2006, at the height of the bubble, Goldman had issued $76.5 billion of collateralized debt obligations (CDOs) comprised of real estate loans, one-third of which were *subprime ... to be disposed of as soon as possible*.

Charles Ferguson, in his book *Inside Job*, recounted one such transaction: *"One of the first asset-clearing deals was a $2 billion synthetic CDO called Hudson Mezzanine Funding 2006-1. The sales promotion for these products was almost a complete hoax. It stated that Goldman's intention was to "establish a long-term relationship with a selection of partners" by creating "attractive property investments"... When the deal had been executed there were cries of euphoria from the deal group: they had achieved a large reduction in risk and $8.5 million in profits were booked*[301]." Goldman Sachs brokers knew exactly what kind of crap they were selling to their clients.

John Paulson *"ran several hedge funds and had enough resources to lose money for a long time. Despite his conviction that an "RMBS meltdown*[302] *subprime" was coming, he was also concerned about the opacity and complexity of mortgage securities. So Paulson looked into the possibility of having an investment bank custom-design one for him, so he could know exactly and even decide what was going on in there. Even Bear Stearns, not exactly a model of ethics in mortgage dealings rejected his request as "dishonest" ... for despite their scant concern for ethical issues they did fear potential fraud prosecutions. Happily for Paulson, Goldman had no such scruples. The fabulous Fab Tourre was in charge of designing the instrument, communicating with investors and overseeing the preparation of promotional materials. To make it easier to sell to long investors, in other words suckers, Tourre needed an independent manager who would supposedly be responsible for selecting the investment assets... In the end, the job was assigned to*

---

[301] Charles Ferguson, *Inside Job, the financial crisis...* Ediciones Deusto, Barcelona, 2012, p. 174.
[302] Residential mortgage-backed securities (RMBS) were very popular in those years, coveted by traders looking for attractive yields, from hedge funds to pension funds to insurance companies. Some RMBS bundled many *subprime* mortgages. The rating processes for CDOs and RMBS were similar. In 2006, subprime RMBS accounted for 72% of CDO composition. (NdT)

ACA Management LLC, which had already taken over the management of Goldman's other businesses. ACA was never informed of the true purpose of the transaction. They knew Paulson was in on the deal, but not that his real purpose was to bet against it. Paulson gave Goldman a list of 123 bonds against which he wanted to short; the list was given to ACA, and there were meetings between ACA, Paulson and Goldman. Although ACA was sometimes surprised by the names Paulson recommended, or at least vetoed, agreement was reached on a portfolio of 90 bonds, which included 55 of the original names proposed by Paulson."

The end result was a $2 billion "synthetic" CDO called Abacus 2007-AC1. The securities were classified into several categories, as in most securitization products: the least risky *"super senior"* tranche ($1.1 billion), 4 intermediate tranches ($700 million) and the riskiest *"equity"* tranche ($200 million). Goldman's marketing service presented the product in an attractive way for investors. The sales prospectus consisted of eighteen pages praising ACA's expertise in credit selection: *"Asset selection based on credit fundamentals... Alignment of economic interests with those of the investor...". None of ACA's CDOs have ever been downgraded*[303]*."* Obviously, none of the CDO's presentation documents mentioned John Paulson, known for betting short on the market.

This Abacus was not the first in the series, as the bank had already created some twenty products of this type. But Abacus 2007-AC1 later became famous because it was at the origin of a complaint filed by the SEC in April 2010, the only complaint to date that was to put Goldman Sachs on the ropes.

Officially, for investors, these mortgages had been selected by ACA Management, an independent third party. But the bank misled ACA Management into believing that Paulson's fund wanted to invest in the Abacus CDO, not bet against it on the downside. The next move is well known: John Paulson paid the bank $15 million to pick the most toxic *subprimes* himself. He would then buy the CDSs that would cover him

---

[303] Charles Ferguson, *Inside Job, the financial crisis...* Ediciones Deusto, Barcelona, 2012, p. 178.

against defaults (products that would increase in value as the risk increased) and then short the Abacus CDOs[304].

Knowing that the product was going to depreciate sharply, Paulson, as a shrewd trader, had started by buying a small part of Abacus himself (the riskiest), to encourage other investors to do the same. Only later would he clandestinely position himself as a seller of the vast majority of Abacus.

It didn't take long for the unwary to arrive. In April 2007, the small German bank IKB in Düsseldorf "guaranteed risk protection" by buying $150 million of *equity*. In May 2007, the Dutch bank ABN Amro "guaranteed risk protection" for the *"super senior"* tranche (the least risky a priori). The Paulson & Co. fund took the position of "protection buyer".

Abacus was not a simple CDO, but a "synthetic" CDO. It was a new product: the fruit of bankers' love for investors. As the number of real estate loans granted decreased with the crisis, it was necessary to find a solution to continue securitization. And the solution was as follows: just use existing mortgage-backed securities as a benchmark or index, and create a two-sided bet. The synthetic CDO is nothing more or less than a bet on the value of a CDO; and in a bet, to make money, you have to find people to bet against you.

On the one hand, an investor would buy the "upside" of a synthetic CDO and receive a sum that reflected the performance of the "real"

---

[304] In finance, short selling, short sale, short position or short position is the financial operation consisting of the sale by a market participant of an asset that it does not own. This asset may be acquired for sale by means of a securities loan. When it comes at a later time to return the securities that were the subject of the loan, identical securities must be purchased. The person carrying out the operation expects to obtain an economic benefit to the extent that the value of the security has fallen because he sells it at a higher price (initial moment) than when he buys them (later moment). If, on the other hand, the securities were to rise, he would suffer a loss. Short selling is betting on a fall in the share price. It consists of selling an asset that you do not own in order to buy it back later at a lower price.

If an airline wants to protect itself against a rise in fuel prices, it can insure itself against this risk by buying oil on the forward contract markets, thus fixing the price of the oil that will be sold to it in six months' time. Using derivatives, this company can also take out an insurance policy against the risk of an increase in this price. In a period of stock market crashes, downward gains can occur very quickly, while in upward periods some patience is required for capital gains to be generated. In the latter case, if a stock is considered overvalued, a short sale has the effect of calming speculation and preventing it from soaring higher.

CDOs (or an index of values of several CDOs). What he earned then came not from the mortgage loans but from the "flip side" of the bet: the payments that someone else agreed to pay in exchange for the right to pick up the spoils in the event of a stock crash. In this case, it was John Paulson who paid an annual fee of 1.5% on $1 billion to protect himself from risk. The investors who bought the Abacus securities were in a sense the underwriters ("protection sellers") who received premiums as long as the bonds did not collapse. If the CDO failed, they would pay the losses.

Thus, a synthetic CDO is not a bond like a CDO but a derivative product of a CDO, in the sense that its benchmark, what defines its performance, is the performance of an underlying CDO. Thanks to synthetic CDOs, it was no longer necessary to raise $1 billion in mortgage loans securitized into bonds to create a bet. It was enough to find someone in the market willing to bet that $1 billion against one. This is the reason why the losses were much greater than what the *subprime* loans represented. Whoever buys the financial product called "CDO" (Collateralized Debt Obligation) will never earn more than the financial flows generated by the aggregate monthly mortgage payments made by the borrowers whose loans constitute the bond security (the actual CDO). But the amount of money that the seller of a synthetic CDO can potentially earn is in principle unlimited: it depends only on the amount of bets that the buyers are willing to accept in exchange for the premiums paid to them. In a bet, there is no limit to the number of bettors, nor to the sum of the bet: the number of bettors convinced that the horse *Bella de Mayo* will win in the fourth race at the Saint-Cloud racecourse is potentially unlimited. The same principle applies to a synthetic CDO[305]. It was thus a matter of betting on the risk of a debt going unpaid, and to make money on this bet, it was necessary to find people willing to bet[306].

---

[305] Analysis by Paul Jorion. Paul Jorion is a Belgian anthropologist and financial expert of some renown who announced the global financial crisis in 2005.
[306] A synthetic CDO (collateralized debt obligation) is a variation of a CDO that generally uses credit default swaps (CDS) and other derivatives to achieve its investment objectives. As such, it is a complex derivative financial security that is sometimes described as a bet on the performance of other mortgage (or other) products, rather than an actual mortgage security. The value and payment stream of a synthetic CDO is not derived from cash assets, such as mortgages or credit card payments, as in the case of a normal CDO, but from premiums paid for the "insurance" of credit default swaps (CDS) on the possibility of default on a defined set of cash asset-based "reference"

Goldman Sachs did not limit itself to betting with CDSs on the losses of the products it sold to its clients; it used this new financial instrument that made it possible to multiply the gains caused by the potential depreciation of a CDO. By selling synthetic CDOs, Goldman Sachs was protecting itself against a depreciation of CDOs that served as benchmarks. The bank endeavored to find as many counterparties as possible willing to play the role of underwriters in exchange for a premium.

This is how the banks managed to prolong the existence of the financial bubble. Synthetic CDOs allowed them to bet against the securities they issued, as Morgan Stanley had done with the Libertas CDO and as Goldman Sachs had done.

The securities created were so opaque and complex that they were incomprehensible to investors and rating agencies. The Abacus marketing document had specified that a counterparty was taking short positions on the underlying CDOs. But investors were unaware that it was John Paulson, known for his aggressive positions in the *subprime* market. Obviously, investors would never have chosen to invest in Abacus 2007-AC1 securities if they had known that Paulson's fund had chosen them.

And what was bound to happen happened: Abacus had the worst performance of all similar products in the market. Investors had bought the product in April 2007 and by January 2008 99% of the Abacus portfolio had been downgraded by the rating agencies[307]. The buyers of these CDOs had been masterfully fleeced. IKB, the Düsseldorf-based regional bank—a usually prudent investor for the middle class—lost its entire stake. Through its investment fund Rhinebridge Capital, it also lost more than 17 billion euros in the *subprime* market. IKB was bought at a bargain price by a US pension fund, but its shareholders, mostly retirees, had lost all their savings. ACA filed for bankruptcy at the end of 2007, and in August 2008 the Dutch bank ABN Amro was bought by the Royal Bank of Scotland, which had preferred to abandon the assets of Abacus by paying 840 million to Goldman Sachs. In the end, Paulson had pocketed close to 1 billion dollars.

---

securities. The "counterparties" buying the insurance may own the "reference" securities and manage the default risk, or they may be speculators who have calculated that the securities will default. (wikipedia. NdT).
[307] Article by Matt Taibbi published in the July 2009 issue of *Rolling Stone* magazine.

In August 2008, the SEC quietly opened an investigation into Paulson. But it was not until 2009, when Greg Zuckerman's book, *The Greatest Trade Ever*, was published, that it became public knowledge that Goldman Sachs had entered into an agreement for the sole purpose of allowing Paulson to short the market[308]. In April 2010, a civil fraud complaint was filed in federal court.

For Charles Ferguson, many of the actors were aware of the *subprime* scam. The journalist was thus opposing the version presented by Michael Lewis, according to whom only a few investors were aware of the risks. Indeed, in his fascinating and highly instructive book, *The Big Bet*, Michael Lewis gives the impression that only *"a small group of crazy, wild and adorably flamboyant vigilantes"* had bet on the collapse of the market. *"With all due respect to Mr. Lewis, the reality was different; the Big Short Bet was a huge business and most of Wall Street knew how to take advantage of it stupendously well."* *"Undoubtedly, thousands of debt buyers, underwriters, brokers, traders and executives knew full well that this story was going to end very badly, but their fortunes increased while it lasted[309]."*

The bankers had every interest in continuing to produce and sell their junk products for as long as possible. Some were not unaware of it, quite the contrary: *"the lack of information was not a problem for the managers of Goldman Sachs, JP Morgan and Morgan Stanley"*. Although *"the latter company started betting against the bubble at the beginning of 2004, but made a strategic mistake that cost it 9 billion dollars"*, i.e. too early and paying CDS for too long. JP Morgan, on the other hand, did not expose itself and kept some distance. *"Goldman Sachs, however, was a separate issue. The firm made billions of dollars betting against the very products whose sale had allowed it to make profits also in the billions[310]."*

---

[308] The speculator John Paulson was not related to the Secretary of State at the Treasury (Henry Paulson). Paulson's father was a certain Alfredo Guillermo Paulsen, born in Ecuador, of a half-French half-Norwegian father and an Ecuadorian mother. But his mother, Jacqueline Boklan, was the daughter of Jewish immigrants from Lithuania and Romania who had settled in New York. John Paulson and Lloyd Blankfein, the chairman of Goldman Sachs, were the two members of the "chosen people".
[309] Charles Ferguson, *Inside Job, the financial crisis…* Ediciones Deusto, Barcelona, 2012, p. 163, 164.
[310] Charles Ferguson, *Inside Job, the financial crisis…* Ediciones Deusto, Barcelona, 2012, p. 164, 165.

Charles Ferguson was blunt: *"Since synthetic CDOs can only exist if there are people determined to bet against the 'long side,' their rapid rise was a clear indicator that Wall Street knew not only that a bubble existed, but that its end was imminent."* And, he insisted, *"And, in any case, this was not at all a small business practiced by a small group of contentious, alternative, and endearing individuals. A reasonable estimate is that, at the end of 2006, the volume of synthetic, or mostly synthetic, CDOs was around $100 billion, while about a quarter of the assets in "conventional" CDOs were also synthetic. During the first half of 2007, just before the collapse of the system, synthetic CDOs almost certainly constituted the majority of CDOs in the market. And no one knew this business better than Goldman Sachs, John Paulson, Magnetar and Tricadia*[311]*."*

Indeed, other funds had been inspired by Paulson. The best known was Magnetar, founded and run by a Jew named Alec Litowitz, who had worked closely with JP Morgan. Magnetar had done about thirty such transactions, worth between $1 billion and $1.5 billion each. But Magnetar had also worked with Paulson.

"Until the securities effectively go bust, the one holding the short position in a synthetic CDO has to periodically make his payments to the long investor. That can get expensive." Paulson and Magnetar were buying the most toxic tranches (the *"equity"* tranche) to reassure potential investors, but also to pocket good returns (often more than 20% per annum). This interest paid for the "short" position (downside bet) until the bubble burst. When the *equity* tranche plummeted, they certainly lost money, but they knew perfectly well that the next tranches would fall soon after and that they would be more than compensated.

The scam was applied on a grand scale: *"Very rough estimates suggest that this hedge fund's short payments alone could have financed a quarter of the subprime mortgage securities market in 2006. Investment bankers charged immense fees for helping to structure the products and put Magnetar in touch with the suckers he was betting against*[312]*."*

---

[311] Charles Ferguson, *Inside Job, the financial crisis...* Ediciones Deusto, Barcelona, 2012, p. 167.
[312] Charles Ferguson, *Inside Job, the financial crisis...* Ediciones Deusto, Barcelona, 2012, p. 181, 182.

"The first to understand this were some of the big hedge funds [investment funds]. Unlike the investment banks, they couldn't do much business securitizing loans and selling CDOs. Consequently, they had to wait until the bubble was about to burst and make money on the collapse... In addition to Bill Ackman, major hedge funds made billions of dollars betting against mortgage securities when the bubble burst, including Magnetar, Tricadia, Harbinger Capital, George Soros and John Paulson. It is estimated that these five hedge funds alone made more than $25 billion in profit, and possibly more than $50 billion, betting short against the mortgage bubble, and they all worked hand in hand with Wall Street to make it happen[313]." Bill Ackman, Georges Soros and John Paulson, three prominent gamblers, were members of the cult.

In fact, in 2007, John Paulson definitely entered the legend by making the largest profits in the history of financial transactions. He had pocketed 3700 million dollars in 2007 betting against mortgage securities, 2000 million in 2008 and 5000 million in 2010[314].

But John Paulson was not just a high-flying speculator, or an unscrupulous swindler. He was also a generous philanthropist and donor. He had donated $15 million to the *Center for Responsible Lending*, an association that provided legal assistance to over-indebted real estate borrowers. During one of the donations, Paulson had these beautiful words full of compassion, *"We are pleased to support those who provide legal assistance to distressed homeowners, many of whom have been victimized by predatory lenders* [315]*."* Delicious and unmistakable chuzpah!

Complaints against Goldman Sachs

The "Bank" had doubly profited from the real estate bubble: first it had swindled the investors who had bought its CDOs, and second it had swindled the taxpayer by making him pay in full what the insurer AIG

---

[313] Charles Ferguson, *Inside Job, the financial crisis...* Ediciones Deusto, Barcelona, 2012, p. 163.
[314] Mutual funds typically keep 20% of annual profits, plus 2% per year of the value of assets under management, but are not affected by losses, leading managers to take risks.
[315] Jean-François Gayraud, *La grande Fraude*, Odile Jacob, 2011, p. 59.

owed him for the CDS on behalf of the State. This bank was the most powerful, but also the most criticized for its practices.

After the housing bubble burst, Goldman Sachs was hit with a wave of lawsuits. New York State authorities pursued the firm and the 25 brokers who had sold piles of toxic CDOs to pension funds of civil servants who had lost $100 million in investments. The Commonwealth of Massachusetts had brought actions on the same grounds, on behalf of 714 holders of "predatory loans[316]". But Goldman had emerged virtually unscathed, agreeing to pay a derisory $60 million—what its CDO department earned in a day and a half during the real estate boom[317].

The SEC (Securities & Exchange Commission), the U.S. financial markets regulator, probably needed to regain some credibility, as in April 2010 it officially launched a series of civil proceedings against the firm. Goldman Sachs was accused of having misled its investors by claiming that the Abacus 2007-AC1 assets had been independently selected by ACA Management, when in fact the Paulson fund was largely involved in the selection of the securities. According to the SEC, ACA Management had acted in good faith. Instead, Goldman Sachs had misled everyone into believing that Paulson shared with them the same interest in the rise of these securities. Goldman Sachs was accused of misleading its clients for the benefit of itself and, above all, its partner Paulson. The managers rejected the accusations: according to them, they had only protected themselves from the risks and claimed that the investors were informed actors who knew perfectly well the risks they were taking.

However, the indictment had featured a November 2007 email from Goldman Sachs CEO Lloyd Blankfein to his staff: *"Obviously, we didn't get out of the subprime real estate credit mess. We lost a lot of money, and then we made back more than we had lost thanks to short positions."*

On April 27, 2010, during a hearing of Goldman Sachs management before a Senate committee (chaired by Senator Carl Levin), several senators had asked whether Goldman Sachs had its clients' interests at heart, as the bank's slogan read: *"Our clients' interests always come*

---

[316] In October 2010, Angelo Mozilo, the president of Countrywide had agreed to pay $87 million for civil fraud as part of the settlement with the SEC.
[317] Article by Matt Taibbi, *Rolling Stone* magazine, July 2009.

first[318]". They did not get an answer. Next, a senator made this observation, *"Do you think when your people think something is crap and then go and sell it, and then your firm bets against it, do you think that makes them trustworthy?"* Or this other very direct question, *"If an employee of yours thinks something is crap, a crap deal, do you think Goldman Sachs should sell it to your clients while you yourselves bet against those products short? I think it's a very clear case of conflict of interest and I think we should do something about it. But I find that you don't see it that way*[319]*."* The firm's leaders defended themselves against any conflict of interest by arguing the perfect impermeability between *trading* activities and advisory activities.

A young French broker named Fabrice Tourre, a 22-year-old mathematician with a degree from Central High School who had been recruited by Goldman Sachs, was a nominal defendant. He was to be the security fuse. His trial, which the business daily *La Tribune* called "the *most emblematic trial of the 2008 financial crisis*," debuted on July 15, 2013. The emails that Fabrice Tourre sent to his girlfriend were unveiled; like this one from January 23, 2007: *"The whole building is about to collapse, at any moment. Only potential survivor, Fab the fabulous."* And this one from March 7, 2007: *"The subprime business is all but dead, and the poor little borrowers won't last long."* On June 13, 2007, he wrote: *"I just sold Abacus bonds to some widows and orphans I passed at the airport. These Belgians love the Abacus product!"* Fabrice Tourre was not Jewish, but apparently he had been contaminated.

Before the court, Fabrice Tourre said: *"I regret these emails that give a bad image of the firm as well as of myself"*. In fact, we learned that the bank itself had translated and leaked the emails to the media. His superior, Jonathan Egol (future CEO) and his subordinate Gail Kreitman, both testified against him, claiming that Fabrice Tourre was running Abacus on his own. Fabrice Tourre had been sacrificed,

---

[318]"*The interest of our customers is paramount. Experience shows that if our clients are satisfied it will result in our success.*" Goldman Sachs: Our Principles (No. 1), in Marc Roche, *The Bank, how Goldman Sachs runs the world*, Ediciones Deusto, Barcelona, 2011, Annexes p. 237.

[319]Charles Ferguson, *Inside Job, the financial crisis...* Ediciones Deusto, Barcelona, 2012, p. 188, 189.

betrayed by his company. He had also been condemned to silence, as the bank also paid a fortune to his lawyers[320].

Goldman Sachs was cleared of the case in July 2010, when a settlement was reached with the SEC: Goldman agreed to pay the sum of $550 million for having *"misled"* its investors. The amount corresponded to a fine of $300 million and the payment of $250 million in compensation to the two damaged banks: Royal Bank of Scotland (which had acquired the Dutch bank ABN Amro, the real victim) and IKB, the first bank to collapse in the *subprime* crisis in Germany in July 2007.

Goldman Sachs had challenged the charges, but had nevertheless agreed to pay the fine and damages in exchange for dropping the legal proceedings. It should be noted that this amount of 550 million represented barely fifteen days of the bank's earnings in 2009. As soon as the settlement with the SEC was announced, the bank's shares rose 2% on the New York Stock Exchange, a gain far greater than the fine.

Criminals at the top of the State

At the end of the 1990s, under the presidency of Bill Clinton ("left"), the US economy was ruled by "the gang of four", namely: Federal Reserve Chairman Alan Greenspan, Treasury Secretary Robert Rubin, former Goldman Sachs executive (26 years at the firm), his deputy Larry Summers, as well as SEC chief Arthur Levitt (from 1993 to 2001). All four were fiercely opposed to the regulation of derivatives markets[321]. In 1999, Alan Greenspan, Robert Rubin and Larry Summers had made the cover of the *Times* magazine, with the headline "The Committee to Save the World". Given that these were three members of

---

[320] It is essential to watch *Arte's* documentary on Goldman Sachs, available on internet video platforms. On August 1, 2013, the jury found Fabrice Tourre guilty of six of the seven counts of the indictment against him, including stock fraud: Fabrice Tourre had to personally pay more than $800,000 (his former employer could not pay it for him). In addition, he was banned from trading on the financial markets for three years.

[321] *"In the 1990s, the chairwoman of the Commodity Futures Trading Commission had called for such regulation, and the need became more pressing when the Federal Reserve Bank of New York set up a rescue plan in 1998 for Long Term Capital Management... But Treasury Secretary Robert Rubin, his deputy Larry Summers and Alan Greenspan were adamant in their opposition and achieved their goal."* Joseph Stiglitz, *Free Fall, the Free Market and the Collapse of the World Economy*, Taurus, Madrid, 2010, p. 192 (and note 4 p. 385). (NdT).

the "chosen people", it was not unreasonable to think of a wink from the newspaper's editorial staff to their friends in high finance[322].

It should be noted that many of the actors in the *subprime* crisis were either members of the sect or former partners of Goldman Sachs. In 2008, during the crisis, the situation within the government administration was no different. In fact, whether the president is a "Democrat" or a "Republican" (from the American "left" or "right") is of no consequence as long as the cosmopolitan advisors and bankers are in place. At that time, along with the governing team of "Republican" President George Bush, Alan Greenspan had retained the chairmanship of the Federal Reserve. Greenspan had largely contributed to creating the *subprime* crisis *by* keeping interest rates very low between 2001 and 2004, thus favoring the growth of the housing bubble before raising them sharply at the beginning of 2005. And he had done nothing to ban predatory lending. In 2006, he was replaced by another member of the sect, Ben Shalom Bernanke[323]. The president's chief of staff, Joshua Bolten was also a son of the "chosen people" and a former Goldman Sachs employee.

The Secretary of State at the Treasury, Henry Paulson, was certainly not Jewish—but a member of Christian Science, one of the numerous Protestant sects infesting the United States, all Judeo-compatible and furiously pro-Israel[324]. Henry Paulson was the former CEO of Goldman Sachs bank, where he had stayed for thirty-two years. If Paulson let Lehman Brothers fail in September 2008, it was probably because of some old rivalries.

Timothy Geithner, who headed the Reserve Bank of New York, was also not Jewish but had been one of the deputies of Robert Rubin, a

---

[322] The "left" was in favor of deregulation: Bill Clinton in the 1990s in the United States, Gordon Brown in the United Kingdom, Romano Prodi in Italy, Gerhard Schröder in Germany, Pierre Bérégovoy in France.

[323] *"Skyrocketing asset prices meant Wall Street was having a party. Orthodox theory says that the Fed should contain that kind of partying—not least because, inevitably, it is others who will have to pay the cost of the cleanup the next morning. But Fed chairmen Greenspan and Bernanke didn't want to be spoilsports, so they had to come up with a series of fallacious arguments to justify standing by and doing nothing: bubbles didn't exist, you couldn't say there was a bubble, even if there was, the Fed was in any case better at cleaning up the mess after the bubble burst."* Joseph Stiglitz, *Free Fall, the Free Market and the Collapse of the World Economy*, Taurus, Madrid, 2010, p. 184.

[324] Read about it in our book *The Eschatological War* (2013).

former Goldman executive and Treasury Secretary under former President Bill Clinton.

The director of the World Bank (2007–2012), Robert Zoellick, was on the other hand a member of the sect; he had also been, in 1997, international affairs advisor to Goldman Sachs Bank. His predecessor at the helm of the World Bank, Paul Wolfowitz, who had later been President George Bush's Assistant Secretary of Defense and one of the hawks who had rushed the United States into the Iraq war in 2003, was also a member of the "chosen people".

When, in October 2008, "Hank" Paulson had Congress approve his $700 billion bailout plan (the TARP), he appointed one Neel Kashari to oversee that immense fortune. That 35-year-old "American Indian", until then unknown, was a Goldman Sachs banker.

It may also be recalled that at that time, the president of the International Monetary Fund (IMF) was another member of the sect: Dominique Strauss-Kahn. As head of the IMF, he was supposed to be one of the best informed men in the financial world. However, on May 25, 2008, he had declared that the crisis was *"behind us"*. Dominique Strauss-Kahn did not last long in office. On May 18, 2011, he resigned following his indictment in a sexual assault case at the Sofitel hotel in New York. On August 23, he benefited from a dismissal of the case despite the evidence and his past in the matter. The following year, a financial transaction had put an end to the civil proceedings, but in 2013 Dominique Strauss-Kahn was again sent before a correctional court for "aggravated procuring in meeting" in the framework of the case of the Carlton hotel in Lille in France.

After the November 2008 presidential election and the election of black President Barack Obama, nothing changed. Ben Bernanke remained at the head of the Fed; Tim Geithner replaced Henry Paulson as Treasury Secretary; and Mark Patterson, a former lobbyist ... for Goldman Sachs, was chosen as Chairman of the Cabinet. It was clear that there would be no sweeping reforms to alter the financial system. In fact, just after his nomination, Tim Geithner declared, "*I have never been a regulator*[325]"

The Secretary General of the presidency was Rahm Emanuel, a Jewish-Zionist of proven pedigree. He had made hundreds of thousands of

---

[325] See Charles Ferguson's excellent documentary: *Inside Job* (2011).

dollars on the board of directors of the real estate lending institution Freddie Mac. And, if that wasn't enough, President Obama had chosen Larry Summers as his first economic advisor[326].

At the head of the New York Fed, William Dudley had succeeded Timothy Geithner. He was a former chief economist at the bank... Goldman Sachs.

Barack Obama had chosen Mary Shapiro, a Jewish-Zionist and former chairwoman of Finra, the self-regulatory body for investment banks, to chair the SEC.

Gary Gensler, another Jew-Zionist, was now the chairman of the Commodity Futures Trading Commission, the regulator of the U.S. forward markets, who happened to be a former co-chief financial officer of the firm... Goldman Sachs.

Despite the economic depression, the three major U.S. banks—Goldman Sachs, JP Morgan and Barclays—were in insultingly good health. *"These groups reign as lords and masters. The people who run them, Lloyd Blankfein, Jamie Dimon and Bob Diamond, are the talk of the press today,"* Marc Roche told us in his book on Goldman Sachs.

Lloyd Blankfein, the head of "the firm," was *"the most powerful banker in the country, the emperor of American capitalism, a figurehead of the financial oligarchy who enjoyed the position of viceroy of the United States."*

Blankfein was born in 1954 in New York; *"originally from a family of Jews who escaped the Russian pogroms at the end of the 19th century*[327]*".* This imminent banker *"surrounds himself only with a small*

---

[326]*"But it turned out that Obama was just another oligarch president. The first disturbing sign was his appointments. Not a single critical or reformist voice got an office... Instead we got Larry Summers, the man who was behind almost all the disastrous policies that generated the crisis..."* Charles Ferguson, *Inside Job, the financial crisis...* Ediciones Deusto, Barcelona, 2012, p. 367. "*The White House's chief economic advisor, Lawrence Summers—former Secretary of the Treasury under Bill Clinton, and, as such, undertaker of the Glass-Steagall Act in 1999.*" Marc Roche, *The Bank, how Goldman Sachs runs the world*, Ediciones Deusto, Barcelona, 2011, p. 228.

[327]The Jewish intellectuals always tell the same story. In reality, the emigration of the Jews had been provoked by the establishment in Russia in 1896 of a State monopoly on alcoholic beverages and the suppression of all private distilleries. This measure aimed at protecting the Russian peasantry *"had dealt a severe blow to the economic activity of the Jews of Russia"* (Aleksandr Solzhenitsyn, *Deux Siècles ensemble*, tome I, Fayard, 2002, p. 326. Read in *Jewish Fanaticism*).

clique of acolytes, former traders of J. Aron [a subsidiary of Goldman Sachs, NDT], *and preferably from New York. Among the many faithful who have emerged from this nursery is his number two, Gary Cohn, an inescapable character whose bonus is equal to his own*[328]*.*

Jamie Dimon, the head of JP Morgan, *"likes to present himself as a "patriot","* Marc Roche told us jokingly, noting that "he is, however, *originally from the upper middle class of Izmir, Turkey"*. Dimon had previously worked closely with Sandy Weill, another member of the sect who presided over Lehman Brothers. This Sandy Weill was a *"family friend and legend of American finance*[329]*."*

As for Bob Diamond, the chairman of Barclays Capital, we are told that he came from an Irish Catholic family. It is possible, after all. We have seen that many top bank managers and big swindlers were genuine goyim. The values of Judaism have penetrated many spirits, especially in Anglo-Saxon Protestant countries, but they have also been able to tarnish that of many Catholics, particularly in the United States. But the surname "Diamond" is a classic of Hebraic onomastics, and we know that Jewishness is often lived in secret or at a distance. The Marranos of Spain in the 16th century and the Frankists of Poland in the 18th century posed as Catholics, while the Sabbateans in the Ottoman Empire were often good Muslims[330].

The awakening of anti-Semitism

One might have thought that anti-Semitism was part of a bygone era. As Marc Roche wrote in his book on Goldman Sachs Bank, *"The last bastion of anti-Semitic prejudice, the New York Stock Exchange, fell in the early 1970s, when Goldman Sachs Chairman and CEO Gus Levy became the first Jew to chair the board of governors of the New York Stock Exchange*[331]*."*

---

[328] Marc Roche, *The Bank, how Goldman Sachs runs the world*, Ediciones Deusto, Barcelona, 2011, p. 211, 107, 88–89, 95. *"He is also a lover of puns, an ace of verbal pirouettes, as when he declares to The Sunday Times: "I am but a banker doing God's work."* p. 88.
[329] Marc Roche, *The Bank, how Goldman Sachs runs the world*, Ediciones Deusto, Barcelona, 2011, pp. 95, 217, 212.
[330] In this regard, read *Psychoanalysis of Judaism*.
[331] Marc Roche, *The Bank, how Goldman Sachs runs the world*, Ediciones Deusto, Barcelona, 2011, p. 184.

However, the Jewish community was concerned that many of those who bore great responsibility for the financial crisis were, in fact, Jews.

"Enough to make the followers of anti-Jewish paranoia giddy and imagine that the world economy is in the hands of the Jews," we read on the "community's" websites.

"The American financial crisis is causing a sharp increase in the number of anti-Semitic messages posted on forums, blogs and websites," said the Anti-Defamation League (ADL, the most important anti-racist association in the United States). *"Hundreds of anti-Semitic messages about Lehaman Brothers and other entities affected by the subprime crisis have been posted on financial discussion forums. The messages attack Jews in general, some accusing them of controlling government and finance, of being part of a 'Jewish world order,' and of therefore being responsible for the economic crisis."*

ADL President Abraham Foxman repeated the usual speech, *"We have learned from modern history that every time there is a downturn in the world economy, there is a rise in anti-Semitism and bigotry, and that is what we are seeing now."*

The ADL website published one of its numerous messages accusing the Jews of *"having infiltrated Wall Street and the government, and of having ruined the United States"*. *"The old clichés about Jews and money are resurfacing,"* Abraham Foxman estimated. *"As we saw after 9/11, as soon as problems and uncertainties arise in the economy or in world events, Jews become the scapegoats."*

On French Jewish websites, the same "ready-to-use" analysis was circulating: *"As if it were an iron law, international crisis situations—especially financial ones—awaken the anti-Semitism always latent in the collective unconscious. The alleged link between "the Jew and money" or "the Jewish conspiracy to dominate the world" are once again fashionable themes."* The accusations were terrible!

Obviously, some Muslims had taken the opportunity to denounce the nefarious role of the "Zionists" in the world economy: *"The anti-Semitic wave accompanying the crisis is in turn fed by the declarations of the Arab leaders of the Muslim world, and the great profusion of anti-Semitic caricatures in the Arab press. Thus we have heard the head of Hamas in Gaza blaming the financial crisis on the "American Jewish lobby", and Iranian President Mahmoud Ahmadinejad declaring "that a handful of Zionists dominate the world"."*

These accusations, coming from another era, once again placed the Jews on the margins of humanity; and one could wonder when their suffering would finally end: *"in four thousand years of suffering[332]"*, as Jacques Attali wrote. There was a lot of suffering in the skyscrapers and in the ministries!

In fact, the resurgence of anti-Semitism, under the pen of Jewish intellectuals, is a multi-secular constant, and the same refrain is regularly repeated in the mainstream media. We have provided not a few examples in our previous books. Just take a look:

At the beginning of November 2003, a European Commission survey of 7500 people designated the State of Israel as a threat to peace in the world. The survey had not been made public, but articles on the subject in the English newspaper *The Guardian* and the Spanish newspaper *El País* had mentioned it. Horror! The State of Israel was indeed designated as the main threat to world peace, even ahead of North Korea! The survey, conducted among 500 people from every fifteen European Union countries, asked the question, *"Tell me in your opinion whether or not this country represents a threat to peace in the world."* And the state of Israel had been selected by 59% of the respondents. The leak of the results had sparked controversy, particularly from the Simon Wiesenthal Center, which demanded at the time that the European Union be excluded from the Israeli-Palestinian peace process, and accused Europe of experiencing *"the worst manifestation of anti-Semitism since World War II."* Rabbi Marvin Hier, the founder of the Wiesenthal Center, had further stated, *"This shocking survey defies logical reason. It is a racist fantasy that only proves that anti-Semitism is deeply rooted in European society, more so than at any time since the end of the war."* And this was in 2003, five years before the financial crisis.

It is probably also anti-Semitic to note that Jewish intellectuals, Jewish politicians and Jewish financiers are constantly pressuring the West to declare war on nations that are not sufficiently subject to the laws of democracy and international finance. This is how Western nations have been dragged into wars against Iraq (1991), against Serbia (1999), against Afghanistan (2001), again against Iraq (2003), against Libya (2011); and they would probably have gone to war against Iran and

---

[332] Jacques Attali, *Un hombre de influencia*, Seix Barral, Barcelona, 1992, p. 11.

Syria in 2013 if Russian President Vladimir Putin had not made a coup on the table[333].

---

[333]The translation of this book is completed one year after the beginning of the Ukrainian war (February 24, 2022). The dizzying eschatological, geopolitical and military escalation seems unstoppable as Israel continues to bomb Syria and Iran with impunity. After the Euromaiden coup in 2013, the US promoted a "democratic" regime change in Ukraine, led by Victoria Nuland's diplomacy. After the conservative and isolationist presidency of Republican Donald Trump, who was dragging his feet too much in the face of US *establishment* pressures, a dubious election returned a Democratic administration to power in the White House. Once again, preeminent Jews occupy the key ministries (Secretaries of State, Treasury, Attorney General, Homeland Security, and National Intelligence) of the presidential administration, led by U.S. foreign policy chief Antony Blinken. It is necessary to tell the story of the creature Zelensky, that lurid comedian and actor-turned-president of Ukraine. The producer of the film Zelensky (a guy who plays a role in a TV series and then plays that role in reality) was Ihor Kolomoiski, alias Bennia (the name of the godfather of the Jewish mafia in Isaac Babel's *Odessa Tales*, a masterpiece of Ashkenazi literature). For this, Kolomoiski received from Ronald Lauder (American billionaire and president of the World Jewish Congress) the television network that propelled Zelensky to stardom. On the other hand, we have a company of the oligarch Kolomoiski, the main Ukrainian gas company Burisma, implicated in the corruption of the Biden clan (see also note 161). This Ukrainian oligarch had also owned the first Ukrainian bank PrivatBank (used by 33% of Ukrainians), from which he directly siphoned off funds equivalent to 5% of the Ukrainian GDP. The money transited via the British Virgin Islands to be reinvested in the U.S. *Midwest*. Kolomoiski is now the largest real estate owner in the State of Ohio, precisely on the lands of the fiefdom of Lex Wexner, another U.S. billionaire closely linked to the Jeffrey Epstein scandal. Thus, behind President Zelensky extends the entire network of a dangerous international mafia (sources: *Faits et Documents, Courrier international, wikipedia.* NdT).

4. The Super Predators

Among the big winners of the crisis was one David Tepper, the founder of the US hedge fund Appaloosa Management, who had earned 4 billion dollars in 2009. At the age of 56, he had entered the *top 50* of the biggest fortunes in the United States. *"Tepper embodies in body and soul this Goldman connection ..., the CEO of the US hedge fund Appaloosa is number one in the hit-parade of the winners of the crisis[334]."*

Le Monde newspaper of January 4, 2014 had published an article about him, entitled: *"David Tepper, the speculator who transforms stocks into solid gold."* His *Palomino* fund, specializing in U.S. stocks had generated gains of 42% in 2013. Tepper had successfully bet on banks, insurers and real estate developers. His remuneration in 2013 had risen to $3 billion, making him the highest paid *hedge fund* manager in the United States. Tepper, we were told, *"began his career at Goldman Sachs in the ruthless junk bond business"* before setting up on his own: *"David Tepper forged his reputation in February 2009, at the height of the subprime crisis. Contrary to his rivals, the speculator had massively bought the securities that nobody wanted from the totally bankrupt American and British banks. Confident in the effectiveness of the government's rescue plan, the hedge fund's main shareholder had bet on the success of the aid program for the big banks on both sides of the Atlantic to get the financial sector out of the quagmire. The market filibuster has built his fortune on a simple idea: buy undervalued stocks, resist fads and ... wait. "I have never lost by listening to my gut." This is the mantra of this bold gambler, sure of his lucky star."* Since its creation in 1993, his company had guaranteed its investors an average return of 27%. Everything this "Crassus" from New Jersey touched turned to gold. You got it, didn't you: David Tepper *"was raised in a jewish family"*.

---

[334] Marc Roche, *The Bank, how Goldman Sachs runs the world*, Ediciones Deusto, Barcelona, 2011, p. 113, 194.

Goldman Sachs in Greece: financial magic

In February 2010, the "firm" was accused of having played a shady role in the financial crisis in Greece. Between 2000 and 2003, Goldman Sachs had helped the country to make up its debt to enable it to meet the criteria for joining the euro currency: a budget deficit of 3% and a public debt of no more than 60% of gross domestic product. However, the country was far from meeting these criteria. Greece, which was ruled out in 1999 when the euro was created, had managed in 2001 to meet the Maastricht requirements and join the euro zone thanks to a financial subterfuge. In order to conceal part of the debt and to boast healthy accounts, the socialist government of Costas Simitis had resorted to the financial creativity of the investment bank Goldman Sachs, thus managing to hide 3 billion euros of debt.

A decade later, in March 2012, two Greek officials in charge of debt management, Spiros Papanicolau and his predecessor Cristoforos Sardelis, provided details about the debt contract that had been negotiated in 2001 with the "firm", which had allowed Greece to hide part of the national debt.

In June 2011, Goldman Sachs had agreed with the Greek government on a "currency *swap*", which allowed Greece to borrow 2.8 billion euros without it being reflected in the official statistics. There are "credit default *swaps*", the famous CDS that we have seen: a quarterly or annual premium is paid to the bank and if the borrower defaults, the bank pays the debt. But there is also the "interest rate *swap*" (the most common): you are indebted at a variable rate and you want to switch to a fixed rate; you pay a fixed rate for a given period and the bank pays the variable interest. Or commodity *swaps*, for example, in order to buy oil at a price and date determined in advance. And then there are currency *swaps*, to minimize the impact of exchange rate volatility.

The operation consisted in exchanging a debt previously contracted by Greece in dollars (issuance of a 10 billion dollar bond over 5 years), for a debt in euros with Goldman Sachs. If the exchange rate was, for example, €1 for $1.3, the bank would pay €7.7 billion to Greece. But if the two parties agree on an exchange rate of $1.15 instead of $1.3, Greece receives 8700 million euros, and not 7700 million. Thus, the

Greek state had received 1 billion euros more in the operation[335]. The bank then paid half-yearly interest to Greece (of the $10 billion), which in turn paid it to its investors (before repaying them the $10 billion due over five years). At the same time, the bank reimburses the $10 billion to Greece, which reimburses it in euros.

Nearly one billion euros of debt had thus disappeared from the radar of Eurostat, the European Union's statistical body. To recover the discounted amount, the bank had this time used an interest *swap*, taking as a basis a rate different from those prevailing at the time. At the time, the rate had seemed very advantageous to the managers of the Greek debt. But the set-up, much more complicated than it seemed at first, had turned against Greece after the attacks of September 11, 2001. Bond interest rates had fallen in the markets and the interest *swap* had suffered losses.

Greek officials then attempted a renegotiation with Goldman Sachs in 2002, and had agreed to use a new derivative product for repayments based on the inflation rate. But as Papanicolau himself confessed, "it was a *very bad bet*."

The Greek authorities had mortgaged the country's airports and freeways to raise desperately needed funds. With the "Eole" contract concluded in 2001 with Goldman Sachs, the Greek state had received immediate funds and had committed to pay the bank future revenues from airport taxes. The previous year, it had been the national lottery revenues that had been swallowed up with a contract called "Ariana". Greece had become a kind of neighborhood second-hand flea market, but on a national scale. The government had classified these transactions as sales, not loans[336].

By 2005, the amount of the principal debt had almost doubled, reaching EUR 5.1 billion instead of the initial EUR 2.8 billion. Cristoforos Sardelis explained that he had not had the possibility to meet with other banks to get counter-offers and evaluate Goldman Sachs' financial set-up because Goldman Sachs had threatened to cancel the contract. Therefore, the deal was kept secret[337].

---

[335] Paul Monthe's February 2010 article in *next-finance.net*. We did not find any explanatory article in the mainstream press.
[336] *New York Times*, February 18, 2010.
[337] March 10, 2012 article by Audrey Dupeyron, in *express.be*

Since this set-up was very complex and customized, Goldman Sachs had billed brokerage commissions far in excess of those billed for more standard transactions. At the time the deal was signed in 2001, Greece owed €300 million on top of the €2.8 billion it had borrowed from the investment bank.

At the end of 2009, Greece's financial situation became a catastrophic scenario. At the beginning of November, the new socialist government of George Papandreou was wondering how it could implement its program of cuts and austerity to reduce the abysmal debt (112% of GDP) in order to convince the financial markets and the European Union. On December 8, 2009, the rating agency Ficht Ibca downgraded the country's debt rating from AA^- to BBB^+, which was equivalent to donkey's ears.

Rumors of a bankruptcy scenario circulated in the market rooms. This was followed by speculation about Greece's debt, with a consequent increase in the interest rates demanded from the government to borrow on the international markets: 6 to 7%, double the German 10-year rate. The Greeks saw the weight of the debt they had to repay increase in addition to the previously camouflaged credits.

Gary Cohn, the number 2 of Goldman Sachs, landed again in Athens with speculator John Paulson. The banker's role was to reassure buyers of Greek bonds (debt) so that the country could continue to borrow on the markets. Gary Cohn presented a financial instrument that would make it possible to postpone the cost of the Greek healthcare system to a distant future.

But at the same time that it was advising the Greek government, the "firm" was speculating in the CDS market against Greece with Paulson behind the scenes, the same man with whom it had been in cahoots during the *subprime* crisis[338]. By buying and advising its clients on CDS on Greek debt, Goldman Sachs was encouraging the increase in interest rates demanded from the country, which was paradoxical for the first bank to advise Athens. The bank did not shy away from any ploy, spreading false rumors that the Greek state was in dire straits. The 300 million euros a year in commissions was not enough339.

---

[338]*Libération*, February 20, 2010.
[339]The firm also placed its pawns abroad. In October 2011, Mario Draghi, a former vice-president of Goldman Sachs, was appointed to the management of the European Central Bank. In the years when Goldman Sachs was most active in Greece, between 2002 and

John Paulson was also prospering. In November 2009, he created an investment fund specialized in prospecting for gold mines. In 2010, after the first announcements of the devaluation of Greek securities by the agencies Fitch and Standard and Poor's, Paulson launched his attacks against an unstable Greek economy. Speculation about Greece's bankruptcy brought him nearly 5 billion dollars. His fortune was now estimated at $12 billion and his funds now managed $32 billion in assets.

In 2009, Goldman Sachs had declared no less than $13 billion in profits. But the firm had only paid $14 million in taxes the previous year. This bank, which had sold hundreds of thousands of toxic real estate loans to pensioners and confiscated tens of billions from the US taxpayer, had only paid $14 million in taxes in 2008 while distributing $10 billion in bonuses to its managers. Its brand new CEO Lloyd Blankfein had received an envelope of $43 million in bonuses[340].

According to Goldman Sachs' annual report, this weak taxation was largely due to changes in *"the geographic distribution of profits"*. In plain English, this meant that their profits were located in tax havens[341]. All this did not stop Goldman Sachs management from boasting of its exemplary ethics: *"Integrity and honesty are at the core of our business. We expect our employees to maintain irreproachable ethics in everything they do, whether in their professional or personal lives[342]."*

George Soros and speculation

The famous George Soros was also a high-flying speculator. This former Wall Street vedete was still in 2008 one of the richest men in the

---

2005, this same Mario Draghi was vice-president of the firm's European branch. He swore to God that he knew nothing about the falsification of the Greek accounts, although there was no reason to believe him. The Draghi family used to spend their vacations in southern Italy in the company of Robert Rubin and his entourage. Mario Monti, the Italian Prime Minister, had worked for many years as an international banking advisor, as had his compatriot Romano Prodi, former President of the Italian Council and President of the European Commission.

[340] Article by Matt Taibbi, in *Rolling Stone* magazine, July 2009.

[341] In fact, in those years, all large multinational corporations had found ways to reduce their taxes to a minimum. Between 1998 and 2005, nearly two-thirds of the large companies operating in the United States paid no taxes at all. And the situation was identical in all countries. See the article *Cinq astuces des multinationales pour ne pas payer d'impôts*, at www.challenges.fr.

[342] Goldman Sachs: Our Principles (No. 14), in Marc Roche, *The Bank, how Goldman Sachs runs the world*, Ediciones Deusto, Barcelona, 2011, Annexes p. 239.

world. His personal fortune was estimated at 20 billion dollars in 2012, according to the *Forbes* magazine ranking (22nd fortune in the world). He was also a symbol of international speculation. His investment fund Quantum Fund was domiciled in Curaçao, in the Dutch Antilles. This was a tax haven that allowed him to evade taxes and hide the identity of his investors. In 1992, he had achieved one of the best financial coups of the century, pocketing more than 1 billion dollars.

Explanations: In March 1979, the countries of the European Economic Community adopted a new exchange system: the EMS, or European Monetary System. European currencies now had a fluctuation margin of 2.25% around a fictitious currency, the ECU (European Currency Unit), defined as a weighted average basket of the different European currencies and serving as a reference for all of them. Whenever the maximum percentage variation was reached (i.e., plus or minus 2.25%), the central banks had to intervene in the markets to prevent the exchange rate from going outside the fluctuation band, buying currency in the event of a fall in the central reference exchange rate (ECU), or selling the affected currency in the event of a rise.

By limiting the volatility of currencies, this system favored trade within the Union, and companies avoided exchange risks. This implied interventions by central banks in order to maintain parities, as well as a relative homogeneity of economies.

When a currency diverges from the central exchange rate, the central bank of the country in question must then either raise interest rates or use its foreign exchange reserves. A rise in interest rates leads to an increase in demand for the currency. If in France, for example, rates rise from 2 to 5%, then foreign investors will demand more francs to take advantage of the country's more advantageous interest rates. The country's national bank can also sell part of its foreign exchange reserves, for example, by converting its deutsche marks into francs. A fall in the demand for marks and an increase in the demand for francs will result in an appreciation of the franc against the mark and the ECU.

In 1990–1991, Great Britain was experiencing higher inflation (price increases) than other European countries. The Bank of England had then raised its interest rates, thereby strengthening its currency and reducing the prices of imports—especially raw materials and energy—and moderating inflation. Interest rates were very high at the time, and sterling was overvalued.

In 1992, Europe was in recession. The reunification of Germany was costing DM 150 billion every year, and to combat the ensuing inflation, the Bundesbank had raised its rates, causing the mark to appreciate sharply. The other European countries were forced to raise their interest rates to defend their currencies, or to devalue them, as Italy and Spain did. The Bank of England's interest rate was already above 10%; a further rise would increase the unemployment rate in a period of recession (less investment). As for a further devaluation of sterling, that was out of the question: apparently it would affect the pride of the UK... Norman Lamont, the Chancellor of the Exchequer then decided to do nothing.

George Soros took advantage of this indecision and managed to convince other investors that the pound could fall in the event of a massive and coordinated attack. He borrowed £7 billion of overvalued sterling, and, on September 16, 1992, his investment fund Quantum launched its attack by shorting the pound in a "short sale".

The operation was carried out at a good pace together with the Caton Corp and Jones Investment funds, as well as the US banks JP Morgan, Citicorp, Chase Manhattan and Bank of America, which considerably amplified the attack. The exchange rate of a currency depends on the supply and demand of each currency in the foreign exchange market. The pound sterling began to devalue and the mark and franc to appreciate.

To counter the massive sales of pounds, the Bank of England first used its reserves (foreign exchange in other currencies) to buy back the pounds in the market, but the amount of foreign exchange reserves available was limited and the Bank of England eventually had to capitulate.

The next day, Britain announced its exit from the EMS and a 15% devaluation. George Soros and all the funds and banks that had participated in the attack were able to repay their loans in pounds, but with a devalued pound that they were able to buy afterwards. The British Treasury estimated its losses at 3.4 billion pounds, but George Soros had earned 1.1 billion dollars after the operation. After this speculative episode, the other European currencies were devalued one after the other, and on August 1, 1993, the fluctuation margins of the EMS went to 15%[343].

Cosmopolitan billionaires

Greed for money and lust for wealth are probably the most common character trait that comes to mind when thinking about Judaism. Certainly, there are poor Jews, but the fact remains that Jews are vastly overrepresented among the planet's billionaires (in billions, billions).

In a 2004 book entitled *The Jewish Century*, a Jewish historian named Yuri Slezkine, noted the triumph of the Jewish spirit in the world. Undeniably, they were also the wealthiest citizens: *"Jews are now the most prosperous religious community in America, he wrote... Jewish household income is the highest (72% above the national average). Jews are three times more self-employed than the national average. They are also the best represented community among the wealthiest Americans (according to Forbes magazine, in 1982, about 40% of the forty wealthiest individuals in the United States were Jewish). Even new immigrants from the Soviet Union begin earning more than the national average within a few years of their arrival."*

Jews were vastly overrepresented among influential men: *"In October 1994, Vanity Fair published the biographies of twenty-three media moguls, described by the magazine as the "new establishment," namely "the men and women who dominate the worlds of entertainment, telecommunications and computers, and whose ambition and influence made America the true superpower of the information age." Eleven of them were Jewish, or 48%*[344].*"*

In March 2007, on an English Jewish website[345], a certain Leslie Bunder analyzed the annual *Forbes magazine* ranking of the largest fortunes, and drew some conclusions about Jewish billionaires. According to the American magazine, there were then 946 billionaires (in billions) in dollars in the world. The richest Jew in the world was casino king Sheldon Adelson, who "weighed" 26.5 billion dollars. He was the sixth richest man in the world. In eleventh position (the second richest Jew in the world), was Oracle owner Larry Ellison, with a

---

[343] Article by Jacques-Marie Vaslin published in *Le Monde* on September 17, 2012.
[344] Yuri Slezkine, *Le Siècle juif*, 2004, La Découverte, 200, p. 391.
[345] www.somethingjewish.co.uk

fortune estimated at 21.5 billion. Then came Russian oil tycoon Roman Abramovitch (18.7 billion) and Google co-founder Sergey Brin, with 16.6 billion. At 33, he was then the youngest billionaire on the planet. Michael Dell, the owner of the computer giant Dell, was 30th, with a fortune of 15.8 billion. Right behind him was Steven Ballmer, CEO of Microsoft, with 15 billion. A Russian oligarch, aluminum magnate Oleg Deripaska, weighed in at $13.3 billion. Other Jews had amassed fortunes of close to $10 billion: Sumner Redstone, the owner of Paramount movie studios (8 billion); British Philip Green, owner of BH and Top Shop (7 billion); banker Joseph Safra in Brazil with 6 billion and his brother (2.9 billion). Esther Koplowitz (5600 million) was "Spanish". Her sister Alicia "weighed" 5 billion, as did the American stylist Ralph Lauren (born Ralph Lifschitz) and the South African diamond magnate Nicky Oppenheimer and New York Mayor Michael Bloomberg. It would be pointless to continue with this list, which varies greatly from year to year.

A February 26, 2008 *Jerusalem Post* article informed us that Jews were the wealthiest religious group in the United States, with 45% of "six-figure incomes" per year, or at least $100,000, while the U.S. average was 18%.

In October 2009, we discovered the Forbes ranking of the 400 richest men in America, commented by Jacob Berkman: *"Some quick statistics: we are reasonably certain that 139 of the 400 richest Americans are Jewish, including 20 of the 50 richest.*[346]*.."* For a population that represented 1.5% of the total population, these figures were quite significant.

Billionaire Sam Zell was one of the biggest real estate speculators in the United States, where he owned 10 million square meters and 225,000 apartments. He had also invested in Venezuela, Brazil and Chile, in two power plants in China, one in Bangladesh and one in the Philippines. He was ranked 77th out of 400 in the 2009 *Forbes* ranking, with a fortune estimated at 3.8 billion dollars: In the weekly magazine *Marianne* of April 7, 2007, we read: *"Sam Zell made his fortune by buying up old rental buildings; he upgraded them thanks to his political connections; he raised rents, thus driving out tenants, especially the elderly. He just bought the Los Angeles Times, one of the most*

---

[346] *"Some quick stats: We are reasonably certain taht 139 of the richest 400 Americans are Jewish, including 20 of the richest 50."*

prestigious newspapers in the United States. Long live the American model." What bastards these "Americans" are!

In Australia, the same scenario. The *Jewish Telegraph Agency* of June 10, 2008 published this information: Frank Lowy, an Australian Jew, became *"the richest man in the country"*. He was, we were told, a Holocaust survivor who had fought for the State of Israel in 1948. He had then built his fortune by building shopping malls in the United States, the United Kingdom, Australia and New Zealand, although he had had some trouble with the Australian tax authorities. He defended himself by claiming that much of his money had been donated to charities in the State of Israel. Very patriotic, Lowy had founded in 2006 the Institute for National Security Studies in... Tel Aviv.

In 2009, we learned that the three largest family fortunes in Canada were Jewish: the Belzbergs of Vancouver, the Bronfmans of Montreal (now U.S. citizens) and the Reichmanns of Toronto[347].

We know that in the Russia of the 1990s, after the collapse of the Soviet system, a handful of oligarchs had grabbed almost all of the country's wealth. In his book *The Jewish Century,* Yuri Slezkine wrote: *"When the market economy was introduced, the ranks of private entrepreneurs, the liberal professions and all those who claim to prefer professional success to job security quickly swelled. Of the seven leading oligarchs who built huge financial empires on the rubble of the Soviet Union and dominated the Russian economy and media during the Yeltsin era, there was one son of a senior Soviet foreign trade official (Vladimir Potanin) and six Jews (Pyotr Aven, Boris Berezovsky, Mikhail Fridman, Vladimir Gusinsky, Mikhail Khodorkovsky and Aleksandr Smolensk) who built their fortunes "from scratch"*[348]*."*

By the end of 2008, with the financial crisis, several Russian billionaires had fallen down the ranks. According to the Russian daily Izvestia, Oleg Deripaska, the aluminum tycoon, Russia's richest man and the world's eleventh-richest, had seen his wealth melt down from more than 20 billion euros. Russia's second richest man, Roman Abramovitch had seen his portfolio of assets go from 23.5 billion to 3.3 billion dollars in six months. The fortune of the oligarchs was

---

[347] Edward S. Shapiro, 1992, *A Time For Healting: American Jewry After World War Two,* p. 117.
[348] Yuri Slezkine, *Le Siècle juif,* 2004, La Découverte, 200, p. 385. On the plundering of Russia, read *The Jewish Mafia.*

calculated according to the value of the shares they owned and the Moscow stock exchange had lost 65% that year. The "Russian" billionaires, who had built their empires thanks to bank loans guaranteed by their shares, were forced to sell their shares in companies at the worst possible time in order to repay their debts, estimated at 110 billion. Cornered by the banks, they even had to ask the Kremlin for $78 billion in advance to get through the crisis[349].

The *Forbes* ranking of March 2011 established that for the second consecutive year, the richest man in the world was not American but Mexican Carlos Slim (74 billion), ahead of Bill Gates (56 billion). In one year, the Mexican telecommunications king and his family had increased their wealth by more than 20 billion dollars. In third place was the famous investor Warren Buffet, with $50 billion, followed by the luxury industry with Bernard Arnault (France) ($41 billion), followed by Larry Ellison (United States) and Lakshmi Mittal (India).

For the powerful of the planet, the crisis had been forgotten, as the total number of billionaires was now 1210, an absolute record since this ranking existed. The United States was still in the lead with 413 billionaires, but now accounted for only 33% of the list compared to 40% in 2010 and 50% previously. Europe, in second position in 2010 with 248 billionaires, was overtaken by the Asia-Pacific region, with 332 billionaires.

Forbes magazine is usually published in different editions, such as Forbes Israel, which ranks the richest Jews in the world. In 2012, Larry Ellison, co-founder and Chairman of Oracle, topped the list with $36 billion. Behind him was Sheldon Adelson ($24.9 billion), who ranked fourteenth among the world's wealthiest. Next in order were New York Mayor Michael Bloomberg, the famous speculator George Soros, and Google co-founders Sergey Brin and Larry Page, whose mother is Jewish ($18.7 billion each; 24th in the world ranking). In the sixth and tenth position of the richest Jews, there was now the young Mark Zuckerberg, the founder of Facebook, followed by Michael Dell, etc. The article went on to name the Jewish billionaires residing in Israel: Roman Abramovitch (12.1 billion), Lev Blavatnikm, Ralph Lauren, Ron Lauder, David Azrieli and Haim Saban (2.9 billion each). According to Forbes, eighteen Israelis were billionaires in 2014.

---

[349] *Le Figaro,* December 26, 2008

The famous *Vanity Fair* magazine—owned by the Jewish Newhouse family—regularly publishes a list of the most influential, but not the richest, personalities in the United States (*"The new Establishment"*). On October 11, 2007, following the publication of a special issue, the *Jerusalem Post* published an article by Nathan Burstein, who wrote the following: *"This is a list of the most powerful people in the world. And of the hundred or so bankers and entertainment and media moguls who condition the lives of billions of humans, more than half (53%) of them are Jewish."* Burstein evoked the *"predominance"* of Jews, who made up less than 2% of the U.S. population. Seventeen of the surnames were actors, TV hosts who owed their notoriety to media owners.

American nationalist Michael Collins Piper shed some light on the matter: at the top of the list for the second year in a row was media baron Rupert Murdoch, whose mother was Jewish, although he never professed his Jewishness, despite being a fervent supporter of the State of Israel. Flanking his empire were the Rothschild, Oppenheimer and Bronfman families. Close behind is Warren Buffet, who, although not Jewish, is a close collaborator of the Rothschild family. Behind, in second place, was Steve Jobs, the (non-Jewish) co-founder of Apple and Pixar (a cartoon production company). The next Jews were the co-founders of Google, Sergey Brin and Larry Page.

Joseph Aaron, editor-in-chief of *The Chicago Jewish News*, wrote that it was a list of which his paper's readers could *"take special satisfaction and pride. It can be said that we are accepted in this society—yes, and it can be said that we have a lot of power... You have to talk about anti-Semitism as a thing of the past, and say that Jews should no longer be afraid to be visible and influential."*

Visible and influential" billionaires

These billionaires have a huge influence on the democratic game board, as they always know how to influence the candidate who will best defend their interests. In the United States, their influence is very visible during presidential elections, since the campaign can be financed by citizens or companies.

Thus, in 2008, the billionaire Sheldon Adelson, real estate developer and owner of large casinos, had contributed to the presidential campaign of John McCain, the Republican candidate opposing the Democrat Barack Obama. In the 2012 election, Adelson had pledged a total of $100 million to install Republican Mitt Rommey in the White

House. On that occasion, his running mate, Paul Ryan, had literally been summoned to the *Venetian* hotel-casino in Las Vegas: the billionaire wanted to evaluate the young congressman from Wisconsin. *"It is very likely that the subject of Israel has been put on the table,"* commented a close associate of the tycoon. The *Le Figaro* journalist added: *"Since Adelson demands that the candidates he helps become staunch defenders of the Jewish state, Ryan had to swear allegiance to Nevada's slot machine king[350]."* According to the Israeli daily *Haaretz*, the Las Vegas tycoon had created in 2007 the free daily *Israël Hayom*, with a daily circulation of more than 200,000 copies, with the main objective of supporting Israeli Prime Minister Benjamin Netanyahu, the head of the Israeli hard right.

As discreet as Sheldon Adelson, the brothers David and Charles Koch had also financially supported Mitt Romney's presidential campaign with all their financial might. With their $50 billion from oil revenues, they were America's fourth-largest fortune. David and Charles Koch were the founders of the *"Americans for Prosperity"* movement, close to Paul Ryan and the *"Tea Party"* movement which they planned to finance with 400 million dollars. On July 4, 2012, they had organized a sumptuous party at their family estate in the Hamptons, east of New York, on Long Island, which had brought together the entire Republican *establishment* of the East Coast, far from the cameras and the media hustle and bustle.

In 2008, the Democratic candidate, African-American Barack Obama, had been able to count on the support of other billionaires, most of them Jews from the Democratic fiefdoms of New York and Hollywood. From the time he ran for the Senate seat in 2004, Barack Obama had been sponsored by dozens of billionaires: Bill Gates of Microsoft, the richest man in the United States; Warren Buffet, Larry page (Google), Steve Balmer (Microsoft), filmmakers Steven Spielberg and George Lucas, Ken Griffin and Penny Pritzker (Hyatt Hotels), etc. Penny Pritzker, the finance director of his campaign, had raised $745 million.

Let us repeat: all the billionaires on the planet are not Jews, far from it; but Jews are vastly overrepresented compared to their proportion in the general population. They are also the fiercest speculators and financiers. More than a century ago, the Yiddish writer Sholem Aleichem rightly wrote in 1913: *"The biggest beasts and sharks of the stock market are*

---

[350] *Le Figaro*, August 24, 2012

mostly Jews. You can even count their surnames on the fingers of your hand: Rothschild, Mendelssohn, Bleichroeder, Yankl Schiff[351]."

Cosmopolitan bankers and socialist revolutionaries

We know that in Jewish families the weight of tradition and prohibitions force children to marry within the community. Even today, when a member of an orthodox family marries a gentile, the family celebrates a rite called *shib'ah*, a gathering that usually occurs after a death. To do *shib'ah*, means to declare that the person is considered dead in every way[352].

Jewish bankers, perhaps even more than the rest, give the impression of wanting to protect themselves from bad marriages, in order to preserve their secrets and estates. Some families are so suspicious that they promote marriages only within the extended family. The 1905 edition of the *Jewish Encyclopedia* informs us that of the 58 marriages in the Rothschild family, half (29) were between cousins.

The Warburg family was one of Germany's great banking dynasties at the beginning of the 20th century[353]. Based in Hamburg, the Warburg bank financed most German businesses, placed international loans and had worldwide links with other Israeli bankers.

A well-known Sephardic intellectual, Jacques Attali, has followed the evolution of the Warburg family by writing a biography of one of its members. In the mid-19th century, Attali wrote, *"the family now spreads its ramifications throughout Europe through an exceptional*

---

[351] Cholem-Aleikhem, *La Peste soit de l'Amérique*, 1913, Liana Levi, 1992, p. 295.
[352] Read in *Psychoanalysis of Judaism*.
[353] The Warburg family probably originated in Venice, where it was known as the family *of the Bank*. It is said that this same family was founded by the Spaniard Anselmo de Palenzuela. Anselmo *del Banco* was one of the wealthiest Sephardic Jews of the early 16th century. In 1513 he had obtained a letter from the Venetian government allowing him to lend money at interest, an activity especially restricted due to the prohibition of usury in the Catholic world. *From the Bank* he left with his family after new restrictions were imposed on Venetian financial institutions and the city's Jewish community. The family then moved to Bologna, and from there to the German city of Warburg, adopting the name of that city as their surname. Thus, the first known ancestor of the Warburgs was Simon von Kassel (1500–1566). After the Thirty Years' War, the Warburgs moved to Hamburg (wikipedia. NdT).

network of relations and a series of well-planned marriages: the Schiffs in Vienna, the Rosenbergs in Kiev, the Günzburgs in St. Petersburg, the Aschkenasi in Odessa, the Oppenheims, the Bischoffsheims and the Goldschmidt in Germany itself, are its relatives and associates." In 1870, Sigmund Warburg *"maintains excellent relations with Lionel Rothschild in London, with Pereire in Paris, with Günzburg in St. Petersburg and with Salomon Loeb in New York*[354]*."*

In 1871, Abraham Kuhn, who had founded a bank in New York with Salomon Loeb, returned to Germany to retire in Hamburg. There he met an ambitious young man, Jacob Schiff, whose father was a money changer in Frankfurt. As Jacob Schiff wished to settle in the United States, Abraham Kuhn introduced him to Salomon Loeb. Three years later, in 1875, Jacob Schiff married the latter's daughter, Therese, and became his main partner. He quickly established himself as the true owner of the "Kuhn Loeb" bank. And he remained so for half a century, becoming *"one of the richest men in America"*. In 1893, Jacob Schiff *"is the most celebrated Jew in New York, and one of the richest men in the world*[355]*."*

But back to the Warburgs of Germany: Charlotte Esther and Moritz Warburg had five children, including Max, Felix and Paul. At the age of thirty, Max asserted himself as the heir to the bank's business. He became a close friend of an influential Jew, Albert Ballin, who was then head of the large shipping company Hamburg-America Linie and confidant of Emperor Wilhelm II himself[356]. Paul, the younger brother, was the intellectual of the family, while Felix traveled the world. In 1893, in Frankfurt, Felix met one of Jacob Schiff's daughters who was vacationing in Europe with her family. The wedding between Felix Warburg and Frieda Schiff took place in New York in 1895. There, another idyll blossomed between Felix's brother Paul Warburg and Nina Loeb, the young sister of Frieda's mother. Paul would thus become his brother's uncle. A year later, Paul moved to New York and became a

---

[354] Jacques Attali, A man of influence, the life of Sigmund Warburg... Seix Barral, Barcelona, 1992, p. 45, 50.
[355] Jacques Attali, *A Man of Influence*, Seix Barral, Barcelona, 1992, p. 52, 59.
[356] *"The banker and the Hamburg shipowner take advantage of their respective relationships, and do not separate. The first private telephone line installed in Germany connects their respective offices. The two, from Hamburg, influence a powerful Empire, and make a lot of money by arranging loans and opening shipping lines for the benefit of the Reich."* Jacques Attali, *A Man of Influence*, p. 72.

partner in the Kuhn Loeb bank. Paul would have a son, James, who would become the sixth generation of Warburg bankers.

"Their alliances are therefore still very carefully studied: they marry among bankers, Jews in the case of those who are, in order to extend the empire, to prevent it from fragmenting, to keep the secrets of business within the narrowest circle. This rule is rarely overturned, and always with drama. In particular, a Jew or Jewess very rarely marries a non-Jew, even if he or she is a nobleman[357]."

Felix, very spendthrift, received all the New York high society in his Tudor castle, or in his five-storey palace on the prestigious Fifth Avenue, where the paintings of the great masters, the Dürer, the Rembrandt and the Boticcelli were piled up. He thus became the friend of Albert Einstein, among others. Paul, on the other hand, took his work very seriously, and worked closely with his brother-in-law Jacob Schiff.

The Warburgs were evidently very attentive to any manifestation of anti-Semitism in the world, especially in Russia. Jacques Attali wrote: *"They detest even more what they read from the pen of journalists or writers like Dostoevsky: 'Today, the Jew and his bank dominate everywhere, Europe and the Enlightenment, all civilization, socialism above all, for, with their help, the Jew will eliminate Christianity and destroy Christian civilization. Then there will be nothing left but anarchy. The Jew will rule the universe[358]...'"*

Max had remained in Germany and ran the house of origin: *"He feels German and only German,"* Attali tells us without joking, *"he was the very type of the court Jew, more German than the Germans, super-patriotic."* This façade patriotism, which we often find in Jews, essentially corresponds to the hatred they feel towards those who oppose their power; in this case it was fundamentally the Russian monarchy: *"The Jewish conscience of the family, somewhat dormant, awakens and becomes hatred towards the "Russian devil"."* The German Emperor Wilhelm II had been taken in by this very particular patriotism, being influenced by Max Warburg and Albert Balin. During his first interview with the emperor in 1903, Max Warburg had begged him to protest to the tsar against the "pogroms" in Russia. *"Otherwise,"* he tells him, *"the fragility of the Romanov dynasty will come to full light and revolutionary threats will spread. The emperor shrugs his shoulders,*

---

[357] Jacques Attali, *Un hombre de influencia*, Seix Barral, Barcelona, 1992, p. 69.
[358] Jacques Attali, *A Man of Influence*, Seix Barral, Barcelona, 1992, p. 62.

absolutely skeptical. The interview ends dryly[359]*."* But after the insurrectionary strike of 1905 which had shaken the power of the Tsar, the German Emperor called Max Warburg and admitted him into his circle of closest advisors[360].

In New York, Jacob Schiff, president of Kuhn Loeb and Co., was also working to overthrow the Russian monarchy, guilty of not giving the Jews the place they felt they deserved. Since 1894, "he has been *striving to organize a financial blockade of the Tsar, whom he calls "the enemy of humanity"*," wrote Jacques Attali. In 1905, he lent money to Japan in its war against Russia. *"He accepts with pleasure to finance this war*[361]*".* He also proposed to Max Warburg to jointly launch a loan to the German population for the war. A few months later, Japan's victory was complete and Japan took control of Manchuria and Korea.

In August 1914, at the beginning of World War I, the Kuhn Loeb Bank naturally chose the German side against Russia and raised the necessary credits. For his part, Felix Warburg was in charge of federating the main charitable organizations and, in 1916, he created the *Joint Distribution Committee*, which organized aid to the Jews of Eastern Europe (Jews only). The Kuhn Loeb bank had also provided funds to Lenin and Trotsky in order to travel to Russia and undermine their regime, considered by Jews around the world as the priority enemy. Collusion between bankers and Jewish revolutionaries was therefore natural[362].

The defeats of the Russian army against Germany precipitated the events, and in February 1917, the revolution broke out. On March 2, 1917, the Tsar abdicated. The priority enemy—i.e. the least democratic country and the least permeable to international financiers—was now the Empire of Wilhelm II. Curiously and almost by chance, a short time later, in April, the democracies finally succeeded in convincing the US

---

[359] Jacques Attali, *A Man of Influence*, Seix Barral, Barcelona, 1992, p. 71, 62, 72.
[360] A good prince should never surround himself with Jews, nor with people who have contacts with them.
[361] Jacques Attali, *Un hombre de influencia*, Seix Barral, Barcelona, 1992, p. 77.
[362] On December 12, 1918, the U.S. Navy Secret Service report on Paul Warburg read: "Warburg, Paul: New York City. Naturalized German citizen, 1911. He was decorated by the Kaiser in 1912, was vice chairman of the Federal Reserve Board. Large sums handled went out through Germany to Lenin and Trotsky. He has a brother who is a leader of the espionage system in Germany." "Kuhn, Loeb Company's documentation of the commitment to the establishment of Communism in Russia is too extensive to be cited here...", Eustace Mullins, *The Secrets of the Federal Reserve*, Ed. Digital White Moon, 2014, p. 197, 196. On the Bolshevik revolution read *The Planetary Hopes*.

government to declare war on Germany [363]. All the American newspapers controlled by the Jews turned against Germany and changed the American public opinion, until then pacifist. From good and peaceful, the Germans were now portrayed as ferocious beasts capable of cutting off the hands of innocent children. In Germany, the Jews suddenly changed their jackets: this was the famous "stab in the back", a famous phrase coined by the Germans. Everywhere, in all the cities of the Reich, socialist agitators from the ghettos proclaimed the world revolution. In November 1918, the situation was totally insurrectionary, even though no Allied soldier had set foot on German soil.

In June 1918, shortly before the armistice, Max Warburg was introduced to Friedrich Ebert, the future Social Democratic president of the Wiemar Republic. Jacques Attali himself revealed the duplicity of the banker, supposedly a "super patriot": *"Max impresses him. Ebert did not expect to see him so critical of the imperial regime, nor to agree with someone he has known as the emperor's most listened-to financial advisor for fifteen years[364]."*

We even see the evident complicity of the cosmopolitan bankers and the Jewish revolutionaries come to light: *"On November 5, 1918, a revolutionary committee takes power in Hamburg. Max Warburg's aura is of such a magnitude that the committee, having taken him hostage and pressured him to tell where the city's money is, protects his family, invites him to lunch in the Town Hall and listens to him as an advisor[365]."*

A few days after the November 11 armistice, Friedrich Ebert, as president of the provisional government, asked Max Warburg to head the German financial delegation at the peace treaty negotiations in Versailles.

---

[363] On the power of the lobby in the United States in 1917, read the testimony of Pierre Antoine Cousteau in *Jewish Fanaticism*. The entry of the United States into the war had been prepared since October 1916 by Lord Lionel Walter Rothschild, who was negotiating in exchange the establishment of a "Jewish home in Palestine" with England. On November 2, 1917, the British Foreign Secretary, Arthur James Balfour, wrote a letter to Lord Rothschild expressing Britain's support for Zionist projects. These negotiations nullified the peace initiatives launched by Germany in 1916. Read Benjamin Freedman's speech at the Willard Hotel (Washington DC) in 1961.
[364] Jacques Attali, *Un hombre de influencia*, Seix Barral, Barcelona, 1992, p. 100.
[365] Jacques Attali, *Un hombre de influencia*, Seix Barral, Barcelona, 1992, p. 101.

The Federal Reserve fraud

Paul Warburg was at the origin of the creation of the Federal Reserve in 1913. A few years earlier, in 1907, after a stock market crisis, he had published a small book entitled *Plan for a Central Bank*; the main objective was to ensure that there would always be a supply of credit available. Paul Warburg had given numerous lectures on the subject, and his efforts were becoming more and more concrete. In 1910, after receiving U.S. citizenship, the New York Bankers Association had officially endorsed his project, and in 1912 the newly elected President Wilson asked him to draft a text for submission to the nation's representatives. The bill, submitted to the Senate by Robert Owen and to Congress by Carter Glass, became known as the Owen Glass Act, adopted in December 1913.

The next day, December 24, 1913, the *New York Times* ran a headline in all caps on its front page, *"Wilson Signs Money Bill!"* It followed with another headline, *"Prosperity to be free. Will Help Every Class."* But on the inside pages, the paper summarized in a brief quote from a speech by Congressman Charles Lindbergh, the father of the celebrated aviator: *"The bill would establish the most gigantic Trust on earth."*

In his speech to the House of Representatives, Lindbergh had actually been much more blunt: *"This Act creates the most gigantic Trust in the land. When the President signs this bill, invisible government through the money power will be legalized. The people may not know it immediately, but the day of reckoning is only a few years away... The worst crime of the legislative of the ages is perpetrated by this banking bill... This is an inflation bill, the only question is the magnitude of the inflation."*

That same day, Jacob Schiff had written to Colonel Edward Mandel House, President Wilson's closest friend and most trusted advisor: *"My dear Colonel House: I want to say a word to you for the quiet, but undoubtedly effective work you have done in the interest of money legislation and congratulate you on the measure. I with good wishes, faithfully yours, Jacob Schiff*[366]*."*

The Owen Glass Act created twelve regional banks to defend the economic interests of their territories. But it was the New York Federal

---

[366] Eustace Mullins, *The Secrets of the Federal Reserve*, White Moon Digital Ed, 2014, p. 81, 83–84.

Reserve that set interest rates and controlled the daily supply of money and its price. The shareholders of this bank were therefore the real masters of the whole system. For many years, the identity of these shareholders had remained hidden, like a mystery. In his instructive book, *The Secrets of the Federal Reserve*, published in 1952, the researcher Eustace Mullins provided some clarifications:

"The Federal Reserve Bank of New York issued 203,053 shares, and, as filed by the Controller of the Currency, May 19, 1914, the large New York City banks took more than half of the outstanding shares. The National City Bank controlled by Rockefeller Kuhn, Loeb took the largest number of shares of any bank, 30,000 shares. First National Bank took 15,000 shares. When these two banks merged in 1955, they owned en bloc almost a quarter of the shares in the Federal Reserve Bank of New York which controlled the whole system and so they could appoint Paul Volckler or whomever they chose to be Chairman of the Board of Governors of the Federal Reserve."

The shareholders of these banks, who owned the shares of the New York Federal Reserve, de facto controlled the country. They were the *"Rothschilds of Europe, Lazard Frères (Eugene Meyer), Kuhn Loeb Company, Warburg Company, Lehman Brothers, Goldman Sachs, the Rockefeller family and JP Morgan interests. These interests have merged and consolidated in recent years, so control is much more concentrated[367]."*

"Not only did the Morgan-Kuhn, Loeb alliance buy dominant control of the stock of the Federal Reserve Bank of New York, with nearly half of the stock owned by the five New York banks under their control ... but they also persuaded President Woodrow Wilson to appoint one of

---

[367] Eustace Mullins, *The Secrets of the Federal Reserve*, White Moon Digital Ed, 2014, p. 94–95. [In the book, the author argues that there was a conspiracy involving Paul Warburg, Edward Mandell House, Woodrow Wilson, J.P. Morgan, Benjamin Strong, Otto Kahn, the Rockefeller and Rothschild families, and other European and American bankers, which led to the founding of the U.S. Federal Reserve System. Mullins argues that the Federal Reserve Act of 1913 contradicts Article 1, Section 8, Paragraph 5 of the U.S. Constitution, as it establishes a "central bank of issue" for the United States under the domination of international bankers and empowered to set U.S. interest rates. Mullins argues that World War I, the agricultural crisis of 1920 and the Great Depression of 1929 were provoked by international financial interests hoping to profit from conflict and economic instability. Mullins also recalls Thomas Jefferson's stubborn opposition to the creation of a central bank in the U.S. (wikipedia, NdT)].

the group, Paul Warburg, to the Federal Reserve Board of Governors[368]."

Each of the twelve Federal Reserve Banks had to elect one member to the Federal Advisory Committee that would meet with the Board of Governors of the Federal Reserve four times a year in Washington in order to be instructed on future monetary policy. This seemed to ensure good representation. But in practice, the president of the Saint Louis or Cincinnati bank would never contradict Paul Warburg or JP Morgan, *"when a scribbled note from either of them would be enough to plunge his little bank into bankruptcy."*

The Federal Reserve Bank, which was neither a "reserve" (since its task was to create the currency and not to hold it) nor "federal" (being owned by private shareholders), acquired enormous power: that of issuing laws to fix the interest rate, the money supply and the exchange rate of the currency.

During World War I, the fate of the nation rested in the hands of three members of the "chosen people": Eugene Meyer, appointed to head the War Finance Corporation; Bernard Baruch, who headed the War Industries Board; and Paul Warburg, the governor of the Fed. These three Israelites were the triumvirate that wielded unparalleled power in the country. They financed Woodrow Wilson's election campaign and got him re-elected in March 1917. And thanks to their advice, the peace candidate became an ardent warmonger.

When Paul Warburg resigned from the Board in 1918, he was replaced by Albert Strauss, a partner in the Seligman bank. Warburg had returned to his business at Kuhn Loeb Bank, although he continued to influence Fed policy as chairman of the Federal Advisory Committee. In December, President Wilson sailed for France with a delegation to attend the Peace Conference. He was accompanied by, among others, Bernard Baruch, JP Morgan, Thomas Lamont, Albert Strauss, Walter Lippman, Felix Frankfurter, Justice Brandeis of the Supreme Court, and Paul Warburg as chief financial advisor. In Versailles, where the peace treaty negotiations were taking place, he was able to meet his brother

---

[368]Eustace Mullins, *The Secrets of the Federal Reserve*, White Moon Digital Ed, 2014, p. 106–107. *"The Morgans had always been associated with the House of Rothschild."* Eustace Mullins, The Secrets *of the Federal Reserve*, p. 131.

Max, who was leading the German delegation, accompanied by businessmen[369].

In 1935, the ten-year term of the members of the Board of Governors of the Federal Reserve was extended to fourteen years. Thus, despite not being elected by the people, the CFOs remained in office for a cumulative period of three presidential terms.

With the "Owen Glass Act", the Federal State had abandoned to a cartel of private banks the right to issue its own currency. While the normal function of a central bank is to provide a public service of issuing money free of charge to the country's administration for the proper functioning of the economy, Paul Warburg's system had imposed a banking cartel that had arrogated to itself the right to mint the currency and lend it at interest to the State.

From now on, when the U.S. Treasury needed $1 billion, it would be obliged to borrow it from the big private banks. As Congressman Patman phrased it, *"The Federal Reserve gives a billion in dollar credit to the Treasury per bond, and has created out of thin air a billion dollars in debt which the American people are obliged to pay back with interest[370]."*

The indebtedness of the State makes the fortune of the bankers. Since the early 1990s, the US government debt has increased exponentially: $16.7 billion in 2013, 20% of which was held by the Federal Reserve. But the debt was actually more than $50 billion, if we added health care and pension expenses, which represented twenty times more than the country's annual budget. Obviously, this colossal amount, which continues to grow steadily, will never be repaid, but it allows high finance to dictate its law to the American people.

Since 1971, with the abandonment of the gold standard, the dollar was no longer convertible into gold and its value depended only on the confidence of investors in the government. In short, from now on, the credibility of the dollar rested solely on the political and military might of the United States. Needing the prestige of the State to establish the

---

[369] Eustace Mullins, *The Secrets of the Federal Reserve*, White Moon Digital Ed, 2014, p. 107, 218.
[370] Eustace Mullins, *The Secrets of the Federal Reserve*, White Moon Digital Ed, 2014, p. 325 (Money Facts, House Banking and Currency Committee, 1964, p. 9).

credibility of its currency, the bankers turned a blind eye to the exponential increase in its indebtedness and supported successive governments, contributing the sums necessary to finance wars and maintain the hundreds of military bases scattered around the planet.

5. A singular mentality

The vast majority of normally constituted human beings are content with little: taking care of their family, buying a small house, a summer vacation, some hobby or passion and doing sports and/or spiritual upliftment, satisfies them amply. Almost all of humanity—on all five continents—lives with little money and does very well that way. Only a tiny minority of human beings on this earth worship money, talk about it day and night or sleep dreaming of bathing in gold coins and bank bills. And for centuries, these people have essentially co-opted themselves into a small sect well known for its commercial fervor, its greed and its thirst for power.

Greg Smith was not part of this small sect. Originally from South Africa, a former scholarship student at Stanford University in the United States, he had nevertheless worked his way up the hierarchy at Goldman Sachs, where he rose to the position of "executive director of derivatives markets" in Europe, the Middle East and Africa. During his career, he had advised two of the world's leading *hedge funds*, five of the largest U.S. portfolio managers and three of the largest Middle Eastern and Asian sovereign wealth funds. His clients represented "*a total portfolio of over $1 trillion.*" But Greg Smith had gradually experienced some scruples about continuing to swindle them, so he decided to resign in March 2012. And he did so with a bang, announcing his departure in an article published in the *New York Times*. The newspaper *Le Monde* of March 14, 2012 picked up the story with the headline: "*Why I am leaving Goldman Sachs*". Greg Smith explained that he "*could not look the interns in the eye*" when he had to praise the work of his bank. He accused Goldman Sachs managers of taking clients for suckers, cretins, cash cows, and of only seeking to enrich themselves at their expense. He directly blamed the bank's CEO, Lloyd Blankfein, and its chairman, Gary Cohn, for having fostered this culture of contempt that could only, he said, lead the company to ruin. "*People who only care about making money can't keep this business afloat—nor keep the trust of their customers—for much longer.*"

Because of their upbringing, and also the old Christian background, the Goyim tend to have more scruples than Jews when it comes to swindling their fellow man, and they are also less likely to amass money. The hoarding fever that reigns on Wall Street has certainly tainted spirits—numerous managers of large banks are not Jewish—but it is clear that this predatory frenzy is not a legacy of our old European traditions, and even the most Judaically steeped Goyim seem restrained by old moral principles buried deep within them. Jews, on the other hand, are not restrained by any sort of "anti-commercial" morality. Their financial inventiveness and appetite for riches even seem to be enhanced by the pleasure they take in swindling a client or a competitor. Since they do not believe in hell, life after death or reincarnation, they are probably less subject to moral obligations than other peoples on Earth and more inclined to invest in their earthly sojourn.

Blessed are the gold coins

At the end of the first part of this book, we have seen how the Jews could consider the goyim in their holy book, the Talmud, which contains the teachings of the rabbis. In the Torah—i.e. in the divine word supposedly transmitted to Moses at Sinai and transcribed by him for the people of Israel (Genesis, Exodus, Leviticus, Numbers and Deuteronomy)—one can also find an explanation of this thirst for wealth that seems to animate many Jews. Jacques Attali, one of the main representatives of intellectual Judaism in France, gave us some explanations on the occasion of the release of his book entitled *The Jews, the World and Money*. In the magazine *L'Express* of January 10, 2002, he presented his work in this way: *"In the Bible, he explained, wealth is a way of serving God, of being worthy of him. One of the foundational texts says: "You shall love God with all your strength," and one of the commentaries* [midrash, Talmudic Gemara, NDT] *specifies: "This means with all your wealth." Therefore, "The richer you are, the more means you will have to serve God"... God asks him [Abraham] to be rich to serve Him. That is why Genesis (XIII, 2) proudly measures the progress of that wealth: Abraham was very rich in flocks, silver and gold... Isaac and Jacob confirm the need to become rich in order to please God. Isaac accumulates animals. "He grew richer and richer until he became extremely wealthy. He had large flocks of sheep, large herds of cattle and many slaves" (Genesis XXVI, 13–14). Next, Jacob "became very rich, he had many flocks, maidservants and menservants, camels and donkeys" (Genesis XXX, 43). God blesses his fortune and allows him to buy his right of entailed estate from his brother Esau, proof that everything is monetized, even for a plate of lentils371..."*

And to get rich nothing better than importing and exporting, and lending at interest. These two activities are closely related, and it is well known that from time immemorial the Jews played a prominent role in them. Long before the Christian era, Jewish bankers flourished throughout the Mediterranean. After the fall of Jerusalem in 586 B.C., *"we find then in Alexandria, together with some very powerful Jewish bankers, numerous communities,"* wrote Jacques Attali, confirming this widespread idea that Judaism is the source of the capitalist spirit: *"Their dispersion to Babylon and elsewhere makes them the ideal agents of international trade, and therefore of money lending, intimately linked to it... Some of them associated with the Phoenicians, had also the control of loans to international trade expeditions... In the archives found of one of the first credit houses of the world, in Babylon, the "house of Murashu", we find seventy Jewish names as well as contracts signed in equality between Jews and Babylonian businessmen372."*

Then, in the Muslim world, the situation would not change. The famous Jewish historian Leon Poliakov mentioned *"Arab sources about the bankers Josef ben-Pinchas and Aaron Ben-Imran who prospered in Baghdad under the caliph Al-Muqtádir (908–939). Ben-Pinchas and Ben-Imran ran a banking firm and enjoyed a large clientele of wealthy Jews, but also non-Jews, who gave them their capital on deposit."* They organized *"transactions and fruitful speculations"* and *"commanded the capture of black slaves on the coasts of Africa... Kings of finance in Baghdad and bankers to the Caliphs for a quarter of a century, Ben-Pinchas and Ben-Imran, although they were the first, were not the only ones373."* In Persia and Egypt, indeed, Jewish bankers and merchants exercised a similar dominance. Jacques Attali wrote: *"The caliphs recruited their advisors and economic experts only from among the*

---

[371] Jacques Attali, *Los judíos, el mundo y el dinero*, Fondo de cultura económica, 2005, Buenos Aires, p. 21-22, 23.
[372] Jacques Attali, *Un hombre de influencia*, Seix Barral, Barcelona, 1992, p. 18. "Thus, from the dawn of the coin ... the Jewish communities are installed along the lines of force of money. And when the Roman Empire is sighted, they organize themselves around the empires of the East, and become financiers of their commerce, and enlighten the capitalism of risk and profit, deploying calculation and reason and putting them at the service of an abstract form."
[373] Leon Poliakov, *Histoire de l'antisémitisme*, 1981, Calmann-Lévy, 1991, Points Seuil, vol. 1, p. 81, 82.

Jews374" A few centuries later, the Jews still dominated world finance with an iron fist. Attali wrote: *"In the Byzantine Empire, shortly after the heart of the world, the Jews become moneylenders with bail or with guarantee of precious stones, they control the minting of money, exchange, deposits and credit; later they are entrusted with the collection of taxes, an unpopular task if ever there was one. And having at their disposal, from community to community, the best information networks of the time, in Baghdad, Cairo, Alexandria or Fez, they impose themselves as advisors to the princes*[375]*."*

From the other side of the world, the Venetian merchant Marco Polo mentioned the prosperity and influence of Jewish establishments in China (1286). Some Arab travelers' accounts from the 9th century already told the same story[376].

In 12th century Spain, the situation was identical, for we see how in the deed of the Cid—that masterpiece of the popular Spanish epic—two Jews, Raquel and Vidas, are financiers and usurers. In the 14th century, wrote Leon Poliakov, *"the great Jewish financiers of Toledo and Seville, who controlled all the financial circuits of the kingdom, remained all-powerful at the court of Castile*[377]*."*

Abraham Leon, a Jewish Marxist intellectual born in Poland (his real surname was Wajnsztok), had studied this subject. In his book *The Materialist Conception of the Jewish Question*, he surrendered to the evidence: *"In Christian Spain, in Castile, the Jews are bankers, tax collectors, suppliers of the king. The royalty protects them because they provide it with economic and political support."*

Jews were less numerous in France, but still very influential as well: *"With the advent of King Philip Augustus (1180) and during the first years of his reign, the Hebrews were rich and numerous in France... In the 12th century, usury seems to be the main economic function of the Jews of France."*

---

[374] *L'Express*, January 10, 2002, p. 56-65.

[375] Jacques Attali, *A Man of Influence*, Seix Barral, Barcelona, 1992, p. 19. "There *is no more money lending than Judaizing, it is exaggeratedly said everywhere, and in many languages of the time "Judaizing" even means "charging interest", and this is not a very kind expression."*

[376] Leon Poliakov, *Histoire de l'antisémitisme*, 1981, Calmann-Lévy, 1991, Points Seuil, vol. 1, p. 13.

[377] Leon Poliakov, *Histoire de l'antisémitisme*, 1981, Calmann-Lévy, 1991, Points Seuil, vol. 1, p. 144.

In England, they were few thousands but enough, apparently, to raise tensions with the population. *"In England, at the time of King Henry II (in the second half of the twelfth century),"* wrote Abraham Leon, *"the Jews are already fully engaged in usury. They are generally very rich and their clientele consists of large landowners. The most famous of these Jewish bankers was a certain Aaron of Lincoln, very active at the end of the 12th century. King Henry II owed him £100,000, a sum equivalent to the annual budget of the kingdom of England at that time. Thanks to extremely high interest rates—ranging from 43% to 86%—an immense amount of land of the nobility had passed into the hands of Jewish usurers. But they had powerful and demanding partners. The kings of England supported Jewish business because it represented an important source of income for them. All loans contracted with Jews were levied with a 10% tax in favor of the royal treasury[378]."*

In Germany, they also practiced the slave trade from the East. *"The mainly commercial period extends to the middle of the 13th century. The Jews connected Germany with Hungary, Italy, Greece and Bulgaria. The slave trade was flourishing until the 12th century. So in the customs tariffs of Wallenstadt and Koblenz it was often stipulated that Jewish slave merchants had to pay for each slave 4 dinars. A document of 1213 said of the Jews of Laubach "that they were extraordinarily rich and that they trade with the Venetians, the Hungarians and the Croats"[379]."*

In Poland, *"the demands of the nobility and the clergy against Jewish usury became more and more pressing. An ecclesiastical congress held in 1420 asked the king for measures against the "great Jewish usury". In 1423, Ladoslas Jagellon promulgated the "Statute of Warta" prohibiting Jews from mortgage lending[380]."*

In Tsarist Russia, before the Bolshevik revolution, *"more than half of the credit, savings and loan institutions were in the Zone of residence"*, wrote Aleksandr Solzhenisyn, and *"in 1911, 86% of their members were Jews[381]"*. Thus, the situation was identical wherever there were Jews.

---

[378] Abraham Léon, *La Conception matérialiste de la question juive*, 1942, Chapitre 3, La période de l'usurier juif.
[379] Jews have always been, in all ages, the main slave traders. Read *The Jewish Mafia*.
[380] Abraham Léon, *La Conception matérialiste de la question juive*, 1942, Chapitre 3.
[381] Alexandre Soljenitsyne, *Deux Siècles ensemble*, Tome I, Fayard, 2002, p. 175, 333-335. This was confirmed by the Sephardic sociologist Edgar Morin: "Seventeen Polish banks out of twenty were Jewish-gentiles in the mid-nineteenth century" (*Le monde*

One could never finish evoking the role of Jewish financiers in history, from ancient Egypt to the triumph of the partners and managers of Goldman Sachs, through the saga of the famous Rothschild brothers who had established their dominance over the business world in the 19th century. The prodigious wealth of the Rothschild family was proverbial, and a topic of conversation throughout Europe[382].

Of the suffering of being a banker

Jewish intellectuals often use the excuse that Jews were forced into these financial activities, that the doors of the noble professions were closed and that, for centuries, they would have had no choice but to practice the profession of financier in order to survive. The famous physicist Albert Einstein also expressed this belief. He denounced the *"terrible injustice that has afflicted us since the Middle Ages. And it is that in those times the Jews were forbidden to engage in directly productive professions, forcing them to the purely mercantile[383]."*

Michel Wieviorka is one of those sociologists pampered by the French republic and the media. He is director of research at the Ecole des Hautes Etudes en Sciences Sociales: it is a comfortable and well-paid job. In his new book *Anti-Semitism Explained to Young People* (2014), this brilliant intellectual wrote about the situation of Jews before the French Revolution of 1789: *"Jews have no right to belong to corporations, to exercise some trades. They are confined to certain professions, for example in the pecuniary professions (lending at interest, forbidden to Christians). Sometimes they must wear a distinctive mark*384."

---

moderne et la queston juive, Seuil, 2006, p.117). On the Zone of residence, read *The Jewish Fanaticism*.

[382]"*James Rothschild's wealth had reached 600 million marks. Only one man in France possessed more. That was the King, whose wealth was 800 million. The summed wealth of all the bankers in France was 150 million less than that of James Rothschild. This naturally gave him incalculable powers, including the magnitude to overthrow governments whenever he chose to do so. It is well known, for example, that he overthrew the Cabinet of Prime Minister Thiers.*" Eustace Mullins, *The Secrets of the Federal Reserve*, White Moon Digital Ed. 2014, p. 143. Mullins was quoting David Bruck, *Baron Edmond de Rothschild*.

[383]Albert Einstein, *My view of the world*, speech delivered in London, Titivillus digital ed. 2016, p. 105.

[384] Michel Wieviorka, *L'Antisémitisme expliqué aux jeunes*, Seuil, 2014, p. 23.

The prolific Jacques Attali, who was an advisor to Socialist President François Mitterrand before becoming an advisor to Liberal President Nicolas Sarkozy, also fed this thesis: *"The corporations, which have become omnipotent, exclude them from the artisanal professions, even from the least sought-after trades... Then, in many parts of Europe, there is practically nothing left for them but the horse trade, the butcher's trade and, above all—tragic quagmire—that of moneylender, a strategic trade in this phase of nascent capitalism and the constitution of nations. As they are forced to exercise it, they are going to do it to the point of exhaustion. To their greatest misfortune. Once again, they will be useful and they will hate them for services rendered[385]."*

We also see him shed some tears for the poor Jewish bankers of the Middle Ages. They were *"by the force of things forced to lend money to the princes to attract their protection, at the risk of being creditors of the powerful to guarantee their freedom, knowing that they multiply at the same time the risk of ending up as scapegoats, and having learned, in four thousand years of suffering, to articulate a moral and an action[386]."* All Jewish historians repeat this fallacious discourse ad nauseam.

However, the truth compels us to say that no one has ever prevented the Jews from cultivating the soil, from being carpenters, or blacksmiths. Indeed, it is the Talmud that forbids them to cultivate foreign soil, and their own traditions impel them to engage in import trade and usury, and not any unknown prohibition of Gentile societies. But readers of our previous books know that Jewish intellectuals, driven by their *"chutzpah"*—that immeasurable impudence that is foolproof in every way—never hesitate to utter the greatest falsehoods to deceive the goyim.

In his perfectly documented study entitled *The Jews and Economic Life*, published in 1911, the eminent German historian Werner Sombart denounced the *"myth according to which the Jews would have been forced, during the European Middle Ages and especially "since the Crusades", to engage in usury because all other professions were forbidden to them. The two-thousand-year history of Jewish usury, prior to the Middle Ages, suffices to demonstrate the falsity of that*

---

[385] Jacques Attali, *Los judíos, el mundo y el dinero*, Fondo de cultura económica, 2005, Buenos Aires, p. 167.
[386] Jacques Attali, *Un hombre de influencia*, Seix Barral, Barcelona, 1992, p. 11.

historical construction." Sombart then presented some examples: *"During the Middle Ages and later, we often see governments endeavoring to steer Jews into other careers, but without success. This is what happened in England under Edward I, in Posnania in the 18th century, where the authorities tried by means of bonuses and other means to encourage Jews to take up other careers*[387]*."*

But despite all those efforts, the Jews had remained merchants and usurers.

Abraham Leon had the honesty to admit it: *"In many writings about the economic life of the Jews in the Middle Ages, it is said that they were excluded, from the beginning, from craftsmanship, from the trade of goods and that they were forbidden to own real estate. These are but legends... It is just as false to assert that Jews could not be admitted to craft guilds... Certainly, there were few Jewish blacksmiths or carpenters among the craftsmen in the Middle Ages: the Jewish fathers who gave their sons to apprenticeship in those trades were very few. Even the guilds that excluded Jews did not do so out of religious animosity or racial hatred, but because the professions of usurers and peddlers were reputed to be "dishonest". Corporations excluded the children of Jewish businessmen, usurers, and peddlers, just as they did not accept into their midst the children of simple laborers, boatmen, and linen weavers*[388]*."*

The great Russian writer Aleksandr Solzhenisyn recalled that several government measures had been taken to promote Jewish agriculture in Russia. At the beginning of the 19th century, the authorities had allocated more than 30,000 hectares for this purpose. These were lands in southern Ukraine, some of the most fertile in Europe, which had been given to them in hereditary ownership. Each Jewish family had received 40 hectares of land from the State, when in Russia the average peasant's plot rarely exceeded ten hectares. In addition, they had been granted money loans and offered to build them wooden izbas. This program was however cancelled in 1810. In 1812, it turned out that of the 848 families settled, only 538 remained. The tools had been lost, broken or pawned, the oxen had been slaughtered, stolen or sold, and the fields sown too late. Solzhenitsyn thus explained to us the mentality of some

---

[387] Werner Sombart, *Les Juifs et la vie économique*, 1911, Payot, 1923, p. 401. His economic study is a reference, but his chapter on psychology seems to us mediocre.
[388] Abraham Léon, *La Conception matérialiste de la question juive*, 1942, Chapitre 3, La période de l'usurier juif.

of these "shock" farmers: they feared that if it was demonstrated that the Jews were *"capable of working the land,"* they would end up *"by forcing them to do so389."*

Already in the 13th century, in his Summa Theologica (1273), the great Catholic theologian Thomas Aquinas had written, after careful examination, *"It would be better to force the Jews to work for a living, as is the case in some regions of Italy, rather than let them live in idleness and enrich themselves only by usury[390]."*

The purchase of a protection

Naturally, as everyone knows, we find Jewish financiers and their usury throughout the history of anti-Semitism. From time immemorial, Jews have been expelled from everywhere, from all countries, from the highest Antiquity. Among the accusations against them, we always find the practice of lending at interest, fraud, theft and swindling, in addition to their incessant mockery of the dominant religion. They hoarded wealth, ruined the peasants, took their property without scruple, always trying to buy the favor of the princes, asking them in return for their protection against the common people, always eager to disembowel them.

The Jews were expelled or massacred by the Egyptians, by the Babylonians, by the Persians, as well as by the Greeks and the Romans. And in the following centuries, Christian states and Muslims acted in the same way towards them. They were expelled from England in 1290; expelled from France in 1306, but reintroduced by a weak king and again expelled in 1394. They were expelled from Spain in 1492, from Provence at the same time, from the Italian cities and states, from Hungary, Austria and all the German principalities, although they managed to return shortly afterwards. The Ukrainians massacred them in the following century. They were again expelled from Moscow in 1891, before returning as lords and masters in 1917. Only the great constituted States (England, France and Spain) had managed to get rid of them permanently. Most of the time, in fact, the Jews managed after a few years to reintroduce themselves in the square, usually thanks to a

---

[389] Alexandre Soljenitsyne, *Deux siècles ensemble, Tome I*, Fayard, 2002, p. 79-86. Read in *Jewish Fanaticism*.
[390] Quoted in Leon Poliakov, *Histoire de l'antisémitisme*, 1981, Calmann-Lévy, 1991, Points Seuil, vol. 1, p. 282.

weak king or a power vacuum. That proves how much interest they had in returning, despite the hostile environment.

Jewish historians are in the habit of making us believe that the Jews were indispensable, and that the people demanded their return and welcomed them with tears in their eyes, asking for their forgiveness. Listen to the "great" historian Leon Poliakov tell us about those *"once helpful and familiar moneylenders whose return the people demanded."* Sometimes Jewish intellectuals turn the equation around and pretend that the princes expelled the Jews and then called them back just to get money. *"The kings of France expelled and took in Jews several times to confiscate their property[391]"*, wrote Abraham Leon.

Obviously, such remarks should be taken with a smile. Throughout their history, the Jews always tried to corrupt the princes in order to buy the right to return to the country and continue—under the protection of the authorities—to practice their favorite activity which was usury (i.e. lending with abusive interest). After a few decades, the same script was repeated: popular exasperation broke out in the form of an insurrection against the vampires and the Jews were expelled once again ... while waiting for a new readmission by paying a good amount of gold coins. This tragicomic story, as ridiculous as it is pathetic, has been repeating itself for 3,000 years...

The states that relentlessly expelled the Jews experienced a period of splendor: France expanded until the Revolution; Spain experienced a golden age after 1492. On the contrary, Poland, which had welcomed Jews expelled from everywhere in the Middle Ages and in modern times, finally collapsed completely and was torn to pieces by its neighbors at the end of the 18th century.

The Jewish historian Abraham Leon rebelled against the thesis of the German Werner Sombart, who tends to believe that the prosperity of a city or a nation depends on the presence of Jewish merchants, because undoubtedly Jews have also played and continue to play a crucial role in the history of capitalism. The commercial and financial power of the Netherlands in the 17th century was due, if not entirely then in large part, to the presence of all those Sephardic Jews expelled from Spain with all their assets.

---

[391] Abraham Léon, *La Conception matérialiste de la question juive*, 1942, Chapitre 3, La période de l'usurier juif....

The great French historian Fernand Braudel, who had represented in his time the Annales School (a historical school that studies civilizations in the long term, as opposed to the history of events[392]), had given an account of this evidence. In his voluminous work *Material Civilization, Economy and Capitalism, 15th-18th Centuries*, Braudel wrote about those Jews expelled from Spain in 1492 and refugees in Amsterdam: *"The Sephardic Jews, in particular, contributed to the progress of Holland. Nobody doubts that they provided a serious support to the city, in the field of the changes and still more in that of the stock market speculations. They were masters in these activities, and even their creators*[393].*"*

But Abraham Leon rightly noted that the great majority of the Jews expelled from Spain in 1492 had taken refuge in the Ottoman Empire (Salonica, Istanbul, etc.). *"It is there that the "capitalist spirit" of the Jews should have produced its greatest effects."* However, this was not the case. "Therefore *Sombart's theory is completely false*," concluded Abraham Leon, perhaps a bit hastily.

In Germany, the Jews had remained very influential. The Holy Roman Germanic Empire, which was divided into 350 quasi-independent principalities, had not been able to rid itself of its Jews as radically as England, France and Spain had done: Jews who were expelled from one principality immediately found refuge in the neighboring duchy or kingdom, and waited for the right moment to return in exchange for hard cash. By the 17th and 18th centuries, some Jews had risen to prominent positions thanks to their financial skills. Among the so-called "palace Jews "(*Hofjuden*), the most famous was undoubtedly Joseph Ben Issachar Süß kind Oppenheimer, who lived in the first half of the 18th century and was the chief advisor to the Duke of Württemberg (opposite Alsace). Already at that time, this individual had been the

---

[392] The *Annales* School is a historiographical current founded by Lucien Febvre and Marc Bloch in 1929, which has dominated practically all French historiography in the 20th century and has had an enormous diffusion in the Western world. It is named after the French journal *Annales d'histoire économique et sociale* (later called *Annales. Economies, sociétés, civilisations*, and again renamed in 1994 as *Annales. Histoire, Sciences sociales*), where his approaches were first published. The "Annales Current" develops a history that is not interested in the political event and the individual as protagonist typical of the work of contemporary Historiography, but in processes, social structures, and then in a wide range of topics whose approach with the methodological tools of the Social Sciences allowed him to study. (wikipedia, NdT).

[393] Fernand Braudel, *Civilización material, economía y capitalismo, siglos XV-XVIII*, volume III, Alianza Editorial, 1984, Madrid, p. 150.

target of numerous pamphlets denouncing his actions and his crimes. Before World War II, the propaganda services of the National Socialist regime made a film about this financier, inspired by the novel published in 1925 by a Jewish writer named Lion Feuchtwanger. In this book about the life of the "Jew Süss", written by a member of the sect that tried to hide or minimize some aspects of the "Jewish problem", we could read the following:

"Süss had confidants and spies everywhere, and whoever rose up against him could be sure to spend the rest of his life locked up in a gloomy dungeon in Neuffen Castle... Süss already publicly flaunted his power and showed it clearly, just as he flirtatiously and boastfully displayed his mastery of the courtly and society arts... Apart from this, he made a great effort to be the center of courtly events. There was no foreigner in the States who came to Stuttgart and did not pay his respects to the all-powerful favorite... Ministers and high officials had before him a slavish respect. They feared him almost more than the duke. At a whistle from him, they all rushed to him. At the slightest resistance he threatened to have them locked up or flogged or buried under the gallows... Of course, Süss also had the duke in his power... So he blindly followed any advice of his director of finance... He had relations with all the financiers of Europe and through his innumerable agents, mostly Jews, Swabian money flowed through the most complicated channels... He controlled industry and commerce in every nook and corner of Europe, and an important part of the entire German patrimony passed through his chests[394]*"*

In the second part of the novel, we also find these considerations: *"With a grim and boundless ironic arrogance, he managed all those around him and made the ministers run as if they were fried lackeys. He emanated from him a violent and sarcastic contempt for everything that meant human dignity, freedom and responsibility... He plundered, openly and without measure, the ducal treasury. He attributed commissions to himself and sold to the duke, at a colossal price, valueless objects. He imposed on the duchy, groaning and exhausted,*

---

[394] Lion Feuchtwanger, *El Judío Süss*, Edhasa, Barcelona, 1990, Editorial Sudamericana (Pdf), p. 97-100.

new burdens, and what he extracted from it he deposited without concealment in his private coffers and not in the duke's[395]."

Thus, fatally, a reaction was to be expected, which our present-day politicians would describe as "anti-Semitic". And what was bound to happen happened: Joseph Süss Oppenheimer met with stiff resistance, appeared in court and ended his life hanging from a rope.

The author of the novel, Lion Feuchtwanger, told us on the other hand that: *"In the cities on the shores of the Mediterranean and the Atlantic Ocean, the Jews were great and powerful. They were the intermediaries in the exchange between East and West. They reached beyond the sea[396]."*

We do not know if they were already importing Chinese frying pans, canapés and leather jackets to Europe at that time, but their political, commercial and financial practices were certainly not very popular on the continent.

The palatial Jews, bankers and advisers to the princes should not make us lose sight of the fact that the vast majority of Jews lived much more modestly. However, it remains true that the Jews, today as in the past, are generally and proportionally richer than the rest of the population. Werner Sombart demonstrated with statistics that in Germany, in the seventeenth and eighteenth centuries, Jews were *"several times richer"* than Christians. *"Especially instructive are the figures referring to the towns of Upper Silesia or the city of Posen, where the Jews are six times richer than the rest of the population."* And Werner Sombart added: *"Even in Russia and Galitzia where the Jewish communities are generally very poor, they are always richer than the Christian population among whom they live[397]."* Werner Sombart finally pointed out this evidence: *"From King Solomon to Gerson Bleichröder and Barnato, Jewish wealth runs through history like a golden thread."*

---

[395] Lion Feuchtwanger, *El Judío Süss*, Edhasa, Barcelona, 1990, Editorial Sudamericana (Pdf), p. 215-216.
[396] Lion Feuchtwanger, *El Judío Süss*, Edhasa, Barcelona, 1990, Editorial Sudamericana (Pdf), p. 121.
[397] Werner Sombart, *Les Juifs et la vie économique*, 1911, Payot, 1923, p. 243.

Interest-bearing loan

Jewish historians never tire of repeating that Jewish financiers were indispensable to the proper functioning of the economy because lending at interest was forbidden in Christendom and in the Muslim world. It is true that in the Christian Europe of the Middle Ages, lending at interest was frowned upon. The Fathers of the Church, and after them theologians, relied on the Old Testament (Exod. 22, 24; Leviticus, 25, 33–37; Deuteronomy, 23, 20; Psalms XV) and on the Gospel of St. Luke (lending without expecting anything in return).

"To a foreigner you may lend with interest, but to your brother you shall not lend with interest," one can read in Deuteronomy. Jews interpret the text in the simplest way in the world. Naturally, Jacques Attali evoked lending with interest several times in the pages of his book. In essence, he said: *"There is no reason to prohibit lending with interest to a non-Jew, since interest is nothing more than the mark of the fertility of money. On the other hand, among Jews, one should lend without interest, in the name of charity. It is even prescribed, respecting the very poor, to lend at a negative rate of interest."* But beware: *"Wealth is a means, not an end[398]."*

Lending with interest is practically an obligation for Jews, recommended by their sages. Of the 613 commandments (*Mitzvah*) of

---

[398] *Interest (which is called neshej, or "slice, bite") is forbidden within the community, because in the community, lending is considered a form of solidarity between brothers, not a commercial operation"; "Outside the community, which demands solidarity and charity, interest is authorized because there is nothing immoral about it". No one is obliged to consider the stranger as a potential pauper. Nor do non-Jews run the risk of being expelled."; "For Jews to obtain interest on money is not immoral; and if it should not be done among Jews, it is out of a sense of solidarity, not because of moral prohibition. Like cattle, money is a fertile wealth"; "(...)To lend at interest to non-Jews is, for all Jews, an obligation, a moral duty. The Talmud authorizes in all cases lending at interest to non-Jews"; "The judges then authorize Jewish moneylenders to group together to raise the funds they must lend to Christians. Thus, lending at interest between Jews becomes possible, provided that the ultimate borrower is a Christian."; "For Rabbi Judah Loew, the right to lend at interest stems from the fact that the numerical value of the word "interest" (ribit) is 612: in his view, this proves that in itself lending is tantamount to obeying the 613 obligations of the Law."; "(...) wealth is a means to better serve God ... money can be an instrument of good ... anyone can enjoy well-earned money ... to die rich is a blessing, if the money was acquired morally and one has performed all one's duties towards the poor of the community...".* In Jacques Attali, *Los judíos, el mundo y el dinero*, Fondo de cultura económica, 2005, Buenos Aires, p. 45, 66, 91, 121, 144, 233, 90.

the law that a pious Jew must obey, commandment 545 obligates him to lend with interest to the goyim, inversely to how he must treat his "neighbor": *"To the gentile you shall inflict a usurious bite and to your brother you shall not inflict a usurious bite,"* one can read in the Talmud[399].

To the foreigner it is therefore permitted, even recommended, to demand interest, since he is not a brother or a neighbor. For Christians, on the other hand, the text is read differently, since Jesus Christ came to proclaim the law of universal love. In Christianity all human beings are considered as brothers, there is no longer any distinction between the fellow citizen and the stranger.

In 325, the Council of Nicaea forbade any kind of pecuniary traffic to clerics. The prohibition gradually became generalized and was extended to the laity. At the end of the 8th century, in the chapter of 82 articles called *Admonitio generalis* (general exhortation), promulgated on March 23, 789, the emperor Charlemagne imposed the prohibition of lending with interest. The Third Council of Latran (1179), the Fourth Council of Latran (1215), the Second Council of Lyon (1274) and the Council of Vienna (1311) consolidated these principles over time. But long before the Christian era, Aristotle had already condemned lending at interest: *"As for lending at interest, it is rightly hated, because it derives its profit from money itself and not from that for which it was introduced. Money, in fact, was made for the sake of exchange, but in the loan we say interest multiplies money. (By this property interest has received the name it has, for as children are similar to their parents,*

---

[399] *"The prohibition against paying interest to one's brother is explicitly written in the continuation of the same verse in Deuteronomy: "Thou shalt not lend to thy brother with interest." Therefore, it is not necessary to learn this halachah [Jewish law] from inference. The Gemara answers: It is necessary in order to teach that if one pays interest to a Jew, he violates both the positive mitzvah of paying interest to a gentile but not to a Jew, and the prohibition against paying interest to a Jew. The Gemara answers: It does not mean that borrowing money with interest is a mitzvah; rather, the verse mentions paying interest to a gentile to the exclusion of your brother, to teach that although one may pay interest to a gentile, one may not pay interest to a Jew... One may borrow money from them and lend them money with interest. Similarly, with regard to a Ger Toshav [foreigner residing in Israel], one may borrow money from him and lend it to him with interest, since he is not a Jew. The mishnah indicates that a Jew may lend money with interest to a gentile from the outset."* Talmud Bava Metzia 70b, at www.sefaria.org. (NdT).

interest turns out to be money money). Of all the species of traffic it is therefore the most contrary to nature[400].*"

However, it did not seem possible to envision an economic growth of society without recourse to credit, especially since monetary circulation in the Middle Ages was very small. In the absence of Christians, Jews, who were not subject to these prohibitions, played the role of creditors. But very soon, some Christians invented forms and operations that circumvented the measures against usury, through a disguised system of pledge credit or through the solution of the "dead man's guarantee", an agreement by which the debtor ceded an inheritance to the creditor in compensation for the interest on the debt and for which the lender could receive income.

In Charlemagne's time, long-distance commercial transactions were rare; but later, with the commercial awakening of the West, it became indispensable to resort to forms of payment that did not involve the transport of large sums of cash. It was in Genoa, in the middle of the 12th century, that the exchange contract appeared, and here too the interest was concealed[401]. The system was very simple: by means of a notarial contract, an Italian merchant-banker advanced to a merchant visiting a trading post—especially the Champagne fairs—a sum of money in foreign currency in exchange for Genoese denarii; the sum in foreign currency was always specified in round numbers: one hundred, two hundred, three hundred ... denarii of Provins, a fair currency. In this way, the commission or interest on the transaction did not appear. Thus, these merchants were sometimes bankers themselves, with capital mainly of family origin, to which would later be added deposits from private individuals, which they would be responsible for bringing to fruition. At the end of the 12th century, the Piedmontese merchants

---

[400] Aristotle, *Politics, Book One, III.*

[401] The contract of exchange was at the origin of all banking activity and bills of exchange. This is demonstrated by the documents and writings of jurists and theologians who have dealt with the question of usury and the exchange contract. The most common at the beginning was the *cambium minutum* or manual exchange. The *cambium minutum* was practiced mainly by money changers who exchanged gold coins for money or foreign currency for local money. In exchange for his services, the money changer received a commission that was very modest and was called "ventaja camba". Exchange contracts in the Middle Ages were holographic documents, i.e., written entirely in the drawer's handwriting, but they were not negotiable and did not circulate in the form of an endorsement until the early 17th century in Flanders. Prior to the early 17th century, bills of exchange were not discounted, but were bought and sold at a price determined by the exchange rate. (NdT)

were joined by Tuscan, Sienese and then Florentine merchants. Italian merchants from Lombardy arrived at the Champagne fairs, where they met merchants from the northern countries, the Flemish and Germans. The term "Lombard" came to designate an Italian merchant who engaged in the practice of money trading, later becoming synonymous with usurer. His financial activity included both capital transfers and bank loans, to the great scandal of the Church, but with the complicity of the King of France and the great men of the kingdom. St. Louis and Philip III, hostile to the Jews, had favored and encouraged these merchant-bankers to take their place, while the ecclesiastical authorities did not fail to condemn them to the flames of hell[402].

The practice of lending at interest developed progressively with the commercialization of the economy and the rise of the bourgeoisie, although the princes always exercised their authority in the matter. From the 15th century onwards, banks, trading companies and manufactures were able to pay interest on borrowed funds, with the king's permission.

In the 16th century, the Protestant theologian John Calvin was the first in Christendom to admit lending at interest. This practice spread like lightning throughout Calvinist cities and countries such as Geneva, the Netherlands and England.

Imbued with Old Testament ideas and fascinated by Judaism, Protestants—especially Anglo-Saxon and Dutch Calvinist Protestants—in turn thought that the accumulation of wealth was a divine blessing.

In his essay entitled *The Protestant Ethic and the Spirit of Capitalism* (1905), Max Weber noted that, in Germany, the richest families were the Jews, followed by the Protestants and finally the Catholics. In the year 1895, in the State of Baden, an income subject to income tax was

---

[402] In Perugia, in 1462, some Franciscan monks had succeeded in convincing the city's wealthy to set up a pawnshop, the *"Monte di Pietà"*. This lent money for free or at a very low interest rate. The "Monte di Pietà" spread throughout Italy and Europe. The French and Spanish term comes from a bad translation of the Italian *"monte di pietà"*; from *monte* (value, amount, sum) and *pietà* (piety, charity). It should have been translated as *"credit of charity"*.

calculated at 4 million marks for 1000 Jews, 954,060 marks for 1000 Protestants, and 589,000 marks for 1000 Catholics[403].

Among Calvinists, the propensity for commercial and banking professions and enrichment by all means was an even more evident reality. Werner Sombart quoted a passage from a 17th century *"burlesque pamphlet"*—from 1608—entitled *The Jewish Mirror of Calvinism*, the content of which shows the spiritual links between Puritanism (Calvinism) and Judaism. The author, apparently, knew how to handle irony: *"If I am to say on my honor and in all truth why I became a Calvinist, I must confess that there is no other reason than this: no other religion comes so close to Judaism in its way of solving religious and life problems."*

The author then quoted *"half seriously, half satirically,"* wrote Werner Sombart, the similarities between Judaism and Calvinism: *"The Jews hate the name of Mary, and only put up with her when she is made of gold and silver or stamped on coins; we too have little regard for Mary, but we are far from despising the coins on which her image is reproduced, and we gladly sell her gold and silver statues in our stores."*

And also, *"Jews sneak into every country to deceive people; we do the same: we leave our homeland and go to other countries, where we are unknown, so that we can, with our trickery and lies, exploit people all the more easily because they do not distrust us*[404]*."*

This alliance of the Anglo-Saxon Puritans and the Jews, which was nourished by the sap of the Old Testament, was the true matrix of the capitalist, liberal and cosmopolitan society which tends, today, to expand over the whole planet. The triumph of the cosmopolitan spirit is due to this symbiosis, at once religious and vilely materialistic, which represents contemporary cosmopolitanism, that is to say the Jewish and Protestant realism of capitalism which maintains that profit is the motor of Creation[405].

---

[403] Max Weber, *La ética protestante y el espíritu del capitalismo* (1905), Alianza Editorial, Madrid, 2001, note 4 page 44.
[404] Werner Sombart, *Les Juifs et la vie économique*, 1911, Payot, 1923, p. 322.
[405] On the links between Protestantism and Judaism, read *Jewish Fanaticism* (2007). And on Jewish contagion in Protestantism, read *The Eschatological War* (2013).

Pathological rapacity

It would be naive to think that the tendency of some Jews to accumulate wealth depends solely on the teaching of religious precepts. The truth is that this religion is the expression of ancient pre-existing dispositions, the origin of which must be sought in the very particular history of the sect: money is for them above all a means of corrupting the authorities in order to ensure their survival in a hostile environment. But in order to understand the root of the problem, one must study the psychological background that determines these accumulative impulses in the Jews. Indeed, there exists in the depths of the Jewish soul a latent paranoia that leads them to build walls to protect themselves from the hostility of millions of goyim living around them, who apparently have only one desire: to kill Jews! This mentality was very well summed up by this comment by a certain Christian Boltanski: *"The war in France has taught me that our neighbor has only one desire: to kill us. That our neighbor, extremely kind and sympathetic, can murder us the next day, that the same man who embraced his children in the morning can kill others in the afternoon*[406]*."*

Twenty years earlier, community leaders did not see the world differently. In 1978, for example, *Le Droit de vivre,* the organ of the *League against anti-Semitism* (Licra), carried a front-page headline: *"Defeating anti-Semitism to avoid the worst"*. In 1991, its president declared: *"We have a right to be worried. I have the impression that we are in 1934 or 1938*[407]*."* In our previous books, we have shown that this Jewish restlessness was chronic and permanent for centuries, and that the cause should be sought not only in its history, but above all in psychoanalysis[408].

Jewish literature offers several examples of characters animated by greed and the unbridled pursuit of power. Irene Nemirovsky, a novelist originally from a family of Jewish bankers, left us in her books the portrait of powerful characters she had met in her native Ukraine. In her novel *David Golder*, published in 1929, she described an émigré banker in Paris (like her own father) thus: *"In London, in Paris, in New York,*

---

[406] *L'Arche*, *"Le mensuel du Judaïsme français"*, June 1995 issue, in *The Mirror of Judaism*.
[407] In *The Mirror of Judaism*, chapter *The Jewish Jeremiad*.
[408] Read the third parts of *Psychoanalysis of Judaism* (2006) and *Jewish Fanaticism* (2007). And *The Mirror of Judaism* (2009).

when David Golder was named, people thought of a tough old Jew who had been hated and feared all his life, who had crushed everyone who had crossed his path[409]."

David Golder did business with another Jew by the name of Soifer. This was the kind of man the writer described: "*Soifer, an old German Jew, an old acquaintance from Silesia whom he had lost sight of and with whom he had met again a few months before, came to play cards with him. Soifer, once ruined by inflation, had made up for all his losses by speculating in the franc. However, he had been left with a permanent distrust, which grew from year to year, towards a money that revolutions and wars could transform overnight into worthless paper. Little by little, he turned his fortune into jewels. In a safe deposit box in London she kept diamonds, magnificent pearls, emeralds so beautiful that even Gloria in her best times would not have dreamed of possessing... However, she was stingy to the point of obsession[410]*."

Let us now look at a passage from a book by the famous Yiddish writer Isaac Bashevis Singer. In his novel entitled *Meshugah* (Yiddish for "crackpot"), Isaac Bashevis Singer (who is well known to our readers) drew a portrait of a character named Chaim Joel Treibitcher: "*The latter was still a very rich man. The empire of his business in America surpassed in importance what it had once been in Europe. He slept exactly four hours a night, plus three quarters of an hour during the day—not a minute more. When he was in bed, he was still scheming new ways to increase his wealth. In America, during the thirties, he had bought houses and factories as well as stocks, and the value of the whole was steadily increasing. In Miami Beach, he owned land worth a fortune. Long before Israel became a Jewish state, he had acquired land and real estate in Jerusalem, Haifa and Tel Aviv. Everything he touched was transformed into gold[411].*" On page 135 of the novel, a Jewish prostitute related that Harry Treibitcher, Chaim's nephew, had committed suicide. "*He ran after prostitutes,*" was "*a hustler and gambler. He bet on races and drove a Rolls Royce.*"

After the Second World War, the famous "Holocaust survivor", Martin Gray, recounted in his book *In the Name of All My People* how he had become rich. He had settled in the United States, in New York, where

---

[409] Irene Nemirovsky, *David Golder*, Ed. digital jugaor, Lectulandia.com, p. 76.
[410] Irene Nemirovsky, *David Golder*, digital ed. jugaor, Lectulandia.com, p. 85.
[411] Isaac Bashevis Singer, *Meshugah*, Edition L'Empreinte, 1994, p. 86.

he had been reunited with his family and had been frantically busy earning a lot of money: *"I multiplied my activities, gambling, sales, services, shows. I accumulated dollars. At night, I would lie down on my bed.* He then threw himself into the antiques trade, especially porcelains, raiding everything he could find. He traveled to Europe, which was trying to recover from the ruin of war. *"My principle was to buy and sell early. A small profit multiplied produces a big profit. The merchandise arrived. Berlin became for me a distant suburb of New York. For months I wandered thus, from continent to continent... I soon added London to my itinerary. I shopped, phoned, jumped from cab to plane... In Berlin the market was getting tough... All the antique dealers of the United States had fallen upon Berlin, emptying the city and the whole of Germany of its porcelains*[412].*"* To remedy the shortage, Gray began to manufacture fake real 18th century porcelain. *"I accumulated dollars, invested, sold... I was now rich, a citizen of the United States, importer, manufacturer, had opened a branch in Canada and another in Havana. I owned houses; I put my money in the stock market. I was going from capital to capital, for me Paris and Berlin were suburbs on the outskirts... Never did my business go better: I cashed, invested, bought, cashed again*[413].*"*

We can also mention Peter Rachman (1919–1962), born Perec Rachman, in Lvov, Poland, son of a Jewish dentist. After the war, he had built up a real estate empire in West London. His housing stock consisted of a hundred blocks of flats that housed a number of nightclubs. The houses he bought were sometimes subdivided for prostitution (Rachman was twice convicted of pimping). But most of the time he was content to expel the tenants by making their lives miserable (noise, construction work, etc.). The "blanquitos" who had a legal protection of old rent were thus replaced by more malleable African and Caribbean immigrants. His "wikipedia" file, on the internet, indicates that he had become famous for his stinginess and that the word *"Rachmanism"* had been included in the *Oxford English Dictionary* to designate a greedy and dishonest landlord.

---

[412] This is how the defeated Germany was plundered from top to bottom. In this regard, read the testimony of Samuel Pisar in *Psychoanalysis of Judaism*.
[413] Martin Gray, *Au nom de tous les miens*, Robert Laffont, 1971, Poche, 1984, p. 365–393 and *In the Name of All My Own*, digital edition at https://es.scribd.com. Read in *The Jewish Mafia* and in *The Mirror of Judaism*.

Naturally, not all Jews possess this trait, and not all greedy, rapacious and ruthless individuals are Jews. But we are forced to note that this inclination to amass great fortunes occurs more in this community than in any other, and that all too often these fortunes are built at the expense of others.

"The Jew is a pike in a carp pond," wrote the merchants of the Prussian town of Stendal in 1734, who thus complained to the authorities.

A 1765 injunction from the merchants and merchants of Paris read as follows: *"The Jews can be compared to hornets that enter beehives to kill the bees, open their bellies and extract the honey from their entrails."*

After the French Revolution of 1789, emancipated Jews were also able to pursue political careers. One of the great historians of Judaism, Leon Poliakov, rightly explained: *"Having always excelled in the race for riches, the emancipated Jews applied themselves to it with double the ardor, and the political and economic transformations of the time facilitated many spectacular promotions[414]"*.

At the end of the 19th century, Bernard Lazare, a Jewish intellectual very famous in France at the time for his involvement in the defense of Captain Dreyfus [415], naturally recognized some defects of his community: *"The Jew is undoubtedly better endowed than any other to achieve success... He is cold and calculating, energetic and flexible, persevering and patient, lucid and exact, and all these qualities he has inherited from his ancestors the ducat handlers and dealers. If he engages in commerce and finance, he benefits from his secular and atavistic education, which has not made him more intelligent, as his vanity declares, but more apt for certain functions[416]."*

At that time, the French dictionary *Littré* gave this definition of "Jew": *"3° Fig. Colloquial: One who lends usuriously or who sells exorbitantly dear, and, in general, anyone who seeks to make money by hard[417]."*

---

[414] Léon Poliakov, *Histoire de l'antisémitisme*, tome II, 1981, Points Seuil, 1990, p. 134.
[415] The Dreyfus case had as its origin a judicial sentence of allegedly anti-Semitic court, on a background of espionage and anti-Semitism, in which the accused was Captain Alfred Dreyfus of German shepherd Jewish origin, and which, for twelve years, from 1894 to 1906, shocked the French society of the time, marking a milestone in the history of anti-Semitism. (NdT).
[416] Bernard Lazare, *Anti-Semitism, its history and its causes, (1894)*. Editions La Bastille, digital ed. 2011, p. 159.
[417] Leon Poliakov, *Histoire de l'antisémitisme*, 1981, Points Seuil, vol. 1, p. 337.

Edgar Bronfman, who served as president of the World Jewish Congress for 26 years beginning in the 1980s, was well aware of the importance of interest-bearing loans. Shortly before his death, a journalist had asked him what he thought was the greatest invention of mankind. Bronfman had answered quite matter-of-factly: *"Lending at interest!418 "*

His predecessor in the post, Nahum Goldman, founding president of the World Jewish Congress, had expressed the same idea. In his book *The Jewish Paradox*, published in 1976, he wrote: *"Jewish life is composed of two elements: amassing money and protesting419."*

Today, with their billions, the Jews control the press, television, the film industry, and have the power to destroy the reputation of any politician. They advise ministers, frequent deputies and senators, dictate their slogans to police commissioners and take their adversaries to court, where they are sure to win their lawsuits.

In these conditions, we understand that money is the best protection. It guarantees you that the police will be at your side the day the rioters try to penetrate your homes in order to recover your property and take revenge for all the humiliations.

Terrible prejudices

It seems admissible that a historian—Jewish or not—can mention the immeasurable wealth of Jewish bankers or merchants in Antiquity or the Middle Ages. But let a goy dare to point out the extraordinary financial power of Judaism in today's society, and then the Jews jump to the fore to denounce the inadmissible "violence" of such statements, the "prejudices" of another era, "the resurgence of anti-Semitism", or the "darkest hours of our history420", etc.. The cries, the tears, the shouts of the Jewish intellectuals impress the Frenchman so much that

---

[418] Quoted by Israel Shamir in his article *Banquiers et voleurs (Bankers and thieves)*, October 2001.

[419] Nahum Goldman, *Le paradoxe juif*, Paris, Stock, 1976, p. 67 (Read in *El Espejo del Judaísmo*). [*La paradoja judía*, Editorial Losada, Buenos Aires, 1979 (out of print), p. 67).

[420] "The darkest hours" (*Les heures les plus sombres*) is an expression coined and used by the French cultural and media sphere that refers to the 1930s and the Second World War. It is a sort of reminder invocation on the memory of the public whenever it is pronounced. (NdT).

at first he wonders what was said that was so shocking, since it was nothing more than a truism. Then he quickly understands that there is only one thing left for him to do if he wants to keep his job: to get down on his knees and ask for forgiveness421.

The importance of the wealth and power of the Jews should not therefore be exaggerated. Jacques Attali, noticing this strong prejudice in 16th century Holland, wished to emphasize it: "*Amsterdam has become the temple of speculation, the place where financial "bubbles" are formed. As the community builds a magnificent synagogue, the city comes to exaggerate the wealth of the Jews... In fact, the fortune of the Jews is more apparent than real.*"

Likewise, one should not believe that in the 19th century the Rothschilds were really rich. It would be a crass mistake to think so, since such lies feed anti-Semitic propaganda: *"The Rothschilds are not comparable to the hundredth British fortune, and Fred Krupp remains, beyond dispute, the richest German of his time ... in France, no Jew has a fortune close to that of the Morny or the Hottinguer. They constitute a cultural rather than a material elite*422." It is well known that Jews are weak and vulnerable. The "Jewish finance" is a myth of the anti-Semitic and reactionary propaganda to deceive the masses and throw them against the eternal "scapegoats". Jews are poor, very poor. To say otherwise, or to insinuate that among the billionaires of the planet the Jews represent an exaggeratedly disproportionate share is an anti-Semitic opinion. And as they say nowadays: *"This is not an opinion, it is a crime"*, or *"a criminal opinion"* if you prefer.

One would have thought that Jewish domination of the world of finance had ended a long time ago: from the 11th century, Jacques Attali affirmed in all seriousness, *"more than a thousand years of almost absolute, and totally involuntary, Jewish domination of international banking came to an end. From this time on, their power remains immense, but they are no longer the main financiers of capitalism ... and the Jewish financiers partly give way to other merchants and bankers*423."

---

[421] The "great emotional fragility" of Judaism and its "intolerance to frustration" belong to the clinical picture of hysterical pathology (read *Psychoanalysis of Judaism*).
[422] Jacques Attali, *Los judíos, el mundo y el dinero*, Fondo de cultura económica, 2005, Buenos Aires, p. 262-263, 324.
[423] Jacques Attali, *A Man of Influence*, Seix Barral, Barcelona, 1992, p. 20.

How to explain then that they were subsequently expelled from everywhere? Jacques Attali answered this question very simply: the Goyim do not understand to what extent the Jews are useful to them. Listen and marvel: *"In Baghdad they had already had that experience in the ninth century, or in London in the twelfth, in Cordoba in the thirteenth, in Seville in the fifteenth, in Frankfurt in the eighteenth: the more they were hated the wider the spectrum of services they rendered"*. We goyim are very ungrateful people. After the great expulsion from Spain, Attali wrote: *"Poor and rich depart together, without goods or almost without them, and without understanding why they are thrown out424."*

Abraham Leon, also trained in the Talmudic arts, had found some ingenious and original solutions to dismantle the anti-Semitic "theses": *"The definitive expulsion of the Jews took place at the end of the 13th century in England; at the end of the 14th century in France; at the end of the 15th century in Spain. These dates reflect the difference in the extent of the economic development of these countries. The 13th century is the time of England's economic heyday. In the 15th century, the Spanish kingdoms began to grow richer and to develop their trade... Feudalism gradually gave way to the exchange system. Consequently, the field of activity of Jewish usury is constantly shrinking. It becomes more and more unbearable because it is less and less necessary. The more money abounds, as a consequence of the more intense circulation of merchandise, the more ruthless becomes the struggle against an economic function which has hardly found economic justification except in the epoch of economic immobility, when the usurer's treasury constituted the indispensable reserve of society... The Jews, as a source of income, lose more and more interest in the eyes of the kings (not to mention that the expulsion of the Jews was always an extremely profitable operation). Thus, the Jews were progressively expelled from all Western countries."*

In short, if we understand it correctly, the Jews would have been expelled when they were losing all their power; at the moment when they were at their weakest. *"Here and there, small Jewish communities managed to maintain themselves in certain subordinate economic functions. The Jewish banks are no longer more than pawnshops, pawnbrokers, pawnbrokers, where misery borrows. It is a total*

---

[424] Jacques Attali, *Los judíos, el mundo y el dinero*, Fondo de cultura económica, 2005, Buenos Aires p. 327, 218.

breakdown. The Jew becomes a petty usurer who lends against small pledges of little value to the poor of the cities and the countryside. And what can he do with the unpaid pledges? He has to sell them. The Jew becomes a small peddler and rag-picker. The old splendor is completely gone. The era of the ghettos and of the worst persecutions and humiliations begins... As managers of the Monte de Piedad, merchants of old clothes, peddlers and ragpickers, they lead a miserable life in dark ghettos, being the target of the hatred and contempt of the common people[425]." Life was always very hard for the Jews.

Hannah Arendt, an obligatory figure of postwar intellectual Judaism, took up this bizarre explanation in her book *The Origins of Totalitarianism*. In the third part of the book, entitled *Anti-Semitism*, she showed that the rise of anti-Semitism in the 19th century did not correspond at all to the prodigious increase of Jewish power in European society since its emancipation, as superficial spirits had hitherto believed, but—paradoxically—to a loss of power of Jewish financiers [426]. In the course of the 19th century, after the social transformations brought about by the French Revolution, citizenship had been granted to Jews in almost all countries of Europe, with the notable exception of Russia and Romania. In Germany, Hannah Arendt explained, the "palace Jews" lost their power and influence. "*In the first decades of this evolution the Jews lost their exclusive position within public finance to imperialist-minded entrepreneurs; their importance as a group declined, even if some Jews retained their influence, as financial advisors and as inter-European intermediaries*427." So that "*it can be observed that anti-Semitism reached its peak when the Jews had similarly lost their public functions and influence and were left with only their wealth. When Hitler came to power, the German Banks were already almost entirely Judenrein (and it was precisely in that sector that the Jews had held decisive positions for over a hundred years).*"

The naivety and credulity of the Goyim is such that Hanan Arendt allowed herself to go even further: "The *same can be said of almost all the countries of Western Europe. The Dreyfus affair did not break out*

---

[425] Abraham Léon, *La Conception matérialiste de la question juive*, 1942, Chapitre 3, La période de l'usurier juif....
[426] The word "paradox" appears frequently under the pen of Jewish intellectuals; this, of course, is no coincidence.
[427] Hannah Arendt, *The Origins of Totalitarianism, Antisemitism*, 1951, Taurus-Santillana, Madrid, 1998, p. 37.

under the Second Empire, when French Jewry was at the height of its prosperity and influence, but under the Third Republic, when the Jews had almost completely disappeared from important positions (though not from the political scene). Austrian anti-Semitism did not become violent under Metternich and Franz Joseph, but in the post-war Austrian Republic, when it became clear that no other group had suffered such a loss of influence and prestige by reason of the demise of the Habsburg monarchy428."

Anti-Semitism, which was constantly on the rise in Germany, France and Austria, was the work of "conspiracy nuts," always ready to take it out on the poor and vulnerable because they are too cowardly to target the truly powerful. *"The anational and inter-European [cosmopolitan] Jewish element became the object of universal hatred precisely because of its useless wealth and of contempt because of its lack of power."* The anti-Semites, who personify *"human baseness,"* do not attack the powerful, but *"groups devoid of power or in danger of losing it*429." The truth had to be told!

It must be understood that the thesis of Abraham Leon and Hannah Arendt is only ridiculous for anti-Semites, because the ordinary goy is always ready to swallow this kind of Talmudic lucubrations. Readers of our previous books know this perfectly well: Jewish intellectuals do not back down from anything and are always ready to deny the evidence and contradict reality. This explanation of anti-Semitism, which postulates that it would have been unleashed against a community weakened by its loss of power in the 19th century, is obviously totally contradicted by the overwhelming reality, namely that the emancipation of European Jews was the beginning of a considerable increase in their influence in all spheres of society. The image of the fabulous power of the five Rothschild brothers dominating 19th century Europe remains the reference of the legendary *"anonymous and vagabond fortune"*.

Marc Roche is another Jewish intellectual. In his book on Goldman Sachs—rather mediocre by the way—he surpassed Jacques Attali, Abraham Leon and Hannah Arendt, achieving the feat of making Jewish financiers disappear purely and simply from the equation, as if by magic—or witchcraft, as it were. Marc Roche thus denounced the

---

[428] Hannah Arendt, *The Origins of Totalitarianism, Antisemitism*, 1951, Taurus-Santillana, Madrid, 1998, p. 29.
[429] Hannah Arendt, *The Origins of Totalitarianism, Antisemitism*, 1951, Taurus-Santillana, Madrid, 1998, p. 37, 88. Read in *The Planetary Hopes* (2005).

alleged racism that reigned on Wall Street, and evoked *"the difficulties experienced by racial minorities in finding their place in such a white universe430."*

The Jewish bankers have disappeared: only racist Whites remain, the bleary-eyed "wasps" who plunder the Third World and hoard the world's wealth. Marc Roche used the well-known "accusatory inversion", so dear to Jewish intellectuals, which consists in projecting onto others what they probably feel guilty about. Read what he wrote to denounce the financial oligarchy, especially the "oligarchs" who had monopolized all the wealth of Russia in the 1990s: *"Oligarchy: political regime in which sovereignty is held by a small group of people, a restricted and privileged class. The word has been updated to define the "Cossack capitalism" that has taken over Russia after the collapse of communism431."* And God knows that Cossacks are rapacious, violent, deceitful and unscrupulous people.

The author was visibly determined to make his readers understand that Jewish finance was a myth, since he ended his book with a passing glance at this question. Thus, at the end of his book, he once again dotted the i's and crossed the t's: *"Until 1945, there was real segregation on Wall Street between Jewish and Protestant banks. Today, Goldman Sachs is no longer really a Jewish bank, just as JP Morgan no longer cultivates its Protestant roots. Yet the prejudices of public opinion are hard to overturn432."*

Roger Cukierman, former president of the Crif (Representative Council of Jewish Institutions in France), was also indignant against these hateful prejudices and denied the evidence, thus respecting the traditions of his community: *""Jews have money!" There always appear these so trivialized and terrible anti-Semitic prejudices which, in the end, bring the worst consequences433."*

---

[430] Marc Roche, *The Bank, how Goldman Sachs runs the world*, Ediciones Deusto, Barcelona, 2011, p. 168.
[431] Marc Roche, *The Bank, how Goldman Sachs runs the world*, Ediciones Deusto, Barcelona, 2011, p. 97. On the plundering of Russia by the Jewish oligarchs in the 1990s, read *The Jewish Mafia*.
[432] Marc Roche, *The Bank, how Goldman Sachs runs the world*, Ediciones Deusto, Barcelona, 2011, p. 233.
[433] Roger Cukierman, *Ni fiers, ni dominateurs*, Edition du Moment, 2008, p. 97. In *El Espejo del Judaísmo* (2009)

Now you know the truth: Jewish finance is a myth. Perhaps it existed in Babylon thousands of years ago, perhaps also in the 19th century, or ephemerally at the beginning of the Goldman Sachs adventure, when this bank was in its infancy. But that story is definitely over. What your eyes see does not correspond to reality. Your eyes are closed, your eyelids are heavy... You are completely relaxed... You are now fast asleep.

There is no "Jewish lobby", contrary to the fallacious and slanderous allegations of the anti-Semites. Listen to what this Meir Waintrater told us about the "Jewish lobby" in the Jewish magazine *L'Arche* of October 1999 (page 10):

"Anyone who is even minimally familiar with Jewish affairs knows the futility of such a question. The Crif, which is the only organization that can speak on behalf of the Jewish community in the political arena, is a small organization that relies almost exclusively on volunteerism. It only intervenes openly, in the form of press releases and meetings with national and international leaders. It has neither the vocation nor the means to exert pressure on politicians or the media, which is what characterizes any pressure group? (And I am not talking about the Israeli embassy, whose information service is undoubtedly one of the poorest and most ill-equipped of all the diplomatic representations in Paris; nor about the World Zionist Organization, decayed and periodically condemned to disappear, whose few delegates in France are exclusively concerned with spreading Hebrew culture and helping candidates to emigrate to Israel). In a word: the concept of "Jewish lobby" lacks any basis in reality." And that is precisely the reason why, every year, almost all the cream of the French political world, political personalities and ministers of the left and the right, are invited to the famous Crif evenings.

In a similar vein, we can see, for example, the second part of the well-known film *La Vérité si je mens*[434] (France, 2000): some unscrupulous bastards swindle a poor small supplier of the Sentier, leading him to ruin. These bastards are the buyers of the hypermarkets of large-scale distribution, the blue-eyed goyim owners who will be punished at the end of the film. Don't misunderstand us: we are not saying that this cannot happen in reality. It just seems to us that the role of the bastard usually falls, almost exclusively, on white goyim, and that it would be

---

[434] Popular Jewish comedy that was a great success in France in those years.

fairer that from time to time we also see in film fiction some swindling, scamming, evil, imperialist and warmongering Jew, as well as serial killer blacks or rapist Maghrebis. But for that, we will probably have to wait for a new era.

Anti-Semitism is an absurdity, Jewish intellectuals tell us: *"Anti-Semitism is totally incoherent, but that never bothers the anti-Semites,"* wrote the great sociologist Michel Wierviorka. *"Everything has a place in the anti-Semitic discourse, Jew-hatred is fed by contradictory arguments[435]."* How, then, to explain the permanence of anti-Semitism, *"if it is absurd and irrational?"* Michel Wierviorka answered this way in his fictitious dialogue with a goy: *"To tell the truth, I have asked myself this question many times, and I have never found a satisfactory answer. The best one, in my opinion, is the idea that the Jewish people have been constituted throughout history as the figure of evil and misfortune. Their presence among other peoples, where they were never more than a minority, made them the ideal scapegoat."* Obviously, the sociologist was speaking out against *"the absurd accusations that they are conspiring to run the world and lead it to perdition[436]."*

However, all these considerations have never prevented the Jews from giving moral lessons to mankind, like teachers marking their students in an exam. Read the words of Albert Einstein, who wrote with a certain self-importance: *"The situation of our people scattered over the earth is a barometer of the morality that reigns in the political world... The tradition of the Jewish people consists of a will to justice and reason that serves and has served the rest of men, and will serve them in the future[437]."*

Or as one of his congeners, Stéphane Zagdanski, also admirably put it: *"One could develop in every possible tone this ode, this gigantic rhapsody of generosity, selflessness, gratuitousness, and splendorous but useless self-giving that is Judaism[438]."*

Jacques Attali also knew how to display great humor when he reminded us of the moral rules of Judaism: *"Impose a very austere morality, do*

---

[435] Michel Wieviorka, *L'Antisémitisme expliqué aux jeunes*, Seuil, 2014, p. 100.
[436] Michel Wieviorka, *L'Antisémitisme expliqué aux jeunes*, Seuil, 2014, p. 115, 117.
[437] Albert Einstein, *My View of the World, speech delivered in London*, Titivillus digital ed. 2016, p. 104–105. [*"Spinoza and Karl Marx emerged from that tradition."* p. 105.
[438] Stéphane Zagdanski, *De l'Antisémitisme*, Climats, 1995, 2006, p. 327.

not tolerate arrogance or immorality, so as not to create jealousy or pretexts for persecution[439]." It is no laughing matter!

---

[439] Jacques Attali, *Los Judíos, el mundo y el dinero*, Fondo de cultura económica, 2005, Buenos Aires, p. 490.

The Cosmopolitan Project

The truth is that the Jews have a head start in the art and manner of deceiving people and accumulating wealth. It is therefore not surprising, under these circumstances, that they are the champions of liberalism, deregulation and the suppression of borders. States, with their meddlesome legislation, their inquisitorial administration and their more or less "anti-Semitic" police, are for them essentially obstacles that force them into certain financial acrobatics, such as opening bank accounts on the other side of the world, domiciling themselves in tax havens, etc. All this, in order to keep their fortunes away from the tax authorities and justice. Jews, in fact, always feel the imperious need to correct the injustice they believe they have suffered by some extra-legal self-compensatory action.

But Jewish billionaires (in the billions) do not accumulate wealth for the mere pleasure of possessing and enjoying material goods. Like their fellow Jews who really feel themselves to be Jews, they are above all animated by a desire to see the prophecies come true: they are convinced that their messiah must come. But they are also aware that it will not come until peace is established on the face of the earth, a peace that will be absolute, universal and definitive. For generations, Jews have been working tirelessly for this goal of global pacification of humanity. The notion of "Peace" is at the very core of Judaism, and it is no coincidence that this word (*shalom* in Hebrew) appears so frequently in all the speeches of the Jews of the world. It is not just a religious concept, or a belief in the advent of a better world, the work of God in the distant future, but a guiding principle that determines the commitment and the work of Jews in their daily lives. Indeed, Jews, through their work, their actions and their involvement in politics, work every day for the construction of "Peace".

To achieve this peace, Jews work tirelessly to eliminate all sources of conflict, first and foremost the conflicts between nations. Nations are supposedly the generators of wars, so everything possible must be done to weaken them. In the films they produce and make, in the novels they write, in the speeches they repeat in the media and in their academic chairs, the Jews actively militate in favor of everything that contributes to the fading of the feeling of collective belonging. In the name of "equality", of "human rights" and of "tolerance" they encourage with all their might the universal fraternity, the opening of borders, the free circulation of people and goods. In all the countries where they are installed, they favor immigration, encourage miscegenation, exalt multicultural society and identity ambiguity. Traditional societies must disappear; all differences between men must be swept away and suppressed: races, ethnicities, nations, religions. In the end, all the States must merge, fuse into a world government, the only one capable of making happiness and prosperity reign on earth. The unification of the world will also be the prelude to a global pacification of humanity, which is, according to them, the precondition for the arrival of their messiah[440].

In the 19th and 20th centuries, with Marxism and communist ideology, the Jews had tried to suppress social classes at the cost of countless victims, but always wrapping themselves in the garb of great humanitarian ideals: secularism, tolerance, "human rights", "internationalism", etc.[441]. Today, they push their fanaticism to the point of making the differences between men and women disappear[442], trivializing homosexuality in their films and television series, encouraging sexual ambiguity, the dissolution of the referent represented by the heterosexual family, as well as attacking "reactionary" or patriarchal moral values, always with the aim of establishing "Peace" and "Unity" between nations and individuals. Nothing must remain of the old world, everything must disappear! And when there is nothing left to destroy, then the Jews, who will have kept their blood, their law and their religion intact, will be recognized by all as the "chosen people" of God. This is the egalitarian and messianic

---

[440] This is what we have thoroughly demonstrated, from top to bottom, relying on hundreds, if not thousands, of citations in our previous books. On this subject, read particularly *The Planetary Hopes* (2005) and *Jewish Fanaticism* (2007).

[441] Almost all of the Marxist ideologues were indeed originally from this community. See the chapters on this subject in *The Planetary Hopes* (2005) and *Jewish Fanaticism* (2007).

[442] We believe that the current global offensive of transhumanist and transgender politics is inspired by the esoteric doctrines of the Jewish Kabbalah. Read in *Psychoanalysis of Judaism* (NdT).

fanaticism that paves the way for democratic and totalitarian progressivism.

By acting in concert, with a well-defined objective, the Jewish billionaires are thus much more effective than the goyim and exert great influence on political decisions, especially in Western countries.

George Soros, for example, was not only an unscrupulous speculator: he was also a great "philanthropist". After the collapse of the Soviet Union, he founded the *Open Society Institute* in 1993, whose declared aim was to promote the development of democratic and "open" societies. At first, his investments were mainly directed towards developing countries and the countries of the former Soviet Union. But it then poured hundreds of millions of dollars into its foundations, which are present in more than 30 countries.

In his book, published in 2006 (*The Great World Disorder*), we saw how the speculator encouraged immigration to Europe: *"Due to an aging population, immigration is an economic necessity, he wrote. As the prototype of open world societies, Europe must welcome immigration and encourage new members to join."* Soros also revealed some information about his role in the bombings against the small patriotic Serbia in 1999, as well as in the "democratic" (colored) revolutions: in the "Rose Revolution" in Georgia in 2003, and in the "Orange Revolution" in Ukraine in 2004[443]. Ten years later, invited on the set of the US network CNN, on May 25, 2014, the businessman openly acknowledged having financed the opposition to the pro-Russian president in that country. He then designated Russian President Vladimir Putin as the No. 1 enemy to be defeated. The objective being, as always, the establishment of democracies "open" and "tolerant" to globalist interests, thus dissolving the peoples and favoring the establishment of world government. In 2010, Soros had financed the association "Human Right Watch" with more than 100 million dollars. Soros was very concerned about racism and committed to the defense of "human" rights. He called on the European Union to implement a major plan for the integration of the Sinhalese. *"The magnitude of the problems calls for a comprehensive and effective plan for Roma integration on the scale of the European Union."* His foundation had already distributed nearly $150 million in programs and integration of

---

[443]On George Soros and other "Wall Street gurus", read *The Planetary Hopes* (2005) and *Jewish Fanaticism* (2007). (See again note 333. NdT).

Gypsies in Eastern Europe[444]. In 2012, it had donated 35,000 euros to the "Collective against Islamophobia" in France.

In his autobiography, Soros recounted how as a Jewish teenager in Nazi-controlled Hungary he had participated in the spoliation of Jewish property. *"Soros does not feel guilty about it."* The billionaire compared that episode in his life with his attitude to the financial markets: *"If I hadn't done it, others would have done it[445],"* he said. Georges Soros supported all the "liberal" causes in the United States: decriminalization of cannabis, firearms control, euthanasia, etc. In California, he had donated a million dollars to support associations in favor of cannabis legalization, perhaps to lull the population to sleep. The "open society" is in reality a "busted society", in which transnational mafias can operate as they please. This is the globalist project.

The sociologist Edgar Morin is another fairly representative specimen of these cosmopolitan intellectuals obsessed with the advent of their prophecies[446]. For thirty years, he has been repeating the same discourse, almost word for word, and the same ideas in all his books. In 1993, in his book *Earth-Homeland, he* already announced the good news in detail, *"that of the planetary era"*: *"Migrations and crossbreeding, producers of new societies, polycultural seem to announce the homeland common to all humans[447]."* Our task, said Edgar Morin, is to *"reform Western civilization," "federate the Earth"* and *"bring about the era of planetary civility."* We must *"consider planetary citizenship, which would give and guarantee to all earthly rights[448]"*, the sociologist assured us.

Twenty years later, in 2014, in his book titled *Our Europe*, Edgar Morin pounded his same obsessions, his same prophetic warnings: *"We are at the beginning of the planetary era... There is hope that our current societies will undergo a metamorphosis towards a planetary union, towards a world-society, rational demand of a limited and interdependent world... Human beings do not only have a single*

---

[444] *Le Monde.fr*, August 28, 2010.
[445] *Le Point*, September 18, 2008.
[446] Edgar Morin (Paris, 1921), born Edgar Nahum, is a centenarian French philosopher and sociologist of Sephardic origin. He is a prolific and award-winning author, widely translated into English.
[447] Edgar Morin and Anne-Brigitte Kern, *Tierra-Patria*, 1993, Editorial Kairós, Barcelona, 2005, p. 43.
[448] Edgar Morin and Anne-Brigitte Kern, *Tierra-Patria*, 1993, Editorial Kairós, Barcelona, 2005, p. 136, 142, 143.

common parentage. Human beings also have a common destiny... All human beings have a homeland. We are all children of the Earth[449]." And here we go again: *"Unity, diversity and miscegenation must win out over homogenization and withdrawal. Mestizaje does not only constitute blah blah blah blah[450]..."* In his wheelchair, in front of a wall, Edgar Nahum would spend the day repeating the same words.

Jacques Attali is also very representative of these Jewish intellectuals, literally obsessed with universal miscegenation (except for themselves, of course) and the unification of the world. Readers of our books know him well, even in his intimacy! He is probably the writer who expresses most clearly the political project of Judaism, since he has been shamelessly exposing for many years his ideal of planetary unification in his books and on French television sets[451].

In his book entitled *Fraternities*, published in 1999, he already called for the creation of a world government. He projected himself into the future and imagined *"thirteen characters composing the world government created twenty-three years earlier, in 2083"*. Any resistance to its power had disappeared: *"By 2080, no one, or almost no one, denounced the formidable concentration of wealth and power: five financial groups controlled more than half of the world's capital, and a significant part of the rest belonged to organ traffickers[452], clones and virtual brains. Five billion earthlings had hardly anything to survive on."* Peace finally reigned on Earth: *"A new privileged class had been formed, bringing together, regardless of nationality, entrepreneurs of data banks, manipulators of genes, producers of chimeras, organizers of networks and animators of spaces of pleasure... We could see how an open society, generous and respectful of differences, was being established. Everyone took pleasure in cultivating them for the pleasure of all."*

---

[449] Edgar Morin, Mauro Cerruti, *Our Europe, What can we expect, What can we do*, Paidós, 2013, Barcelona, p. 142, 143.

[450] Edgar Morin, Mauro Cerruti, *Nuestra Europa*, Paidós, 2013, Barcelona, p. 145. [The book is full of pearls such as this: *"Europe must, above all, problematize itself. And it must problematize itself by regenerating the constitutive principle of its identity: the principle of unity in diversity and diversity in unity,"* p. 112, 113.]

[451] Jacques Attali is a personality that over the years has become more visible to the Spanish and Spanish-speaking public. Many of his works have been translated into Spanish. One of his most recommended books about the future global society is *Breve historia del futuro*, Ediciones Paidós Ibérica, Barcelona, 2007.

[452] Organ trafficking is a specialty of the Jewish mafia.

The essential, as you will understand, consists in destroying all ancient organic communities, all ancestral traditions, all blood ties and all family or ethnic solidarities. Jewish nihilism knows no bounds, and Jacques Attali openly proclaimed the dissolution of the patriarchal family, speaking of *"multiple and simultaneous marriages, heterosexual or homosexual[453]"*. In the following years, Attali would not cease to repeat this idea ad nauseam in all his works.

In his visions, Attali saw a small elite of *"planetary nomads"* to run the world. The members of this new elite would be *"a planetary hyperclass,"* devoid *"of patriotic references."* Their dream government would be a *"world government,"* *"elected by electronic vote for five years."* *"It had the task of organizing a democracy entirely dedicated to the respect of the human being and the protection of freedoms and rights."* All would go swimmingly in the best of worlds: *"Hunger and misery had been placed universally outside the law."* And planetary citizens blindly trusted their rulers to solve all conflicts: *"The prohibition of the sale of any weapon, including white or hunting weapons, was guaranteed and controlled by a planetary police, justice and regulation ... and genetics did the rest when it made it possible to isolate and neutralize, without infringing on freedoms, the genes linked to violence, envy, jealousy and self-hatred."* The world government would have at its disposal exceptional means: some *"planetary fiscal resources voted by a parliament of the United Nations."* And all the world's gold would finally flow into its hands: *"A single Central Bank controlled the use of the world's only currency[454]."* At the end of the book, Jacques Attali felt that the reader was sufficiently prepared for his ultimate prophecy: *"A planetary central bank would administer the world's single currency.[455]"*

In 2007, Attali unveiled his plans to save the pensions of French retirees. It was simply a matter of *"organizing the arrival of two million foreigners per year between 2020 and 2040, which would translate, taking into account the entire period considered and based on the growth of families, into 93 million immigrants entering our soil; France*

---

[453] Jacques Attali, *Fraternities, a new utopia*, Paidós Iberica, Barcelona, 2000, p. 16, 20, 21 *"To authorize the union between people, whatever their sex and number, so that they can unite their solitudes, take pleasure in helping each other and help others together."* p. 147.
[454] Jacques Attali, *Fraternities, a new utopia*, Paidós Iberica, Barcelona, 2000, p. 20, 21.
[455] Jacques Attali, *Fraternities, a new utopia*, Paidós Iberica, Barcelona, 2000, p. 142.

would then have 187 million inhabitants, 68% of whom would be first or second generation immigrants[456]."

In 2009, in another work of his entitled *The Meaning of Things*, Attali conscientiously continued his work of destroying European values, insisting several times on the *"need for a world government*[457]*"*.

On February 16, 2010, on the television channel *Public Sénat*, in the program *Conversations d'avenirs* dedicated to the city of Jerusalem, Jacques Attali naively evoked that city as a *"planetary capital of a world government"*: "We can dream of a Jerusalem becoming the capital of the planet unified one day around a world government. It is a beautiful place for a world government."

In 2011, after the publication of his umpteenth new book entitled *Tomorrow, Who Will Rule the World*, he proposed *"a planetary executive"* conceived as *"a heptavirate. A Council of seven members elected for seven years, not eligible for re-election—it would symbolize the unity of the world and would exercise the moral authority necessary for the respect of the world Constitution... The presidency of the heptavirate would be annual and rotating. The world government would prepare, propose, vote and execute the world budget*[458]*."* Jacques Attali had the opportunity to present his project on all radio and television channels.

On May 6, 2014, on the French-Israeli billionaire Patrick Drahi's BFMTV television channel, Attali repeated and summarized once again the project so that the Goyim would definitely get the message: *"We need a world government, a world finance, a world bank, a planetary capitalism. We can dream of a Jerusalem as a planetary capital. Jerusalem becoming the capital of the world government would be a beautiful place459."*

---

[456] Jacques Attali, *L'avenir du travail*, Fayard, 2007, p. 118.
[457] Jacques Attali, *Le Sens des choses*, Robert Laffont, 2009, p. 199, 252, 253.
[458] Jacques Attali, *Demain, qui gouvernera le monde?*, Fayard, 2011, p. 311. Read in *La Guerre eschatologique* (2013).
[459] The reader should know that Jacques Attali has a great influence on the French political and media landscape. Since the 1980s, he has been the main advisor to President Mitterrand, and has recently chaired several economic commissions under the presidencies of Sarkozy and Hollande. In the private sphere, he has also developed a remarkable activity as an international banker. In fact, it is well known that Attali publicly sponsored the young Emmanuel Macron, then an employee of the investment bank Rothschild & Co and directly sponsored by David René de Rothschild (member

From then on, thanks to the loan with interest, the single world currency and the planetary Central Bank, all the riches will go to the coffers of the children of Israel. The treatises *Pesachim* and *Sanhedrin* of the Babylonian Talmud assure that, in the time of the Messiah, the treasures of the Jews will be so immense that *"300 donkeys will be needed to transport the keys to each vault[460]."* Then there will no longer be anything to fear. All enemies will have disappeared and the Jews will at last be able to find rest and Peace.

Paris, September 2014

---

of the Council of the World Jewish Congress). Macron was then catapulted to the presidency of the French Republic by the media despite lacking the usual political support, thus being for many analysts the political figurehead of Rothschild and characters such as Attali. With his arrogant and authoritarian style, Emmanuel Macron is implementing in France a globalist policy by leaps and bounds: oligarchic privatization of the French economy, crumbling of the French State and integration into the new world order of the 2030 agenda. (More information in Faits et documents: www.faitsetdocuments.com/). (NdT).

[460]*Pesachim* 118b and 119, and *Sanhedrin* 110b. On eschatology, i.e. the view of the end times in the great religions, read *The Eschatological War* (2013).

OTHER TITLES

PLANETARIAN HOPES — HERVÉ RYSSEN

The triumph of democracy over communism seemed to have opened the door to a new era, to a "New World Order", and to prepare all nations for an inevitable planetary merger.

The idea of a world without borders and of a finally unified humanity is certainly not new...

PSYCHOANALYSIS of JUDAISM — HERVÉ RYSSEN

Judaism, in fact, is not only a religion. It is also a political project whose aim is to achieve the abolition of borders, the unification of the earth and the establishment of a world of "peace".

This book represents the most comprehensive study of the Jewish question ever undertaken.

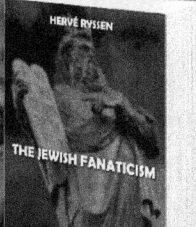

THE JEWISH FANATICISM — HERVÉ RYSSEN

The resulting dissolution of national identity protects them from a possible nationalist backlash against the power they gained, especially in finance, politics and the media.

The Jewish people promote a project for the whole of humanity...

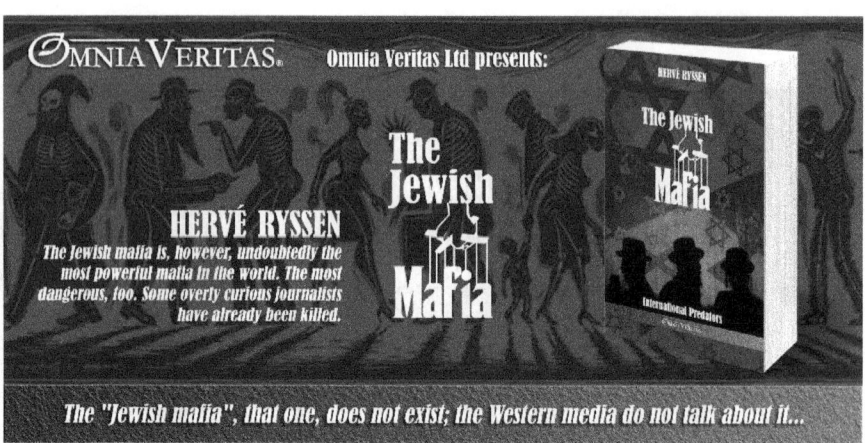

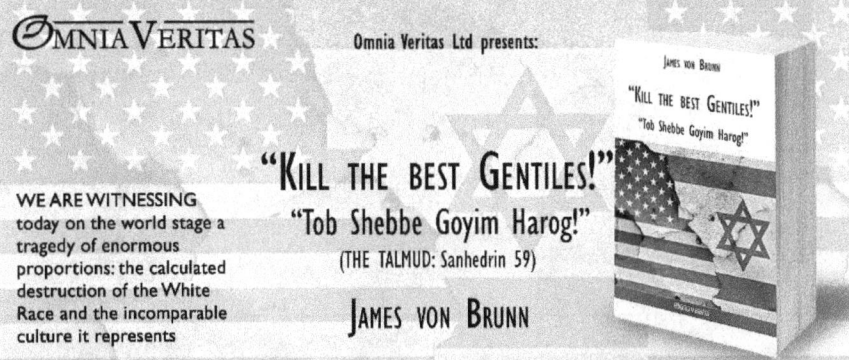

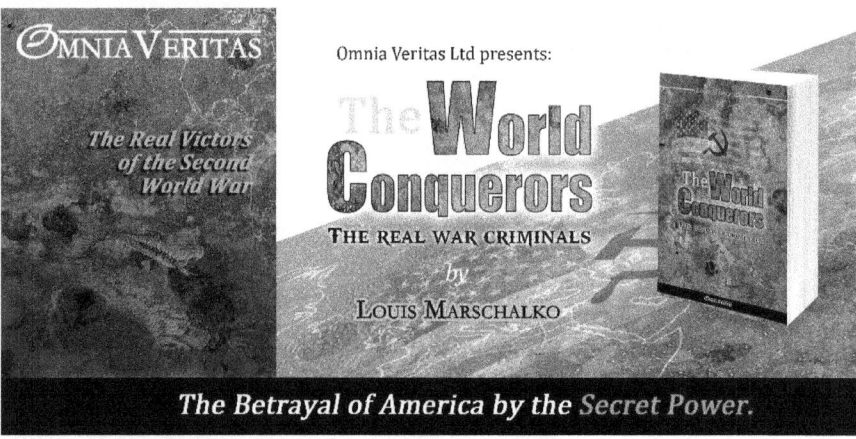

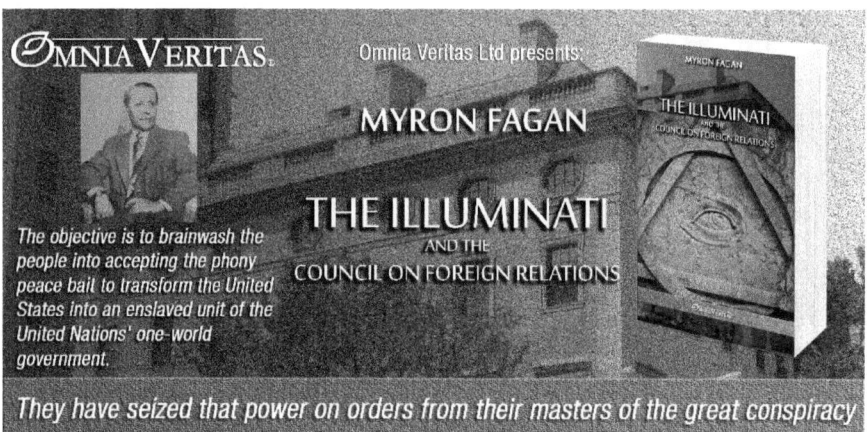

www.ingramcontent.com/pod-product-compliance
Lightning Source LLC
Chambersburg PA
CBHW060112170426
43198CB00010B/864